THE
UNFINISHED
CITY

Also by Thomas Bender

Toward an Urban Vision:
Ideas and Institutions in Nineteenth-CenturyAmerica

The Making of American Society (co-author)

Community and Social Change in America

New York Intellect: A History of Intellectual Life in New York,
from 1750 to the Beginnings of Our Own Time

The University and the City:
From Medieval Origins to the Present (editor)

Budapest and New York: Studies in
Metropolitan Transformation, 1870–1930 (co-editor)

The Anti-Slavery Debate: Capitalism and Abolitionism
as a Problem in Historical Interpretation (editor)

Intellect and Public Life: Essays on the
Social History of Academic Intellectuals in the United States

American Academic Culture in Transformation (co-editor)

City and Nation (co-editor)

Rethinking American History in a Gobal Age (editor)

THE UNFINISHED CITY

NEW YORK AND THE METROPOLITAN IDEA

Thomas Bender

NEW YORK UNIVERSITY PRESS
Washington Square, New York

September 11, 2001

In memory of the victims
In honor of the rescue crews
In appreciation of the city's civic humanity

Published in paperback in 2007 by New York University Press
Washington Square
New York, NY 10003
www.nyupress.org

LIBRARY OF CONGRESS CATALOGING-IN-PUBLICATION DATA
Bender, Thomas.
    The unfinished city : New York and the metropolitan idea / Thomas Bender.
        p.   cm.
    Includes bibliographical references and index.
    ISBN-13: 978-0-8147-9996-3 (pbk : alk. paper)
    1. New York (N.Y.)—Civilization. 2. New York (N.Y.)—Cultural policy.
3. New York (N.Y.)—Intellectual life. 4. City and town life—New York (State)—
New York—History. 5. Popular culture—New York (State)—New York—History.
6. Political culture—New York (State)—New York—History. I. Title.
F128.35.B46   2002
974.7'1—dc21   2002018952

New York University Press books are printed on acid-free paper,
and their binding materials are chosen for strength and durability.

Book design by Kelly S. Too

Originally published in hardcover in 2002 by The New Press.

Printed in the United States of America

p 10 9 8 7 6 5 4 3 2 1

CONTENTS

PREFACE

This book is built upon a series of essays that were written for various purposes, mostly in the 1990s. They have been completely rewritten into chapters for this book. Approaching New York in this manner—with topical essays—is both rich in possbility and frustrating, for the numbers of crucially important topics to be addressed always exceeds the writer's reach. So these essays do not propose to cover the history and culture of the city. Rather than seeking comprehensiveness, the book explores various dimensions and facets of metropolitan culture in New York in pursuit of the illuminating incident, detail, or controversy. What is the character of metropolitan culture in this city, and how has it changed over two hundred years? That is the question posed, explored, and reflected upon.

Most of the essays were originally written when I was either developing or directing and participating in the Project on Cities and Urban Knowledges of the International Center for Advanced Studies at New York University (1996–2001). The essays were rewritten at the conclusion of that multiyear project; they all benefit, therefore, from my experience in that extraordinarily stimulating international, interdisciplinary, and intergenerational intellectual community. I am indebted to some seventy fellows and visiting scholars in residence between 1997 and 2001 for providing me with an advanced—quite advanced—education in the study of cities.

In several cases, editors made important suggestions for the original versions of these essays, and I hope their contributions survived the rewriting. I wish to mention particularly Lynn Garafola, Louis Menand, Irving Howe, Jim Sleeper, James Holston, Engin Isin, Jay Kaplan, Nancy Levinson, and William Saunders. I also have some longer-term debts that go back to an early project on the culture of cities at the New York Institute for the Humanities, where I benefitted from the insights of William R. Taylor, Elizabeth Kendall, Robert Fishman, Anson Rabinbach, Marshall Berman, and Linda Nochlin. More recent colleagues who have commented helpfully on one or more of the essays here deserve thanks, too: Timothy Mitchell, Molly Nolan, and Michael Peter Smith. Twenty years or more of conversations about cities with Gwendolyn Wright, Carl E. Schorske, and Richard Sennett have enriched my understanding of cities and everything I have written on them. It is a pleasure to be able to publish this book with the New Press, and to work with André Schiffrin and Marc Favreau.

It so happened that I was in the midst of writing the introduction and this preface on September 11, 2001. My thoughts and feelings about that event and its implications for the city and the world are not settled yet. But however tragic, the event had its inspiriting moments. Those who gave their lives seeking to save others, and those many who in various ways expressed their solidarity with the victims and the rescue workers all honored themselves and the city. In that spirit, I have dedicated this book about New York to those New Yorkers.

Thomas Bender
New York City
September 2001

INTRODUCTION:

THE UNFINISHED METROPOLIS

In 1903, Herbert Croly, soon to become famous as the author of a classic in American political theory, *The Promise of American Life* (1909), published an article titled "New York as the American Metropolis" in the *Architectural Record*, of which he was an editor.[1] Croly, who later became the founding editor of *The New Republic*, was a child of the city. He was the son of David Goodman Croly, a prominent journalist and leading American proponent of the ideas of Auguste Comte, and of Jane Cunningham Croly, a prolific commentator on women's affairs and the founder of the women's club movement. These prominent parents exemplified engagement in the public life of the city, and Herbert Croly sought to follow in their footsteps.

Edmund Wilson later commented that for Croly, "public affairs" mattered "as deeply as our private affairs do to the rest of us."[2] Yet Croly felt that a vital and effective metropolitan public life demanded that New York be a city of a certain type, something very much like Paris. Its architecture and its concentration of major institutions should impress upon the nation its centrality and legitimate leadership in matters political and cultural. Metropolitanism defined in this way works by demonstration; it is exemplary, a place where the best hopes of the culture and polity are realized and become a national standard. By this means, Croly presumed, the American metropolis would produce a sense of national unity and civic purpose.

New York, in his view, did not quite achieve this. While Croly was surely impressed by the architectural, economic, cultural, and political achievements of New York since the making of Central Park, still he found the city at the turn of the twentieth century wanting as a metropolis. It fell distinctly short of the Parisian model he had in mind.[3] In 1903, he was hopeful that continued development would complete the metropolis; yet by 1909, with the publication of *The Promise of American Life*, he had apparently changed his mind. He denied the capacity of metropolitanism to realize that promise. Instead of the metropolitan ideal, he now proposed a "new nationalism" that was to be premised upon an American "creed." This ideological conception of the nation would provide the unity and the national progress he had once located in the idea of a metropolitan culture. The city had failed him.

The Promise of American Life proposed using Hamiltonian means (national power) to achieve Jeffersonian ends (democracy). While the book is quite urban in spirit, it is not metropolitan in its strategy. Whatever the city might contribute to American progress would be through the nation, which would have the centralized national power necessary to achieve the democratic ideals of Jeffersonianism. New York's Theodore Roosevelt immediately embraced the book and its "new nationalism," which was the rallying cry of the Progressive Roosevelt. These ideas became, as well, the underlying philosophy of *The New Republic*, established in 1914. Croly's enormously influential magazine became perhaps the most important voice of liberalism during the interwar years. But if New York's political ideas and traditions were thus influential—even defining—elements of American liberalism, they did not reflect the metropolitan dominance or the acceptance of metropolitan standards Croly had earlier envisioned. Rather, these ideas and policies infiltrated the nation through a New York–Washington connection that has been reenacted several times in our nation's past. (For example, it has been especially evident in the Jacksonian, Civil War, Progressive, New Deal, and Kennedy-Johnson eras.)

It is interesting and revealing that Croly is rightly remembered for his contributions to American liberalism but not for his writings on New York and cities generally. Few of the commentators who celebrate his *Promise of American Life* and the book that followed it, *Progressive Democracy* (1914), are aware of this earlier career as writer and editor at the *Architectural Record*. There are no doubt many reasons for this loss of memory, but one of them may be the resistance of New York to the kind of metropolitan completion he sought in that phase of his writing. New York is not and will not be Paris.

Those who have Paris or Vienna or Budapest or Mexico City or Buenos Aires (or one of many other cities) in their minds as proper metropolitan centers will be disappointed by New York. From such a point of view New York has not yet completed its progress to full metropolitan status. But that perspective radically mistakes the case. New York's character is to be unfinished. It is not a failed or incomplete example of something else; it is sui generis. One must capture its distinctive metropolitan values and its peculiar role within the United States and beyond. Its very essence is to be continually in the making, to never be completely resolved.

Moreover, the United States is not a nation that welcomes centralization, especially metropolitan centralization. New York had been the administrative center of British North America, and it was in New York that the government created by the Constitution was first assembled in 1789. George Washington was inaugurated as President at Federal Hall on Wall Street, but it was understood from the start that New York would be only a temporary capital. Determining the location of the permanent capital was one of the first orders of business for the new government, and Alexander Hamilton and Thomas Jefferson brokered a political deal that designated a swampy site on the Potomac River as a distinctly nonmetropolitan capital. While there was some disappointment in New York, the city's leaders rather quickly imagined other ways of its being a metropolis. New Yorkers came to appreciate the possibility inherent in representing not the nation but rather its own metropolitan culture and economy. It would be a metropolis without being a national capital or even symbol.

Even in charting its course toward metropolitan standing, New York went its own way. Unwilling to pursue a single line of modernization, New York emerged as a paradoxical modern metropolis. It has been and remains at once a concentrated "slab" city and a dispersed "spread city" of single-family, duplex, and triplex homes; a city of skyscrapers that nonetheless prizes small brick and brownstone houses; a city that builds images of modern urbanity with unprecedented density at the center, yet preserves in that center an absolutely untouchable 800 acres of "greensward." Whether in its physical development or in its social organization, New York refuses a single logic, and it declines any notion of completeness. The city is characterized by a relatively open—one wishes more open—contest over its public definition, always understanding each resolution as temporary, subject to further change. There is not and there is not to be a final truth about itself. In this sense, New York is a pragmatic city, and as such it is necessarily an unfinished city, without final ends. Implicit in the notion of a pragmatic polity is a pluralistic conversation in search of public resolutions—a pragmatic pluralism.[4]

Those who, like Croly, seek a single logic in New York will find in its incompleteness a defect. Contrast Walt Whitman. No one has come closer than Whitman to capturing the soul of New York; his person and poetry (which are nearly indistinguishable) are a part of a collective memory that sustains the city's metropolitan self-definition. As Lewis Mumford once observed, to embrace Manhattan is to embrace Whitman, whether one realizes it or not. But Mumford errs in limiting his comment to Manhattan, for the same is true for the boroughs. Whitman, after all, was of Brooklyn, and his greatest poem, "Crossing Brooklyn Ferry," captures the multiple meanings of that movement between the two parts of the metropolis.

Whitman was self-fashioned—and, like New York, an utterly unpredictable result. Who could have imagined that the undistinguished journalist, carpenter, writer Walter Whitman would or could make himself into Walt Whitman, poet of the city and the continuing fount of American poetry? Yet neither Whitman nor his poem was ever complete. That was his human and artistic strength, as it is New York's. He was always growing, absorbing more, and battling the contradictions that his voraciousness forced upon him. Whitman was the poet of the intentionally unfinished poem. *Leaves of Grass* (1855 et seq.) was never finished or intended to be finished. It was perpetually in revision. So too the city. Both Whitman's poems and the city are deliberately collections of people, sights, things, ideas, feelings. Ordinarily, they seem to be merely miscellaneous, whether in poetry or life. Yet episodically and magically they are fused into aesthetically powerful and morally compelling imageries and practices.

This book records an ongoing search for New York, for the metropolitan culture that is centered in Manhattan. Of course, *metropolitan* is a word of many meanings, ancient and modern. To focus on the modern alone, it has meant the premier city in a hierarchy of cities, and it has meant a city whose influence and connections and identifications extend beyond its locality, even beyond its nation. And there is the notion of metropolitan as a cultural style or psychological quality associated with big-city living, such as Georg Simmel emphasized in his classic essay, "The Metropolis and Mental Life" (1903).[5] I have all of these meanings in mind, and inter alia I explore different aspects of them.

What follows is my personal pursuit, but it engages with and participates in the city's collective experience of finding itself and explaining itself to itself. This endless quest is central to the city's capacity not only to know itself, but also to act on its own behalf and in behalf of its residents and extended constituents. New York is a city of incommensurables, and I have followed no single path of exploration here. I have pursued various lines of inquiry, relying upon different interdisciplinary strategies, from art history to political science.

The result, I hope, is an interconnected series of close studies and sound interpretations that will provide a variety of fresh and illuminating perspectives on New York's history and metropolitan culture. I have examined particulars—either places or people or images or institutions—in order to open ways of thinking about larger patterns and meanings. I find these many stories fascinating and informative as well as building blocks for a more interpretive or academic understanding, and I hope my readers will share that pleasure.

The scale of metropolitan life examined here increases as the book proceeds. I begin with Washington Square, a few acres in lower Manhattan, and the book concludes with a chapter that explores the relation of city, nation, and globalization. The different scales of metropolitan life are crucial to my purposes. Modern metropolitan people live at once in very local enviroments and in giant urban agglomerations that are part of a global economy and culture. The different relations among these different scales and aspects of one's life in the metopolis largely define the constraints and possibilities—personal, social, artistic, political—of metropolitan life.

Places are my focus in Part I. They are special places—selected from a large menu of possible locations—that reveal key transformations in the scale of metropolitan space and in the character of metropolitan life and culture. The historical change I am seeking to track concerns urban perception, the changing ways in which the city is perceived as it becomes more modern. Perception is important because it largely defines the metopolitan experience. As has often been observed, if a situation is perceived as real, it is real in its consequences. We enact metopolitan culture as we internalize these perceptions and organize our lives around them.

In Part II, attention moves from place to the social organization of metopolitan life. Several different issues are addressed: cultural authority and innovation, the self-conscious efforts of artists to capture the social and psychological experience of metopolitan life, and the forming and reforming of intellectual, scientific, and artistic communities. Put differently and perhaps more directly, Part II asks this question: how does one describe the qualities of the metropolis as a place of art and invention? There is a politics of culture in these stories. Indeed, there are two different kinds of politics. First, there are issues concerning institutional power in the cultural realm, whether in museums or arts organizations. The question here is whether all interests are fairly represented and what resources are available to each. There is, however, another more subtle form of a politics of representation running through these chapters. What visual images of descriptive languages fairly represent a city? Whose vision of the city is accepted as real? Why? Here we have a profoundly important cultural contest over perception, values, and interpretation that plays itself out over time and across metropolitan space.

The final part of the book addresses the political history of cities and of New York in a nation historically suspicious of cities. It examines the relation of New York and other cities to their regions, their host nations, and to the larger transnational forms of power conventionally described in the language of globalization. The point of these chapters is to explore the opportunities available to urban citizens for a politics of justice.

Throughout, whether the domain is art or politics, there is a recurring recognition of the incompleteness—or weakness of institutional resolution— in the social and cultural formations in New York. The shifting battle lines and contingent truces that give form to metropolitan culture keep intruding and defining the cultural and political field of the metropolis. Yet however much I emphasize change, contingency, incompleteness, and the like, there are persistent rigidities in the city's history. The most important, especially in the city's modern history, is the persistence of the color line—or, better, color *lines*. It may be that the public culture of the city is more diverse than that in any other city in the country and perhaps beyond. But that said, one does not have to look far for boundaries. More important are the high if, fortunately,

not perfect, correlations that link race to joblessness and economic depriva-
tion; lack of access to adequate educational opportunities, health care, and
housing; and rates of incarceration. These domains are not examined in what
follows, but they cannot be excluded from our awareness as we examine some
of the happier domains of the city's cultural history and present circumstances.

At the center of this story is a paradox of modernity. We often think of
modernity as being revealed in a singular or unified logic. New York, which
has for most of this century been regarded as a symbol of the modern and
modern life, disrupts this notion of what modernity is, what it looks like. New
York offers a richer and more complicated experience of modernity: progress
(or newness) seems to be associated with archaism (or older ways). I want to
argue that this combination is essential to the city's modernity. Modernity is
a conversation with a past, and that past must be present. That is one reason
why the modernity of metropolitan New York must always be unfinished.

Not all commentators would agree. When Le Corbusier visited New York
in the 1930s, he was deeply impressed by the skyscrapers, the new, and he
assumed that the logic of modernity was for the whole of Manhattan to
become a world of skyscrapers. That, indeed, is what happened to São Paulo,
Brazil. But New York's culture and politics are richer and more resourceful
precisely because there are important points of resistance to that modernist
vision of completion: not only Central Park, which Le Corbusier admired;
but also Tribeca, Soho, and Greenwich Village, which he thought an unhappy
example of lag. But anyone who has been to São Paulo will surely appreciate
the alternative scales, pace of life, and change of color represented in New
York by the depressed area between what F. Scott Fitzgerald called the two
"sugar lumps" of downtown and midtown buildings. It is this mixture of the
old and the new, the low and the high, the mixed and the pure, the plethora
of small enterprises and the large corporate culture that gives special meaning to New York, the oldest large city in the United States.

Perhaps the street plan of Manhattan can stand as a closing example of the
city's special and complex way of being modern. The grid that marked out the
new city in 1811, just as a similar grid had marked out the "New Town" in
Enlightenment Edinburgh a few years earlier, seems simple—a commitment
to a modern clarity. But like much in New York, it gets more complex with
examination. As one walks north from the Battery, one moves through and

beyond a medieval street plan, one populated in our time by skyscrapers. When one crosses Houston Street, one enters a new world of "rational" planning reminiscent of the grid devised by Thomas Jefferson to organize the Northwest Territory. Jefferson sought to create identical sections of farmland for his agrarian democracy (in this instance, uncomplicated by slavery, which was prohibited in the territory). Similarly, the commission that created the 1811 plan for New York was also producing republican lots of equal size. Moreover, with a plan that ignored topography, each of the blocks was represented as identical with all others. But of course, the landscape was not undifferentiated, and the social distribution of wealth over the grid gave lie to its possible egalitarian principles.

Indeed, the very uniformity of the plan may have enabled its own subversion. One might think that the grid would produce rational uniformity, even monotony. But it need not, and often has not. The uniform grid has often energized New York by liberating the deviant. The architect Edward Larrabee Barnes grasped this point. At the time when he was designing the skyscraper that meets the southwest corner of Madison Avenue and Fifty-seventh Street at an angle, he observed that the grid enables experimentation and the rejection of its own logic. Since the grid limits the damage done by deviation, one is free to challenge it without risking an intolerable cost. Again, New York defies the logic of closure, of resolution, and that is what produces both its special strengths and its weaknesses. These metropolitan complexities—and the tensions they both reveal and produce—are the concerns of the chapters that follow.

PART I

ICONS OF
TRANSFORMATION

1

WASHINGTON SQUARE
IN THE GROWING CITY

The narrative of Manhattan's development has been shaped by geography. The long, narrow island directed growth north; farms were relentlessly replaced by houses and businesses. This basic narrative was neatly captured in the title of a fine popular history by Charles Lockwood, *Manhattan Moves Uptown: An Illustrated History* (1976). Filling the island was the work of the nineteenth century. Greater New York was created in 1898, and metropolitan growth spilled into the boroughs and suburbs in three states. And of course, when the building lots of Manhattan were seemingly filled, the sky above became the space of ever taller buildings. There is a sense of the inevitable in this metropolitan narrative. Yet even the most ambitious New Yorkers at the beginning of the nineteenth century could not have imagined such growth; nothing like it had ever occurred in the history of cities.

The story of an upward march seems to be determined by the famous 1811 Plan, which ambitiously platted the city from roughly today's Houston Street in the south to 155th Street at the northern end of the island. Certainly the streets were there, supporting a notion of a city with a south-to-north dynamic. Indeed, our sense of New York as a city of movement focuses on the avenues—all too often clogged—and the subways that move us uptown and downtown. The basic motion of New York is uptown and downtown, and it seems that this motion was inscribed in the 1811 Plan. Yet to read the plan in this fashion is to fall into an ahistorical misreading.

The traffic-jammed avenues may offer a clue. If New York was to be a north-south city, why are the avenues so few and far between? Why do the short blocks marking the numbered streets result in so many paths to the east and west edges of the island? Is it possible that an east-west city was envisioned, with the main objective of the street system being access to the water, the key to the city's economy? One of the great changes in the urban perception of New Yorkers was the shift from an east-west orientation to a north-south one.

The origin of the shift can be located, as we shall see, in the development of Washington Square and Greenwich Village. Its incorporation into the spatial perception of the city was accomplished only over the course of the nineteenth century. Yet important traces of the earlier structure of urban perception remained well into the twentieth century. Forty-second Street provides an example. Today, Forty-second Street is a marker of midtown and of our progress (or lack of it) uptown or downtown. But when the United Nations was built, Forty-second Street defined the heart of the city not as a marker but rather as a major crosstown thoroughfare. The UN became one bookend for that public space, while the still vital piers provided the other to the west. Recall the institutions of culture and power that lined the street in the 1950s: the United Nations, the Daily News Building, the Chrysler Building, the Mobil Building, the Chanin Building and Bowery Savings Bank, Grand Central Station, the New York Public Library, the *New York Times*, the Knickerbocker Hotel, the New Amsterdam Theatre, and the McGraw-Hill publishing company. One could add to the list, but the point is that so late as the 1950s (and a few years later the magnificent Ford Foundation building would be added) this east-west line fairly represented the culture and power of the city. Of course, each building had its own unique reasons for being there, but the ensemble is the point, and it gave meaning to Forty-second Street that is no longer present to us. We have lost that meaning of Forty-second Street, though proposals for a trolley could recover it.

My intention here is to interrupt the obvious narrative, enabling us to pause a bit, making it easier to notice the complex imaginings, attitudes, and feelings about the city's growth. It was not so smooth as the commonsense narrative suggests. One way of doing this is to focus on what I call *icons of transformation*. Throughout the history of the city, certain spaces and structures seem to represent a moment when the city becomes something else (or failed to become an expected something else). By examining them closely, one might grasp some of the complexity of development, particularly the weaving together of the familiar and the new, nostalgia and adventure, the archaic and the novel.

We can all reel off a number of such instances beyond the 1811 Plan: the development of South Street, City Hall and City Hall Park, Union Square, Central Park, the subway, Grand Central Station, Times Square, black Harlem, public housing, the World Trade Center, Soho. There are also icons of what did not happen: Audubon Terrace, Columbus Circle, the Bowery and Canal Street approaches to the Manhattan Bridge, the Williamsburg Savings Bank Tower in Brooklyn, Chrystie-Forsythe, and the constantly discussed but never built Second Avenue subway. We could all make our lists. In this and the following two chapters, I have selected three icons to explore phases in the development of Manhattan: Washington Square, the Brooklyn Bridge, and the skyscraper and skyline.

Nothing so charmingly illustrates the complexity of the move uptown than the relation of the new (and present) City Hall, which was completed in 1811, to the famous grid plan of the city adopted in the same year. The City Hall's east, west, and south facades were finished with impressive and expensive white marble. The northern one, the back of the building, was faced with cheaper brownstone. Assuming that a perspective on the City Hall from the north was unlikely for many years to come, a group of city fathers had decided to save the taxpayers' money. The decision seemed reasonable at the time, but events rapidly overtook their assumption. Another group of men, the commissioners appointed to organize the cityscape for future development, had a very different vision. Their plan—the famous grid plan—imagined a Manhattan filled, and they plotted blocks, 2,028 of them, north to 155th Street. Their projection of the city invited ridicule, but they had better grasped the transformation of New York that would follow the War of 1812 and the construction of the Erie Canal.

It is often said that these planners described New York in its modern form. If one considers the cultural assumptions that underlay the map as well as the lines they drew, the modernity of the plan is less clear. In fact, they assumed an eighteenth-century city, one oriented to the waterfront, one in which work and home, employer and employee (apprentice and journeyman) were all in a single building. There was none of the movement to and from work that so shapes the culture and quality of life in the modern metropolis.

The organization of space proposed in the 1811 Plan created the terrain for a reorganization of social life that would transform urban culture, even though the commissioners apparently did not anticipate it. These changes created modern New York, and much of their cultural meaning can be illuminated by reflecting on the relation of the history of Washington Square to the growth of the larger city of New York between 1830 and 1890.

The usefulness of Washington Square's history in this connection does not derive from its representative character. The development around the Square is not a microcosm of developments in the city at large. Though it is representative of the first stage of the creation of the modern city—the development of distinctively residential districts—it does not participate in most of the innovative tendencies that shaped the city after about 1850. In the second half of the century, rather, the Square's development provides an older perspective from which to view the newer ways of growth in New York.

Washington Square was born in death. During the yellow fever epidemic of 1798, in which 1,310 New Yorkers died, the city established an out-of-town burial ground on the present site of the park. Over the next three decades it was a potter's field where the indigent were buried. It was also the burial place for those who met their end on the hangman's tree at the northwest corner of the present park.

Greenwich Village, a sleepy country town, lay to the west of this ground. It was the location of the state's first prison (at the foot of Christopher Street), some farms, and summer retreats for the city's elite, particularly when epidemics hit the city. The severe yellow-fever epidemic of 1822 caused a rather large influx of city people, and after the epidemic subsided, significant numbers stayed. By 1825 the editor of the *New York Commercial Advertiser* could remark that "Greenwich is now no longer a country village. Such has been the growth of our city that the building of one block more will completely connect the two places." Two years later the city government decided to convert the burial ground into a parade ground and to open Fifth Avenue to development. The official opening of the Square took place on July 4, 1828, with a great public barbecue for which two roasted oxen and two hundred hams were prepared.

During the late 1820s and 1830s, residential construction began in the neighborhood of the Square. What James Fenimore Cooper called "second-rate genteel houses" went up in the 1820s in the area now designated the Charlton–King–Van Dam Historic District, while elegant upper-class homes were built on Bleecker Street, especially the block known as LeRoy Place between Mercer and Greene streets, and east of Broadway on Bond and Great Jones streets and Lafayette Place. All this new building represented a revolution in urban life. The development of residential neighborhoods around the Square was the first instance in the city of the modern pattern of life that separates work and residence. It was in the region of Washington Square that an exclusively residential housing market for middle- and upper-class commuters was created. This event marked not only a new spatial order in the city, but a new social order as well. The reorganization of urban space was ultimately bound up with the formation of the modern class system and gender relations.

What happened at Washington Square was generated by changes downtown. By the 1820s the growth of downtown business had overrun residential streets. The volume of commercial activity along the East River grew rapidly, particularly with the opening of the Erie Canal, and commerce spilled from Pearl onto Wall Street. There had long been a few commercial buildings, mostly banking and insurance companies, on the street, but there was nothing about the scale, outward appearance, or even the level of traffic they generated that sharply distinguished these businesses from residences. By the end of the 1820s, however, the general onslaught of commerce had made the street unsuitable for residence. Wall Street became the first fashionable residential street to fall before commerce. As early as 1819 John Pintard, secretary of the Mutual Insurance Company at 52 Wall Street, complained about the changes on the street. The company had provided him with an apartment above the office, and, as the character of the street changed, his rent-free residence became less and less attractive. In a letter to his daughter, he described the discomforts that caused middle-class New Yorkers to seek purely residential neighborhoods. "Our abode," he wrote, "is not very favourable to make domestics contented, being attended with many inconveniences in consequence of the office which supports me." After bemoaning the cost of obtaining a house elsewhere and hoping that perhaps next year prices might fall, he concluded: "Let us live in hope of better accommodations for Mama and Sister, who are nearly prisoners during the hours of business in Wall Street."

Gulian Verplanck, who grew up on Wall Street during the 1790s in a house whose garden abutted Federal Hall, remarked in 1829 on the changes in the district:

> Pine Street is now full of blocks of many tall buildings, which overshadow the narrow passages between, and make it one of the gloomiest streets in New-York. The very bricks there look of a darker hue than in any other part of the city; the rays of the sun seem to come through a hollower and thicker atmosphere. . . . It was not thus thirty or forty years ago. Shops were on each side of the way, low cheerful looking two-story buildings, of light-coloured brick or wood, painted white or yellow, and which scarcely seemed a hindrance to the air and sunshine.

Though Verplanck complains of five-story buildings that we today romanticize, we cannot miss the modernity of the complaint. Dissatisfaction with living conditions was the motive for moving north. We must not, however, discount the rather large sum that one might obtain by selling one's home to a developer who wished to turn it or the site on which it stood to commercial uses. Philip Hone, who in 1836 fled the rapidly developing City Hall area for a new home on Bond Street, complained in his diary of having to move. Yet, as he put it: "I have turned myself out of doors, but $60,000 is a great deal of money."

Domestic life was being transformed, by shifts in cultural sensibility as well as by changes in the economy. New standards of domesticity embraced particularly by women demanded a reform of the household. Finer china and other furnishings marked a new aspiration for family life. These new ideals made the presence of apprentices in the household an anomaly, while commercial activity became unwelcome; not only in the home but even in the neighborhood (a new concept) it seemed incompatible. The culture of sentimentality adopted by American Protestantism and available in a more provocative form in the European novels that the clergy condemned offered the ideal of a purified and feminine domesticity. These developments sharpened gender differences, and they separated the home from the increasingly dynamic and apparently worrisomely amoral capitalist economy.

When, in pursuit of such refinement and purity the middle and upper classes fled the downtown districts, they escaped the din of business in their domestic lives. They also segregated themselves from the working class and impoverished classes who remained downtown. The privatization of family life was advanced, while the range of social experience inherent in everyday life was narrowed, thus creating the spatial arrangement that enabled and required the message later delivered to the middle classes by Jacob Riis in his classic book, *How the Other Half Lives* (1890).

Social etiquette was complicated for the middle classes by the extension of the city beyond the tight, walking city of the eighteenth century. Commenting on his annual New Year's rounds in 1830, John Pintard told his daughter that "our city grows so extensive and friends so scattered that a pedestrian has enough to do to pay his compliments." The spatial reorganization of the city may also have encouraged the gender differentiation of cultural life. Men and women spent their time in different parts of town, and elite cultural organizations that were located downtown and depended on the participation of men and women, like the New York Atheneum, were dissolved, to be replaced by more specialized and gendered organizations.

While the middle classes were establishing themselves in a "suburban" pattern of living, which architectural critic Montgomery Schuyler noted in the 1890s probably provided the cheapest and most comfortable housing New York's middle classes ever had, the working classes and poor found it increasingly difficult to find adequate housing. In the late eighteenth century, apprentices and young journeymen still lived with their masters. But as apprentices were gradually depressed to the status of permanent wage earners, and masters became manufacturers and capitalists, this pattern of social relations came to an end. Living with the master had been a stage in the life cycle of the young apprentice. By the time he was ready to marry, he would be a master himself, could obtain his own house—and take in other apprentices and journeymen. With the breakdown of this traditional pattern of expectations in the emerging capitalist market economy, workers who were low paid and who would remain so had to find cheap housing for themselves and the families they formed.

At first ordinary houses were subdivided. Several unrelated families might live in a house that had earlier housed an artisan's extended household. By the late 1840s, however, New York had invented the tenement house, a new building type that acknowledged the new class structure. There were no tenements around the middle- and upper-class Square, but south of the Square, as Bleecker Street declined in the years following 1850, they emerged in numbers. The tenement replaced the second-rate genteel houses east of the Bowery and created on the Lower East Side a pattern of residence that would accommodate working-class and poor New Yorkers for more than a century to come. While middle-class residences rushed up the avenues after 1869 with the aid of elevated railroads, the immigrant poor were crowded into tenements. By 1876 50 percent of the city's population lived in tenements—residents who accounted for 65 percent of the city's deaths and an appalling 90 percent of the deaths of children under five.

It is no accident or mere coincidence that neighborhoods such as the one around Washington Square emerged at about the same time that the Lower East Side developed into a vast tenement district, extending from Cherry Street, where George Washington resided as president, to Mulberry Street, where Stephen Van Rensselaer in 1816 built a house that still stands, to once-fashionable Tompkins Square, which the *New York Herald* in 1860 described as having that "dusty, dirty, seedy, and 'all used up' appearance peculiar to the East Side of town." These developments are architectural expressions of the new social order. In a curious, perhaps even perverse way, something of the connection between the elegant row houses on Washington Square and the emerging slums was captured in the oft-expressed desire of visitors to the city in the 1840s, including Charles Dickens, to see the houses on the north of Washington Square and the Five Points, the city's most notorious slum, near City Hall.

Beginning in the 1850s the class division of the city was further inscribed in the city's architectural styles. If the tenement was class specific, so was the brownstone. While the brick Federal or, later, Greek Revival house served both merchant and artisan as a residential type (though larger and more richly appointed for the former), the brownstone, which began to be built just north of the Square in the 1850s, as Manhattan moved north, was an exclusively bourgeois residential type. Thus the shift from red brick to brownstone, evident at Tenth Street as one walks north on Fifth Avenue, marks an important transformation in the city's social history.

When, after 1870, the city began to rise above five stories, Washington Square and the Village generally did not follow. Partly it did not for geological reasons, but it was also because the Village was isolated from downtown. Neither Fifth, Sixth, nor Seventh avenues then extended south of Bleecker Street, and the latter two (which do so now) did not until the 1920s and 1930s. Within the Village itself the peculiar street system inhibited circulation. All this limited its commercial appeal.

When New York became the administrative and financial as well as the shipping capital of an increasingly integrated national economy, a new urban building type was needed: the office building. Perhaps the first building constructed in New York exclusively for offices was the Trinity Building, erected by Trinity Church in the 1840s and located just north of the church. It was, however, only five stories high. The first office building to use a passenger elevator was the Equitable Life Assurance Building (1870), and, in the mid-1870s, the Tribune and Western Union buildings near Trinity Church were the first to challenge the church's spire for supremacy of the New York skyline. They marked the city's modernity, a point recognized by T. H. Huxley in 1876, when—spokesman for Darwinism and modern science that he was— he happily noted upon arrival in New York Harbor that these buildings, identified with modern communication and secular enlightenment ("centres of intelligence"), rather than the traditional church spire, defined the city's iconography.

By 1908 lower Manhattan had 550 buildings over ten stories high; dozens exceeded twenty stories. But with one notable exception—the Bayard-Condict Building on Bleecker just east of Broadway (Louis Sullivan's only New York building and one that expresses his artistic ideal for the tall building with remarkable clarity)—the skyscraper form bypassed the Washington Square area. Farther north at Madison Square, the new century saw the rise of the Flatiron Building and the Metropolitan Life Tower; before long, midtown became the site of a second and still-growing cluster of tall buildings. New York's emergence as an administrative center, selling office space— indeed, exporting it as a sort of commodity to national and international corporations—seems to have made no mark on the physical form of the Village. And even today, relatively few employees of this corporate and financial New York have made the Village their home.

The creation of two separate clusters of towers in Manhattan produces a striking visual image. To some the intervening district of low-rise redbrick houses offers a pleasant contrast. But to one of the twentieth century's greatest architects, the Village was an affront. In *When the Cathedrals Were White*, Le Corbusier noted of his visit to New York in the 1930s that "skyscrapers born out of national conditions in Wall Street multiplied . . . first on that site, establishing the mystically alluring city. . . . The skyscrapers then disappear in an area of several miles, an urban no man's land made up of miserable low buildings—poor streets of dirty red brick [only to] spring up suddenly in mid-town." Henry James, who by contrast was offended in 1904 by the "graceless" skyscrapers downtown that "so cruelly over-topped" his beloved Trinity Church, found the "salt that saves" at Washington Square, particularly in the "priceless" house that survived on the corner of Fifth Avenue and Washington Square until it was destroyed in 1950 to make way for the high-rise apartment building at 2 Fifth Avenue.

As people, fashion, and commerce moved up Broadway and Fifth Avenue, Washington Square rather quickly became, as Edith Wharton reminds us in *The Age of Innocence*, "old New York." In the decades following 1850, Fifth Avenue gradually came to be lined with brownstone homes, more charming perhaps in memory than they were in fact. From literature we get a sense of darkened interiors, and from old photographs a sense of a monotonous streetscape. Today, the Salmagundi Club at Twelfth Street, one of the first of the Fifth Avenue Italianate brownstones (and one of the larger ones), is the last survivor on the avenue.

The scale and values of old New York that had established themselves on the Square were further distanced from changes in elite life in the city when the growing post–Civil War millionaire (and multimillionaire) class, led by the Vanderbilts and their architect, Richard Morris Hunt, built a series of houses on Fifth Avenue. With these limestone piles, the color of elite New York turned from brown to white, and the "bourgeois mansion" was, in the words of con-temporary architecture critic Montgomery Schuyler, "expanded into a palace."

The growth of Greenwich Village stopped almost as quickly as it began. By the 1850s the rate of residential growth leveled off in the Village and below Fourteenth Street generally, save for the Lower East Side. In 1850 George Templeton Strong remarked in his diary: "How this city marches northward." As a young man in 1830, living down on Greenwich Street with his parents, he went on his evening walks to the edge of the city, no farther than Fourteenth Street. By 1871, however, the diarist recorded that these walks now took him up as far as the seventies. By 1864 one-half of the city's population resided above Fourteenth Street. In view of the elite character of the Washington Square neighborhood, it is perhaps even more interesting that the rich moved above Fourteenth Street even faster than the general population. When, in 1851, the *New York Herald* published a list of the city's two hundred richest men, it turned out that one–half of them lived above Fourteenth Street, mostly on Fifth Avenue. An earlier list, published but five years before, listed only twenty of the two hundred men living north of Fourteenth Street.

If Washington Square thus became in some degree isolated from the latest tendencies of business and fashion during the second half of the nineteenth century, it had for this very reason a special appeal to some, an appeal that has not entirely vanished, even as we begin the twenty-first century. An eddy in the northward flow of Manhattan life, Washington Square became the physical manifestation of collective memory, of history. In 1857 Alexander Lakier, a Russian visitor to New York, observed that history in the city ended with Washington Square. "It is remarkable," he wrote, "that the streets intersecting Broadway up to Washington Square have historical names but beyond there are numbered 1 to 131, as if history had become exhausted and refused to serve the imagination." What Lakier derived from street names, Henry James deduced from greater familiarity with, and a fuller appreciation of, the texture of the city. Uptown, he reflected in *Washington Square*, the "extension of the city" assumes a "theoretic air." At Washington Square, however, there was the appearance of "having had something of a social history."

In a city defined by movement, energy, and the struggle to be heard, the Square offered relief. Young Walt Whitman, lover of the sights, sounds, and smells of the city, nonetheless cried out in 1842: "What can New York— noisy, roaring, tumbling, bustling, stormy, turbulent New York—have to do with silence?" Three-quarters of a century later, Edith Wharton, so different from Whitman otherwise, similarly but even more succinctly exclaimed: "New York is overwhelming and I am overwhelmed." Speaking of Washington Square in 1880, James noted that "this portion of New York appears to many persons the most delectable. It has a kind of established repose which is not of frequent occurrence in other quarters of the long, shrill city." For Richard Watson Gilder, editor in the 1890s of the prestigious *Century Magazine*, the neighborhood of Washington Square stood as "an island of no pressure, a place to pull out for a while."

The quarter around the Square, known as the "American ward," began to receive an influx of immigrants at the turn of the century. The area had historically been a center of residence for Manhattan's black community, but now as blacks and some of the old white "Americans" moved north, they were replaced by immigrants, mostly Italian. Carmine Street, a historically black neighborhood, became Italian, as it remains, and an Italian church, Our Lady of Pompeii, arose on the site of an earlier black church. It was this Village, marked by both an older feel and new populations, that was so attractive to the city's famous bohemians, and it was this mixed neighborhood that was the subject of Caroline Ware's classic study, *Greenwich Village, 1920–1930*, published in 1935.

The degree to which life in the Village diverged from the Protestant ideal of American culture made it all the more attractive to the cultural innovators who established themselves in the neighborhood before World War I. Enlisting modernism against modernization (with its large organizations and depersonalization), rejecting the genteel and provincial culture of brownstone New York, the self-consciously modern Greenwich Village intellectuals found in this homey atmosphere around the Square what the poet Floyd Dell called a "moral health resort"—right in the middle of the quintessentially modern city. Here they found space for cultural experimentation—in their understanding of the relations between the sexes, in art, and in politics.

The story of Washington Square reminds us that development and citymaking are not the same. Too often that is forgotten in New York. The logic of contemporary development fails to recognize that metropolitan modernity is not monolithic, nor is the making of the modern a wholly linear process. Diversities, complexities, and alternatives are woven into modern city culture. To find the soul of a city is to explore the relations among the different spaces and cultures that urban complexity nourishes. That is what distinguishes the city from the monocultural suburbs and the so-called New Urbanism.

2

BROOKLYN BRIDGE

The 1880s mark the emergence of a metropolitan conception of society in the United States. At about the time of the opening of the Brooklyn Bridge, the United States Bureau of the Census released two fat volumes entitled *Social Statistics of Cities*. While primarily compendia of statistics collected for the 1880 census, these volumes, conceived and authorized by New York City reformer George Waring, develop the notion of metropolitanism. There are two aspects of the concept as he presents it. One, which I will not consider here, concerns the way in which a national hierarchy of cities was assuming the role of organizing American social and economic life. The other concerns the internal development of urban places, the extension and specialization that was increasingly giving character to the great cities of the nation, and to New York in particular.

There are many dimensions to the emergence of New York City as an example of metropolitan culture, and the Brooklyn Bridge, opened in 1883, is closely associated with most of them. However, I will concentrate on changing perceptions of urban culture. I want to explore changes in the structure of urban self-perception, changes in the way the city represented its urbanity to itself and to others from the late eighteenth century to the early twentieth century. The construction of the Brooklyn Bridge falls midway in this long period of American history, and it marks the point when Brooklyn and other non-Manhattan areas became part of the city's self-conception. The Brooklyn

1. General View of the Brooklyn Bridge, East from the Tribune Building, ca. 1890. Courtesy of the Museum of the City of New York

Bridge itself, in its iconography, its technology, and its function, provides in fact a particularly rich example and symbol of this process of urban reconfiguration. (Figure 1)

When one looks at surviving paintings and engravings of late–eighteenth century New York, one finds two related ways in which the city is represented. Always the city is understood as a heightened place, a node, within an agrarian and village landscape. In this context it has an economic exchange function, and it serves as the locale for institutions understood as distinctive to the city, those that manifest either political power or the society's social surplus. The exchange function is portrayed by showing the rural hinterland and the ship-crowded harbor. The specialness of the urban environment is represented by pictures of public architecture, pictures of major political, economic, religious, or cultural institutions, such institutions as Trinity Church or St. Paul's Chapel, City Hall, the Park Theatre, Columbia College. (Figure 2)

It is rare that one comes upon pictures of residences; domestic life did not make city life special, so it was not at this time part of the city's presentation

2. Park Theatre, "A View of the New Theatre in New York," frontispiece image from *New York City Directory*, published by Longworth, 1797. Image by J. Allen and Tisdale. © Collection of the New-York Historical Society

of its urbanity. Nor was the city yet understood as a distinctive sociological phenomenon. In nearly all pictures, people are either absent or marginal; the specialness of city culture is not yet thought to be captured in its unique energy and motion. Nor is it to be found in the color and human diversity displayed in its public places. One begins to get a premonition of this new sense of the city in some of the minor fiction of the 1830s and 1840s. The first example, by Charles A. Briggs, bears the slightly bizarre title, *The Trippings of Tom Pepper* (1847), and like Balzac and Dickens—his contemporaries—Briggs provides glimpses of a vast array of urban types. Of course, a decade later, with *Leaves of Grass* (1855 et seq.), Walt Whitman captures and gives full-throated voice to the manifold dimensions of the new kind of dynamic and diverse human ensemble New York had become.

The modern form of Manhattan above Houston Street dates from the 1811 Plan, which, we now see, had in it the inherent possibilities of such dynamism and motion. But this seems not to have been the way it was understood at the time. Neither the text of the plan nor its visual presentation suggests an anticipation of expansion of spatial experience that comes with the conversion of the avenues into channels of almost delirious movement uptown and downtown. Nor is there any inkling that the streets and ferries would sustain the rich, distinct, and compressed metropolitan culture that so fascinated Whitman and continues to fascinate us all.

The plan assumed a city of houses, an almost infinite increase in the number of houses. The prospect of such a vast increase of population, which the commissioners courageously and presciently predicted, did not seem to imply a new kind of social experience. Growth, as late as the 1820s, when James Hardie published his survey of new houses built in the year 1824, seemed to involve merely quantitative changes, not qualitative ones.[1] Hardie, in the interest of settling a bet about the growth of the city, proposed to resolve the dispute by counting the houses built in the past year. What is striking about his proposal and the resulting book is that he felt so confident that he knew the city so well he would be able to identify every new residence. Equally striking is his assumption, unstated because so obvious, that growth was merely numerical. The city had not yet become, as it would, more complex than such a count could grasp. For him at that time, development was incremental, without apparent cultural implications. The growing city did not get more complex; it was only more of the same. That would soon change.

During the 1830s Broadway came to symbolize the special urban quality of New York, and the Broadway that is represented in picture after picture is marked by dynamic motion, crowding, excitement, and diversity. These pictures speak immediately to us; here is New York as street life, fashion, movement. And the novelty of the urbanity of the 1830s is made even more apparent and more precisely dated when we compare pictures from the 1830s with pictures from about 1820. For example, the visual representation of Broadway at City Hall in 1818 is remarkably static. But fifteen or twenty years later, after the building of the Astor House in 1836, the place became a "hot spot" on the grid of New York—a locale where New York's special intensity was created and represented by the conjunction of major political, religious, amusement, learned, and communications institutions. (Figures 3 and 4) Besides City Hall, there was St. Paul's Chapel, Barnum's American Museum, newspaper row, and the Astor Hotel, the place where all important visitors stopped and the New York elite often dined.

3. Broadway and City Hall, 1818, by Baron Axel Klinkowsrom. Courtesy of the Museum of the City of New York (Bequest of Mrs. J. Insley Blair)

4. Broadway from Astor House, 1850. Drawing by August Kollner, lithograph by Deroy. Courtesy of the Museum of the City of New York (J. Clarence Davies Collection)

By the middle of the century, New York had become largely incomprehensible in traditional terms. The scale and pace of urban development were profoundly disorienting. The city could no longer be grasped in a single walk or in a single view, not even from St. Paul's steeple or the Latting Tower that stood at the site of today's Bryant Park. The city had become multiple environments, unknown to each other. The city as a shared experience was no longer immediate; it was now mediated by the new mass-circulation newspapers. Awareness of the various worlds of the city was now achieved only through the press. New principles of social order began to give a new kind of coherence to the vastly expanded social geography of the city. Transportation lines and public places, the most notable being the new Central Park, made up the cognitive map of the city, something evident in both pictures and guidebooks of the period. It is precisely this strategy that one finds in Horatio Alger's most famous "rags to riches" fiction, the one that established his career: *Ragged Dick, or Street Life in New York* (1867). Dick Hunter, the protagonist, introduces the reader and his middle-class friend who will be his aegis to respectability to the logic of the city. He reveals the secret of this city as he knew it, by following the horse-car lines north from City Hall, to Union Square, to Fifth Avenue, to Central Park.

By the 1860s, six railroads extended up Manhattan. In 1868, the first elevated line was constructed, running up Greenwich Street and Ninth Avenue from the Battery to Thirtieth Street. It was followed by the Third Avenue Elevated in 1878, the Sixth Avenue El in 1879, and the Second Avenue El in 1880. The city in the 1880s was in motion, in linear motion. Many pictures of the era show the elevated lines extending into infinity. (Figure 5)

The final three decades of the nineteenth century saw the undeveloped land of Manhattan largely filled up. By the end of the century, Manhattan had expanded to its horizontal limits. Much of this development was residential. Just as had been assumed in the 1811 Plan, block after block of uptown Manhattan was developed for residential use. But the avenues channeled immense urban energy up and down the island in a way not foreseen in 1811. New forms of technology of transportation and communication enabled this process of urban growth to continue, if not infinitely then at least to a very great extent. In 1879, Frederick Law Olmsted, the planner of both Prospect and Central Parks, wrote a remarkable article in the *New York Daily Tribune* assessing New York's metropolitan prospects. The most serious obstacle to the

5. The "El" on Columbus Avenue, 1879. Courtesy of the Museum of the City of New York

achievement of metropolitan status, he thought, was the incredible crowding faced not simply by the poor but by the bourgeoisie of New York City as well. The 16- or even 18-foot frontage increasingly being used for residential lots produced unacceptable middle-class domestic arrangements. By means of improved transportation and the telephone and telegraph, it was possible, he explained, to vastly extend the residential area of great cities. He saw evidence of a new pattern of metropolitan living that ought to be encouraged. There is, he noted, a modern tendency toward a double movement in cities—a movement "to concentration for business and social purposes . . . and to dispersion for domestic purposes." The first leads to "compact and higher buildings, the other toward broader, lower, and more open building in residence quarters."[2]

This was precisely the context for the annexation of the Bronx. Indeed, the major front-page story in the issue of the *Tribune* carrying Olmsted's article concerned plans for extending rapid transit to the Bronx, or the "Annexed Territory" as it was then called. This was, as well, the logic behind the proposal for the Brooklyn Bridge. Although Brooklyn was the third largest city in the country, it did not envision surpassing New York as a business center. Its ambition was to be part of a metropolis. Its hope—and the hope of the real estate interests behind the Bridge project—was for residential, not commercial growth. As the Reverend Richard Storrs, Brooklyn's most esteemed minister, remarked in his address at the opening ceremonies, the bridge brought Brooklyn "nearer to all that was enriching and endearing in the Metropolis," while it enabled Brooklyn to offer "its broad expanse of uncovered acres . . . for those who wish homes."[3]

The logic for the bridge was the same as the logic for the later consolidation of the metropolis. Indeed, the first "official" proposal for consolidation was made just when the Bridge project was getting underway. In 1868, Andrew H. Green, Commissioner of Central Park and later a bridge trustee, argued for consolidation, hoping that it would generate a "common perception" of the region that would in turn ensure better management of comprehensive development.[4]

In the years between the opening of the Bridge and the consolidation of the city in 1898, one finds a certain pattern in discussions of the emerging metropolis. Three themes recur: there is talk of the parts of the city (that is, business, residence, recreation), talk about public works as a civic responsibility and opportunity, and talk of transportation improvements that would order and connect the whole metropolis. And there is an uncomfortable avoidance of the immigrant masses in the Lower East Side and elsewhere. Underlying this talk and silence there was a rather specific—if a bit schematic—notion of the bourgeois city's social geography: business in lower Manhattan, middle-class homes on Park Slope, and recreation at Central Park and Coney Island. New forms of transit linked them all, thus providing the ligaments of metropolitan urbanity for the bourgeoisie. All of this amounts to a new perception of the city, one that grew more and more prominent in the city's self-understanding as the twentieth century advanced. This perception is different from that of the eighteenth century, which emphasized civic institutions, and that of the mid–nineteenth century, which represented itself in terms of street life.

The linear extension that began in Manhattan with the railroads and elevated lines reached the boroughs soon after the turn of the century. The Brooklyn Bridge was followed by the opening of the Williamsburg Bridge in 1903 and the Manhattan and Queensboro Bridges in 1909. Bridges to the Bronx proliferated: the most important were the Third Avenue (1898), Willis Avenue (1901), University Heights (1908), and Madison Avenue (1910) Bridges. These transportation arteries gave shape to the city. Increasingly, the arterial flow of traffic was seen as the starting point for urban planning. By the 1920s the central preoccupation of the newly developed city planning profession was the management and control of traffic.

But the precedent and meaning of the Brooklyn Bridge for metropolitan New York extends beyond other bridges and roads. The social geography of the modern metropolis derives from a less visible, but equally remarkable technological feat: the subway system. The city we know was defined topographically by the subways; the vast pattern of subway stations gives us an orientation to the metropolis independent of its natural geography. The IRT's 1904 line did not immediately connect Manhattan with the boroughs, but a Brooklyn-Manhattan connection was completed in 1908. The real definition of the city by the subway system resulted from the additions to the system that were authorized by the so-called dual contract in 1913.[5] The expansion undertaken between 1913 and 1917 dotted the boroughs with recognizable place names and gave New Yorkers an extensive cognitive map, shaped by stations rather than local streets or natural topography. (I should say *two* cognitive maps—one for each subway company, each of which denied, in effect, the existence of the city served by the other.) Figures on the increase in single-fare stations during these years reveal the magnitude of the expansion: the number of stations in Brooklyn went from 11 to 193; those in Queens went from 0 to 41; and those in the Bronx from 29 to 75.

The city was unified perceptually and practically on a metropolitan scale for the first time. Subway maps, carried in the minds of New Yorkers, gave definition to the newly unified metropolis. By this time one can say that the greater city, with its 365 square miles and its outlying suburbs, was unified by a complex city and regional transportation system that included railways, street railways, subways, elevated trains, bridges, roads, and until as late as World War II, ferries (which are reemerging today).

Geographical extension, arrayed along and perceived in connection with transportation lines, represents, however, only part of the perceptual transformations associated with the Brooklyn Bridge. If its magnificent span symbolizes extension and horizontal expansion, its great towers point toward the vertical qualities of the skyscraper city that New York had become by the turn of the century. In 1876 the great bridge towers challenged Trinity Church's spire for dominance on the skyline; in the same year the *Tribune* Building and the Western Union Building, two monuments to modern business and communication, surpassed, or in Henry James's phrase "cruelly overtopped," that traditional symbol of religious authority and civic aspiration. By the 1890s the concentration of commercial development at the foot of Manhattan had produced a unique skyline and surely the most widely recognized icon of New York life.

Just as the aesthetic movement of the Brooklyn Bridge is at once vertical and horizontal, so the dynamism and energy of New York City during the half century following the opening of the bridge was both horizontal and vertical. These two movements expressed the urbanity of the city; they represented two intertwined ways of grasping the metropolis.

It is this emerging conception of the metropolis that is crystallized in the famous *Regional Plan of New York and Its Environs*, published in several vol-

6. View of the New York Waterfront, 1876, by J. N. Beals. Courtesy of the Museum of the City of New York

umes in the late 1920s and early 1930s. It was conceived in 1911, on the centennial of the 1811 Plan, and it was intended to provide a metropolitan "framework for growth" for a huge region including three states, 5,528 square miles, and 421 separate communities. Basic to the plan was a notion of the city as a physical structure. The aim of the plan's director, Thomas Adams, was efficiency in locating specialized activities and in moving people and goods around. Transportation improvements made possible the arrangement of business, residence, and recreation over a vast but unified territory. A public-relations pamphlet distributed by the Regional Plan Association in 1929 expressed the vision of the city that they sought to create and assimilate into the city-planning process.

> A city's life is one of movement. People are hurrying about trying to get here and there, to work or to play. . . . Their path must be clear . . . and the right thing put and kept in the right place.[6]

> The essential feature of the Plan is the spreading out of the population over a wider area, with industries, stores, living, transportation, and recreation

facilities so arranged that the existing congestion in the central parts of the Region will diminish and traffic can move. The plan assumes that Manhattan will remain the population center of the Region. . . . [7]

Much of the reconstruction of New York identified with Robert Moses was prefigured in the Regional Plan and even, I suppose I am arguing, in the movement to build the Brooklyn Bridge. The transformation of Manhattan into a financial/administrative center at the cost of manufacturing was a central hope of the regional planners. The plan ranked central city land uses in terms of rents, giving priority thereby to office buildings, luxury housing, and luxury retail stores. The planners sought, on the other hand, to eliminate or decentralize less lucrative land uses, such as loft manufacturing, middle- and lower-class housing, and ordinary retail shopping. Finally, the Regional Plan of New York provided a comprehensive ideological defense of tall office buildings in Manhattan. What the Regional Plan envisioned—and what we got—was a slab city on Manhattan and a spread city over a three-state region.

What we did not get from the Regional Plan deserves a brief mention in conclusion. The modern New York that emerged was driven by investment opportunity; it was not one that proposed to regulate growth by a participatory political process. Writing in the *New Republic* soon after the release of the Regional Plan of New York, the young Lewis Mumford savagely attacked its logic, which he characterized as no more than an extrapolation of existing market forces. He also challenged the particular model of metropolitan regionalism offered by the authors of the plan. The Regional Plan privileged Manhattan; it was the jewel, and, in Mumford's language, the larger metropolitan area was no more than a tributary to it. His own preference was for a more balanced and environmentally defensible regional plan, relying upon the newer technologies of transportation and communication made possible by electricity. The point is not the specifics of Mumford's regionalism—which may have been too hostile to density and Manhattan—but rather his insistence on some combination of market and politics in shaping a metropolis that recognized interests other than finance.[8]

3

SKYSCRAPER AND SKYLINE

(with William R. Taylor)

Any visitor to the residential section of Battery Park City will be struck by architectural echoes. If not a copy of any particular place, it still evokes an earlier New York, with hints of Park Avenue, Gramercy Park, the Esplanade in Brooklyn Heights, and the paved walkways of Central Park. For some, including Herbert Muschamp, architecture critic for the *New York Times*, this evocation of the past is regrettable. Muschamp and his ilk would have a wholly new, avant-garde architecture for major urban design projects. Others, including investors, have found the familiar comforting, and the project undertaken by the New York State Urban Development Corporation during the 1980s in partnership with private developers has been such a financial success that cities around the world sought to imitate it. Whatever one thinks of the merits of the Battery Park City design guidelines developed by the firm of Cooper, Eckstut Associates, the interest, even fascination, inherent in these guidelines is the historical assumption that informs them: there is an older New York that belongs to common memory.

The past inferred by the architects might be styled "Early Modern" New York, a city that was in the throes of dramatic changes, absorbing thousands of immigrants, becoming the administrative center for American corporate capitalism and the center of American intellectual and cultural life. Perhaps most important of all, it was the city of progressive urban reform, which involved as one of its principal aims political and architectural representation of modern forms of public life and culture.

Between the 1890s and 1930, New York acquired its famous skyline, as well as the monumental classical structures that continue to define its public spaces. It is a period when vernacular and modern New York urban aesthetic took form.

In 1981, the urban designers Cooper, Eckstut Associates were again brought in by the Urban Development Corporation. This time the firm was commissioned to address one of the icons of New York metropolitan culture, Times Square, which had fallen on hard times. Again the New York State Urban Development Corporation envisioned a public-private partnership to redevelop the area. The guidelines looked to an architecture that would signify a renewed significance for the street, which the international modernism movement had devalued. How might the street be monumentalized and recognized as a public space at once specific to a place and corporate tenants and inviting to the city as a whole?

Again the architects drew upon an unarticulated history, one that recognized the importance of horizontal lines as opposed to verticality in defining a self-consciously civic space. They recognized that in the history of urban form in New York horizontal monumentalism has implied civic or public purposes, while the tower has represented the power of corporate capitalism. In their guidelines, therefore, they proposed to emphasize the civic or public character of Forty-second Street as a street by maintaining a traditional "five-story building wall" along it. Towers were to be kept well back from this street wall. In doing this, they were making a strong statement for public values, and they made an implicit appeal to the authority of history.

Unfortunately, the guidelines were violated by the designated developer, whose architect, Philip Johnson, proposed massive, bulky towers that ignored and intentionally diminished the street and Times Square itself.[1] Much controversy followed; the design guidelines were scrapped, and so was the Johnson plan. Soon thereafter the Disney Corporation was invited to redevelop the Square, and that is the Square we have today. But again the point is not to make a brief for or against the abandoned guidelines, for my interest concerns the continuing force of history in the controversy.[2] That assumed history will be examined here for what it tells about New York's modernity.

Architectural historians and critics committed to modernism have not been kind to New York, particularly the New York here characterized as early modern. Although New York is arguably the first modern city in the world (or at least one of them), it has not been recognized as a major contributor to the career of the modern movement in architecture.[3] Only the city's parks and parkways received ritual praise. New York between 1890 and 1930 has been treated as stuck in its devotion to mercantile values and Beaux Arts aesthetics. And this criticism continues today with critics such as Muschamp, who is not only hostile to the echoes of this period in more recent architecture, but who also finds contemporary New York as conservative as the modernists found turn-of-the-century New York. Nowhere does one find discussion of the interesting and important tug-of-war that took place between private and civic values, between vertical and horizontal structure, laissez-faire and professional efforts to give a sense of shape and unity to urban public spaces. These contests gave substance to an historically specific early New York modernism.

In no one modernist work has the combined condemnation and neglect of New York's place in the history of architecture and urban design been more clearly registered than in Sigfried Giedion's *Space, Time and Architecture: The Growth of a New Tradition* (1941 et seq.). Displaced now, this classic and highly ideological history presented itself and was received until corroded by the acids of postmodernism as the authoritative cultural history of architecture.

In Giedion's story, late–nineteenth-century Chicago fared very well, since it was there that architectural expression most closely matched structural changes. That city, accordingly, produced more than its share of modernist forerunners. New York, for Giedion, represented neoclassical architectural and planning schemes, sometimes referred to broadly as *Beaux Arts* or *eclectic*, which he scorned as being in the "troubadour spirit, pitting song against the din of modern industry." New York developments were perceived as detours, even perversions, of the logic of modernist architectural progress. He made the dual charge that the Beaux Arts eclectic neoclassicism was not responsive either to technology or to function. In a similar way he dismissed those who engaged in city planning from a neoclassical perspective: "the urbanist, like the popular painter, lost himself in the composition of idylls."[4]

These charges must now be examined skeptically and critically. More than that, it seems appropriate to make a counterclaim. Such a claim would go like this: Buried within the Beaux Arts education and locked into the work of Americans trained in Paris was a preoccupation with "ensemble," with the pattern of construction perceived collectively. This particular concern with ensemble in turn resonated with certain civic attitudes toward the city that have now all but disappeared. In New York, where in the 1890s one finds the greatest concentration of Beaux Arts–trained architects in America and where one finds them developing an evident self-consciousness, this orientation was incubated awaiting the opportunity of the ebullient building spirit at the turn of the century.[5]

A certain preoccupation with what we would call planning was implicit in the way Beaux Arts architectural students were trained to conceive of the buildings they designed. The full implications of this aspect of architectural education have never been adequately appreciated. The Beaux Arts training may not have insisted upon specific sites for buildings, but it did stress siting in general just as it stressed street-level perspectives. To some students, the next step was easy to take. And several of the best students at the Ecole assumed an urbanistic perspective: Henri Proust, Ernest Hebrard, and, most widely known and the only one acknowledged by Giedion, Tony Garnier.[6] This "radical" side of the Beaux Arts tradition was available as well to "provincials" who traveled to Paris, and it is clear that Americans trained in Paris were very receptive to it. The American version appears to have had its most pronounced expression in the architecture and urban design of New York, although Daniel Burnham may well have given it its most concise expression.[7]

The Chicago World's Fair of 1893, identified so often with Burnham and the New York architects, is the crucial event in the historiography of modernism in America. How one interprets that event, located in the American midwest, largely determines, ironically, one's capacity for understanding the urbanistic heritage of New York. The modernist interpretation, much simplified to be sure, is roughly as follows: In Chicago a commercial ethic and new technology had produced in the decades after the fire a steel-frame architecture of tall commercial buildings that exemplified what later became the dictum of modernism: form follows function. When Chicago architect Daniel H. Burnham, who with his partner John Wellborn Root had helped pioneer this new architecture, invited a group of eastern, particularly New York architects to Chicago to design the most important buildings for the World's Fair, the logic of architectural history was perverted. In contrast to the modern architecture being born downtown in Chicago, the neoclassical White City they built in Jackson Park was simply *retardaire*. Louis Sullivan's lament echoes through the history books: The Fair unleashed a "virus" that produced "an outbreak of the Classic and Renaissance in the East. . . . The damage wrought to this country by the World's Fair will last a half century. . . . "[8] According to Giedion:

> At the very moment when the Chicago school gained a mastery of the new means which it had created, its further development and influence was abruptly choked off. The event which directly effected this change was the Chicago World's Fair of 1893 (the World's Columbian Exposition), but influences working in this direction had set in long before in another section of the country. American architecture came under many different influences during the nineteenth century, but none was so strong or came at such a critical moment as the rise of power of the mercantile classicism developed in the East.

Giedion also provided a truncated historical motivation for this anomalous turn of events.

> Public, artists, and literary people believed themselves to be witnessing a splendid rebirth of the great traditions of past ages. The immense appeal of this re-created past in "the White City" can only be laid to a quite unnecessary national inferiority complex. . . . Only Louis Sullivan had sufficient inner strength to hold fast in the midst of a general surrender.

New York, as the home of "mercantile classicism," had a sinister role to play.

> Mercantile classicism had been developing and gaining strength in New York since the eighties, but it won its country-wide ascendancy at the World's Columbian Exhibition of 1893. The spirit behind it had now come to possess authority for American architecture as a whole. The Fair should,

indeed, have stood in New York; it so thoroughly represented the influence of that city.[9]

Yes, there is a sense in which the Fair belonged to New York. But it is important to understand what Burnham and his New York associates were up to and how their achievement was received and interpreted. The Beaux Arts architects of New York brought to Chicago their preoccupations with a unified neoclassical city, and at the Fair, under the leadership of Daniel Burnham, the superintendent of construction, accomplished something that was broadly urbanistic, rather than narrowly architectural. Writing at the time, Montgomery Schuyler, the best architectural critic in America, observed that "the success is first of all a success of unity, a triumph of ensemble. The whole is better than all its parts." This could not be said of any American city at the time, though some hoped it might be. Schuyler went on to point out that this unity derived from two decisions: first, the choice of a neoclassical architectural motif, and second, the regulation of cornice heights, which produced a "visually continuous skyline all around the Court of Honor." It was this horizontal visual unity that gave the Fair its public impact, not the character or architectural expression of individual buildings. Among classicists, at least, this lesson was remembered. In a major article published in *Architectural Record* (1916) under the title "Twenty-five Years of American Architecture," A. D. F. Hamlin acknowledged the "revolutionary" impact of steel framing developed in central Chicago, but he also insisted on the importance of the Fair. It represented, he argued, the first example of American design since Thomas Jefferson's plan for the University of Virginia in which a "monumental group of buildings [was] planned as an ensemble." It was, he continued, "an object lesson in the possibilities of group-planning, of monumental scale, of public decorative splendor and harmony. . . . "[10]

In retrospect, it seems clear that the modernist preoccupation with individual buildings, with overturning the architectural style of surrounding structures, and with historically singling out the new and experimental architectural expression of any age, overlooks the aesthetic lesson that can be learned from the progressivist side of the Beaux Arts tradition. This side of Beaux Arts classicism found its fullest realization not in Paris, but in America, in projects deeply influenced by New York architects. The most important of these projects were the Fair and the plans for Washington (1901) and Chicago (1909). It is probably accurate, moreover, to say that it was Charles McKim, upon whom Burnham most relied at Chicago and who took the lead in the collaboration with Frederick Law Olmsted, Jr., and Burnham on the Plan for Washington (1901) who brought this Beaux Arts ideal, via New York, to Burnham and Chicago, where it was clarified and purified before returning to New York.[11]

This progressive neoclassicism sought to monumentalize and unify the late–nineteenth century city. It moved from the architecture of the buildings to the urbanism of comprehensive planning. It stressed the street perspective, the uniform cornice, the nineteenth-century tradition of the five-story street wall, and it was a functionalist expression of new technologies of urban transportation. Giedion and other modernist historians were able to dismiss the whole enterprise because—despite their ideology of organicism and functionalism—they focused their attention, ironically, on stylistic detail, on surface. The neoclassicists "decorated" buildings; form did not express function, nor did it reveal the building technology. That was enough, apparently, to justify dismissing Burnham and the New York architects. What Giedion, preoccupied with style, did not see was the important urbanistic achievement of the Fair's neoclassicism. Such devaluation of the urbanistic dimension is hard to justify in terms of urban history, for surely the crisis of the industrial city was one of ensemble, not one of style. Most revealing of all, perhaps, is the way in which differences in style made Giedion overlook the remarkable similarities between the *Cité industrielle* of Tony Garnier, the rebel *within* the Ecole and a hero in Giedion's story, and Burnham's Chicago Plan.

Garnier's plan for an "industrial" city, first developed between 1901 and 1904, though published a decade or so later, is architecturally modern in a way that Burnham's contemporaneous Chicago Plan is not. (Garnier, for example, uses reinforced concrete and emphasized functional expression and the cleanness of materials.) Yet as understandings of urban form—and reform—the two are remarkably similar, even though one is the work of a European "socialist" and the other one of American corporate capitalism's most favored architects.

The impulse behind all these plans was a desire to rationalize the perceived chaos in existing cities and to link these sprawling, amorphous conglomerations of population to the countryside and surrounding communities.

It is difficult for us to realize how high a priority such an object could have had, or the price those making such plans were willing to pay for their fulfillment—or even something approaching fulfillment. Transportation and movement was for such planners the fundamental reality of the city. They sought to have these lines of movement converge upon a city "center" at once functional and symbolic, a central axis in a wheel-and-spoke arrangement.

In no city were the issues faced by architects and planners as vexed, the aesthetic tensions as visible, as in New York, where record population growth, commercial and industrial expansion, and novel metropolitan status were heaped upon a restricted island and an old premodern city within the compass of half a century. It is this battleground quality, and the unique character of the aesthetic treaties that resulted from it, that gives New York its architectural interest.

New York has the reputation of being a vertical city, and indeed the tall buildings crowding the battery have long been a spectacular symbol of its modernism. Yet, if we grant modernist legitimacy to certain horizontal impulses and locate New York's verticality in a dialectical relationship to that horizontalism, one finds a far richer heritage of architectural invention than a preoccupation with unrestrained thrust for height suggests.

When Henry James returned to the United States in 1904, he was displeased by the sight of the skyscrapers that had risen over the five-story city he had left twenty-five years before. As was sometimes his wont, James suggested that the thinness of American culture rendered it incapable of resisting such expressions of unrestrained commerce. New York grew skyscrapers, he seemed to say, because it lacked the density of culture required to guide growth away from purely economic and technical considerations, because it lacked, in his words, "the ancient graces." There was no higher aspiration capable of keeping the buildings down.

Another view is possible; one can read New York's development quite differently. One can see technology, economics, and a particular cultural disposition in favor of horizontal urban order interacting to form a distinctive urban form in New York City. One cannot but be struck by evidence of a sustained resistance to a vertical architecture, indeed even to the perception of verticality when it first appeared.

A case in point is the Haughwout Building, a cast-iron building put up in 1857 and still standing on the corner of Broome Street and Broadway, one of New York's most remarkable buildings. It was the first building to have an Otis elevator, and it is a building that Ada Louise Huxtable credited with anticipating all the essential elements of the skyscraper, except that it is only five stories high. But this exception is important because it points toward the essentially horizontal perception of urban form in the nineteenth century. Two illustrations of the Haughwout Building, one a wood engraving made when the building was new, the other a photograph taken when the building was nearly a century old, provide some fascinating evidence (Figures 7, 8). Today, we who have accepted the aesthetic of a vertical city apparently view the building differently from the New Yorkers who first confronted it. The engraving makes the building look flatter, less high, wider than in the photograph. Note also that the engraver faces the building head-on at street level, while the photographer, used to vertical perspectives, chooses a location well above street level to snap his photo. Since New Yorkers were unused to tall buildings in the 1850s, one would have thought that contemporaries would have been struck by the height of a building like the Haughwout. Indeed, might not one expect the engraving to exaggerate its height, thus leaving the photograph with the task of cutting it down to its proper scale? Apparently, the engraver was prepared to perceive the city in terms of horizontal rather than vertical lines. That his perception of this building was part of a collective horizontal perception of the city is suggested by a contemporaneous series of drawings on New York architecture (by many hands) run in *Putnam's Magazine* in 1853. The anonymous author of this series, probably Clarence Cook, verbalized the mid–nineteenth-century urban bias toward horizontalism in discussing A. T. Stewart's famous department store (1846), the Italianate structure still standing at Broadway and Chambers Street. While he admired the building, he worried that it was too tall, or that it gave the impression of being too tall. "This might have been remedied," he reflected, "by making the horizontal lines of the building more prominent than the perpendicular."[12]

This perceptual or, if you will, cultural resistance to verticality or height provides a crucial context for some comments of Montgomery Schuyler concerning the slow development of the skyscraper. Writing in 1909, on "The Evolution of the Skyscraper," Schuyler insisted that technology and economic

7. Haughwout Building, 1857. Courtesy of Otis Elevator Company

incentive were there before tall buildings were materialized. This discussion reveals how the technology Huxtable found in the Haughwout building was fitted into a frame of cultural or architectural perception that stressed not new possibilities of verticality but rather a continuation of the traditional five-story city. The elevator, Schuyler remarked, did not suggest an unlimited number of floors. Rather its "humble office" was simply "to equalize the desirableness of rooms on the fifth floor with that of rooms on the second." Such was the case for nearly a decade. "Such a creature of habit is man . . . that, throughout that decade, it did not occur to anybody that the new appliance might enable the construction of taller buildings." The first building to go beyond five stories with the assistance of the elevator was the Equitable Building (1870). It went to seven. "The addition of two stories now seems timid enough; then doubtless it seemed audaciously venturesome." By the mid-1870s, the *Tribune* and Western Union Buildings not only went higher, but they expressed their capacity to rise above the traditional city in the architectural treatment, particularly in Richard Morris Hunt's *Tribune* Building with its tower. Yet the evolution of the skyscraper in New York remained slow. Schuyler could find no technical reason for the delay in moving beyond the load-bearing wall to steel frame construction several years before it occurred. "Necessity," he remarked, "seems to have been singularly protracted."[13]

8. Haughwout Building, 1952. Courtesy of Otis Elevator Company

The resistance of New Yorkers to tall buildings is an interesting topic in itself, one that has dimensions other than aesthetic; but certain architectural ideas that stressed horizontal, massive, and monumental forms seem to have preoccupied New Yorkers, blunting their capacity to perceive monumentality in vertical terms. It was assumed that an appropriate civic presence, monumentalism, could be best achieved in the context of traditional horizontal lines.

This nineteenth-century configuration of urban monumentalism reached its fullest development with Pennsylvania Station (1906–1913). While retaining the ideal of the nineteenth-century street wall, this massive and magnificent railroad station by McKim, Mead, and White extended itself to cover two entire blocks. In fact, it faces another civic structure, the new post office, that monumentalizes an adjoining grid. Instead of giving the station monumental status by placing it at the termination of a diagonal avenue, as was being done in late–nineteenth-century Paris, McKim, Mead, and White achieved their purpose by framing it by the street.

The nearly contemporaneous Grand Central Terminal (1903–1913) continues the monumentalization of New York civic space along horizontal lines, but it does not so much monumentalize a block in the grid as create a megablock that in certain (but not in other) ways anticipates Rockefeller Center. It moves beyond the block on a massive scale, but rather hesitantly. By placing the station astride Park Avenue, moreover, the planners created a dramatic vista on both sides of the station that acted to monumentalize the avenue and underscore the north-south movement of traffic through the city. The circumferential drive preserves the Park Avenue street flow, while at the same time allowing Grand Central Terminal to monumentalize a perspective. While Forty-third Street is blocked, the municipal authorities insisted that the fenestration on the east and west walls be aligned so that, if necessary, a bridge could carry Forty-third Street traffic through the main concourse. Quite a similar effect was obtained in McKim, Mead, and White's contemporary Municipal Building, which stood in 1911 astride an arch that permitted a clear east-west vista along Chambers Street, once again underscoring the grid, even at the cost of certain neoclassical oddity.

The structure of Grand Central itself does not attempt to maintain the traditional five-story wall, but it saves the general principle, simply raising the height and maintaining a uniform cornice along Park Avenue. In this quarter of Manhattan, the New York Central and its land-holding company created in microcosm fulfillment of the sort of urbanism one finds in the proposals of Garnier and Burnham. Both of them focus on the hubs of rail and street traffic as the site to monumentalize. Modern technology made it possible for the city to accommodate the railroad underground while monumentalizing a unified horizontal perspective above ground.

The lineage just traced from the Haughwout Store to Grand Central outlines the expansion of the horizontal vision of New York before World War I in its most pristine form. Other examples of neoclassical civic architecture could be cited and discussed. Richard Morris Hunt's Lenox Library (1870–75), which Schuyler in 1895 rated as unrivaled when built for its achievement of "monumental dignity," and, of course, one must note Hunt's East Wing of the Metropolitan Museum of Art. While the massive New York

Public Library (1911) is also an obvious example of horizontal monumental-ism, realized with a sense of commodiousness and liberality, a much smaller building, one called by Schuyler "a modern classic," emphasizes that it is not a mere matter of size that is at issue. The Knickerbocker Bank (1904), on Fifth Avenue at Thirty-fourth Street, by McKim, Mead, and White was only three stories high, but according to Schuyler its very restraint in the matter of height gave it strength. With its tetrastyle front, the building was, in Schuyler's words, "ample in scale for purposes of impressiveness. Since it holds its own against the huge mass of the many-storied Astoria, it is not likely to be put out of countenance by any succeeding erection."[14] Finally, as further examples of horizontal monumentalism, we should note the neoclas-sical uptown campuses McKim, Mead, and White designed for New York University and Columbia University in the 1890s.

At Madison Square, however, we can trace a complicated pattern of devel-opment and of perception that brings us closer to the tensions between hor-izontal and vertical lines in the development of New York's distinctive urban aesthetic. When the Fifth Avenue Hotel opened on Madison Square in 1859, it boasted the first hotel passenger elevator in the city. Yet it was architec-turally and urbanistically of a piece with the old Astor House (1836) down-town, the hotel it replaced as New York's most fashionable place to stop and be seen. It remained within the five- to six-story street wall tradition, and it presented itself to the street. Both hotels are on Broadway frontage facing a triangular park, but such siting is clearly more comfortable for the Astor House, located as it was on Lower Broadway, before Broadway came into ten-sion with the grid imposed on New York in 1811. With the Fifth Avenue Hotel we begin to notice some of the complexity involved in imposing hori-zontal order on the New York grid. (Figure 9) Not only is the facade broken, but the multiple lines of movement produced by Broadway, Fifth Avenue, the Park, and the streetcar rails produce not only an aesthetic tension in photo-graphs and engravings, but also personal problems of movement and orien-tation in the city. This tension is multiplied further when one's gaze widens to include the curvilinear pattern of the paths in Madison Square.

Part of the success that was achieved at Penn Station and Grand Central Terminal was the result of responding to developments in transportation technology (electrification) that allowed rail transportation—both subways and trains—to be placed underground where it would not disrupt the grid.

9. Broadway and Fifth Avenue, 1893. Courtesy of Brown Brothers

The triumph of the street-level grid over the underground technology in defining horizontal movement in New York is embodied in the names given the subway stations. The subway lines do not follow a grid pattern, but the system surfaces only at streets on the grid. In contrast to the Paris Metro, for example, which is "place" oriented (very few stations are named for streets, almost all for places, such as L'Opera, L'Odeon), almost all Manhattan subway stops refer to streets. What could easily have been called the Madison Square station is called the Twenty-third Street station. This tension between surface and subsurface legibility in New York is a continuous presence.

When the Fifth Avenue Hotel was opened, Madison Square was a major transportation node. The depots of the New York & Harlem and the New York, New Haven & Hartford railroads were located just off the northeast corner of the Square. In 1873, after the first Grand Central Terminal was opened at Forty-second Street, Barnum transformed the property into a concert garden. In 1879, it was named Madison Square Garden and ten years later the famous Madison Square Garden designed by Stanford White was constructed on the site. (Figure 10) White's building is fundamentally horizontal, but it points to New York's distinctive skyscraper aesthetic. Reminiscent of the tower in Italian city states and following the New York lead of Richard Morris Hunt's Tribune Building (1873–75), White placed an expressive tower on top of a blockish building. Twenty years later, McKim, Mead, and White would do much the same thing, though with the scale vastly increased, with the Municipal Building (1911) that went up across from

10. Madison Square Garden, 1900. Courtesy of the Museum of the City of New York (Byron Collection)

Hunt's earlier Tribune Building. These developments, in effect vertical towers designed to enhance buildings of horizontal monumentality, contain the germinal aesthetic of the New York skyscraper some twenty years later. The aesthetic rationale for the modern skyscraper, ironically, was the campanile fully as much as the steel frame. But we are moving too fast. Actual events moved much slower. Madison Square Garden was not perceived as a precursor of the skyscraper. It was an entertainment center built along horizontal lines as was traditionally appropriate for monumental public architecture.

Ten years later, south of the square, another building went up. The Fuller or Flatiron Building (1901), designed by the Chicago firm of Daniel Burnham, is recognized for its height and for its steel-frame construction as one of the links in the evolution of the modern skyscraper. Yet we must ask how, in the context of the tradition of horizontal urban perception that we have traced, this architectural innovation was perceived. We gain insight into this problem by examining one of the most famous and compelling photographs made of this building, which was taken by Alfred Stieglitz in 1903. (Figure 11) It is one of the few photographs that Stieglitz talked about, and it is worth quoting him.

> In the early months of 1903 I stood spellbound, during a great snowstorm, before the Flat Iron Building. It had just been erected on Twenty-third Street at the junction of Fifth Avenue and Broadway.
>
> Watching the structure go up, I felt no desire to photograph the different stages of its development. But with the trees of Madison Square covered with fresh snow, the Flat Iron impressed me as never before. It appeared to be moving toward me like the bow of a monster ocean steamer—a picture of a new America still in the making. . . .
>
> Recalling those early days, I remember my father coming upon me as I was photographing in the middle of Fifth Avenue. "Alfred," he said, "how can you be interested in that hideous building?" "Why Pa," I replied, "it is not hideous, but the new America. The Flat Iron is to the United States what the Parthenon was to Greece." My father looked horrified. . . .
>
> Later the Flat Iron appeared rather unattractive to me, after years of having seen even taller and more extraordinary skyscrapers—the Woolworth shooting into the sky, and then still others. . . . I no longer considered it handsome, nor representative of the coming age, nor was I tempted to photograph it.[15]

11. Flatiron Building, 1903, by Alfred Stieglitz. J. Paul Getty Museum, Los Angeles. © Estate of Georgia O'Keeffe

There are many things about this passage that are of interest: Stieglitz's father's abhorrence in 1903 of a vertical aesthetic, Stieglitz's almost mystical association of urban structure with destiny, but the evocation of the ocean steamer is of particular relevance here. The image of the ship's prow suggests not vertical but horizontal conceptions of the development of the city and of American culture generally. One thinks of railroads crossing the continent, or of the streetcar lines crossing in front of the Flatiron more easily than one thinks of, say, the Empire State Building. Ships' prows were high, especially since in 1900 passengers and friends walked or rode right up to the bow of the ship at nearly the water line, but they moved horizontally. (Figure 12) The cornice line of the Flatiron building, from this perspective, suggests that there is more to come, hence the plausibility of his speaking of the building

12. Maiden Voyage of the *Lusitania*, 1907. Courtesy of the Museum of the City of New York (Print Archives)

as the leading edge of a progressive American culture. In 1903 the dynamism of American culture and urban development, at least for Stieglitz, was horizontal. Later, after a perceptual shift which we will soon describe, verticality became central to progressivism. And with many taller buildings to be seen, the Flatiron building could no longer be impressive. It was caught in a shift in urban aesthetics from horizontal to vertical. When it was the world's tallest building, Stieglitz and, we assume, others viewed it in terms of the horizontal lines it suggested. When they began to view buildings with a sensitivity to or preference for verticality, the Flatiron was no longer tall enough.

A clearer idea of the evolution of the New York skyscraper and of the perceptual shift we are discussing can be obtained still within the square by turning our attention to the Metropolitan Life Building and Tower designed by Napoleon LeBrun & Sons (business block, 1893; tower, 1909: Figure 14).

The Metropolitan Life Building accommodates the tower by placing it on top of a horizontal business block. This strategy echoes the campanile characteristic of early Renaissance Italian civic architecture, and it was not new in New York in 1909; we have already mentioned Hunt's Tribune Building and White's Madison Square Garden tower. Such a treatment of bulk—often with Italian or French Renaissance architectural detailing—was a New York tradition extending back to the era of the Haughwout Building. And its pervasiveness explains Le Corbusier's remark upon first seeing New York's skyscrapers in the 1930s:

> It is an odd thing that the modern skyscrapers are the weak ones. The Italian Renaissance skyscrapers are of excellent quality, in contradiction with what I imagined before seeing them. For, prior to 1925, Brunelleschi and Palladio were in control. . . .
>
> In New York, then, I learned to appreciate the Italian Renaissance. It is so well done that you could believe it to be genuine. It even has a strange, new firmness which is not Italian but American.[16]

The monumental scale of the Metropolitan Life Building is impressive; it fills a whole block in the grid. It goes beyond the traditional five stories, yet the power of traditional perceptual categories is strong. The architectural treatment divides the facade into six units, thus modulating its break from nineteenth-century urban scale. It is worth noting, moreover, that it is oriented more to the grid than to the park, and its primary public face is the horizontal business block facade on Twenty-third Street rather than as we might have expected, given our later aesthetic assumptions, the tower side facing the park.

If one looks at two pictures of the Metropolitan Life, both taken from *King's Views of New York*, one from the 1909 edition and the other from the 1915 edition (Figures 13 and 14), it is possible to see an important perceptual shift within the city that points toward the eventual acceptance of the tower itself rather than as a campanile. The 1909 view from south of Madison Square emphasizes the business block and shows the tower to be behind it. The 1915 view, by contrast, is taken from north of the square, and the tower is in the foreground and dominates the picture. In the period of six years, monumentalism had come to be more identified with verticality. In 1961, when the tower was renovated, it was visually separated from the business

13. Metropolitan Life Building, 1909, from *King's Views of New York, 1909*. Courtesy of the Museum of the City of New York

block, suggesting two structures rather than one. By then, the tower could stand alone. When those renovations were undertaken, the idea of a free-standing tower caused few aesthetic tensions, but before about 1930 the dominant urban aesthetic in New York could not accommodate such unabashed verticality.

In 1909 the Metropolitan Life Building and the Singer Tower that Ernest Flagg placed on top of a French Baroque business block represented the basic *form* of the New York skyscraper. They differed from the strong expression of uncompromising verticality that Louis Sullivan prescribed for the tall office building and which he achieved to a remarkable degree in his only New York building—the Bayard-Condict Building (1898)—perhaps appropriately, in terms of our argument, hidden away on Bleecker Street on the "wrong"

14. Metropolitan Life Building, 1915, from *King's Views of New York, 1915.* © Collection of the New-York Historical Society

side of Broadway. What Sullivan prescribed in his famous essay, "The Tall Office Building Artistically Considered" (1896), was alien to New York skyscraper architecture. Sullivan wrote:

> What is the chief characteristic of the tall office building? . . . [A]t once we must answer, it is lofty. This loftiness is to the artist-nature its thrilling aspect. . . . It must be in turn the dominant chord in his expression of it, the true excitant of his imagination. It must be tall, every inch of it tall. The force and power of altitude must be in it, the glory and the pride of exaltation must be in it. It must be every inch a proud and soaring thing, rising in sheer exultation that from bottom to top it is a unit without a single dissenting line. . . .[17]

Cass Gilbert's Woolworth Building (1913: Figure 15), the building that Stieglitz mentions in describing his devaluation of the Flatiron Building, achieved a sense of soaring exultation that no earlier New York building had achieved. But he achieved this effect in the context of the New York campanile tradition rather than in the manner prescribed in Sullivan's essay or exemplified in his Bayard-Condict Building.

From Broadway today the Woolworth Building appears to be a tower. We do not see, unless we approach it from the rear, the familiar New York business block base that is prominent in pictures of it at the time it was completed. It is a massive version of the New York campanile. With a difference. Gilbert, for his "Cathedral of Commerce," as it was called during the opening ceremonies, used the Gothic rather than Renaissance motif. If you want to soar, Gothic soars toward the heavens. The height of the horizontal cornice, as well as the tower, surpassed anything previously built in New York, but Gilbert's concessions to the nineteenth-century city are striking. Although the business block is higher than ever before, the architectural detailing continues to associate it with the traditional five- or six-story cornice line. There is an expanded base and cornice, and there are four intermediate horizontal divisions marked by architectural treatment. This decoration of the building may be read as a failure to achieve functional expression, or it may be seen as an intentional and comforting echo of the nineteenth-century urban building tradition. For a narrowly architectural history, the former explanation is appropriate. But for any urbanistic understanding of what Gilbert was doing the latter explanation is compelling.

Until the mid-1920s photographs and paintings reveal resistance to verticality. The most common and striking perspective on New York's tall buildings from the 1890s through 1930 was the view of the skyline across the water. Yet such views, it must be noted, do not really take advantage of the possibilities of verticality. Instead they array the city's tall buildings along a horizontal axis. The city, in such views, is a mountain range; the ensemble is perceptually more important than the individual peaks.

It was not until the few years between about 1925 and 1931, particularly with the publication of the New York Regional Plan volume on *The Building of the City* in the latter year, that the skyscraper as tower got its full aesthetic justi-

15. The Woolworth Building, 1913, from *King's Views of New York, 1915*. © Collection of the New-York Historical Society

fication and its first examples, with the Radiator Building (1925), the Chrysler Building (1930), and the Empire State Building (1931). During these years architects Raymond Hood and Hugh Ferriss, working with city planner Thomas Adams, director of the New York Regional Plan, rejected the skyline as mountain range in favor of distinct towers. (Figure 16) Hood seems to have been the one who initially articulated this understanding of a skyscraper future, but the three rethought the skyscraper's relation to its surround. It no longer had to be diminished; its aesthetic and urbanistic virtues were now understood to inhere in the free-standing tower. Ensemble and horizontal connections were less important. Ferriss, in his book *The Metropolis of Tomorrow* (1929), contrasted the coming skyscraper city with the skyscraper that had been developed during the previous half century. (Figure 17) Acknowledging the visionary thinking of Hood, he wrote of the city represented in his drawings:

> . . . [W]e are struck by certain peculiarities in the disposition of the towers now before us. In the first place, no two of them rise in close juxtaposition to each other. . . . Also, there is a certain degree of regularity apparent in their disposal throughout; while they are not all precisely equidistant, and their relation does not suggest an absolutely rectangular checkerboard scheme, yet it is obvious that they have been located according to some citywide plan.

The bases of these 1,000-foot (or more) towers cover from four to eight city blocks, and they are located at express entry stops. In between the towers, in the "wide districts . . . which make up the greater area of the city—the buildings are comparatively low. The average six stories. . . ."[18]

With Harvey Wiley Corbett, designer of One Fifth Avenue, the dialectic evaporates and one finds a complete—and amusing—assimilation of verticality and beauty. Writing in the *Yale Review* in 1928, Corbett explained that the vertical is always more attractive than the horizontal; it provides an effect of slenderness that is more pleasing. "We have vertical stripes on our clothes because we think they add to our appearance. And, conversely, how are ugly clothes—clothes that we do not want copied, the uniforms of convicts—how are such clothes designed? They have broad horizontal stripes. No one would willingly wear anything so hideous. In his buildings, too, man has liked lines that accentuate heights and carry the eye upward."[19]

16. Two Views of the New York Skyline. From p. 111 of *The Regional Plan of New York and Its Environs: The Building of the City*, by Thomas Adams. © Collection of the New-York Historical Society

Verticality had been accommodated into a new urban aesthetic. And photography could celebrate it in a way that Stieglitz did not and could not in 1903. The new fascination with verticality is apparent in New York photography of the 1930s, in the cropping done by Berenice Abbott in *Exchange Place* (Figure 45), or in the exploration of the vertical lines of the Empire State Building in *The Maypole* by Edward Steichen, or in the choreography and cinematography in the 1930s movie *42nd Street*.

17. *Imagining Metropolis*, by Hugh Ferriss. From *The Drawings of Hugh Ferriss*, by Jean Ferriss Leich. Courtesy of the Avery Architectural and Fine Arts Library, Columbia University, New York

Yet we must not exaggerate, even in the 1930s, how far New Yorkers moved from the neoclassical civic vision of Burnham at the turn of the century. The New York Regional Plan, which incorporated the ideas of Ferriss and Hood, was a direct offspring of the Chicago Plan. The two individuals most responsible for the establishment of the plan in New York under the auspices of the Russell Sage Foundation, Charles Dyer Norton and Frederic Delano, had been actively involved earlier in the Chicago Commercial Club's sponsorship of the Chicago Plan. There are, it is true, more towers (Burnham and Garnier proposed one each in their plans, while the Regional Plan—and Ferriss and Hood—proposed many), but it is, like Burnham's, an attempt to express civic unity by producing a neoclassical urban form for the modern American city.

There is more to be said about the persistence of the horizontal civic tradition. If the Empire State Building is the premier example of the skyscraper as a block-filling tower, it is important to remember that its street wall is only six stories, as the authors of the Forty-second Street guidelines remembered in specifying the relation of tower to street they desire. And recall that the public or civic extension of Rockefeller Center's Promenade is flanked by the low-rise French and British Pavillions that terminate in a six-story street wall. It was undoubtedly this historical low-rise horizontal tradition for civic architecture that Lewis Mumford was drawing upon when he complained in the forties of the unabashed verticality of the United Nations Secretariat building, comparing it unfavorably with the New York Public Library.[20] Finally, to mention a more recent example of New York civic architecture, the neoclassical horizontalism of Lincoln Center further underscores the persistent interest in horizontal monumentality. Indeed, the relation of Lincoln Center to the street, the gridiron, and the transportation center at the convergence of Broadway and Ninth Avenue recall all of the tensions over the horizontal cityscape that marked Madison Square at the turn of the century.

The distinction we make between civic horizontalism and corporate verticality was recognized, in a strikingly paradigmatic way, in the Regional Plan in 1931. In the course of a discussion of New York's architectural distinctiveness, the authors of the plan presented two pages of pictures. The first portrays public buildings, the second business structures. All of the former are horizontal, while all of the latter are vertical.[21]

Business has appropriated the tower as a means of expressing corporate power. The feeble but not yet extinguished expression of civic life continues to find limited expression at the street level. Indeed, the particular pattern of civic "contribution"—of public space—exacted by the City Planning Commission (in return for allowing businesses to make their symbols—and profits—of "private" power higher) derives from the New York tradition associating civic purpose with the five-story street wall, horizontalism, and street access.

Today, while giant skyscrapers crowd in the center, the question of public space has moved to the river edges of not only Manhattan but Brooklyn and Queens also. Again it is the street-level and horizontal connections, and this time it is as well the connections between the water and nearby neighborhoods. There is a highly contested and tenuous agreement that private development of the waterfront whether commercial or residential, will be limited, that public access is a civic good that cannot be sacrificed. The struggle for civic authority and public space in the city will not, one hopes, be fought in the streets; more likely there will be other forums for debate, but the issues will continue to be defined at the street level and will be about an older tradition of connectivity.

PART II

ART, INTELLECT, AND
PUBLIC CULTURE

4

PUBLIC CULTURE AND

METROPOLITAN MODERNITY

Is there a key that opens the cultural meaning of the modern metropolis? The proliferation of difference that characterizes metropolitan modernity is so great that it seems unlikely that there is a single "text of the city," the explication of which would reveal the city's cultural script. New York is particularly difficult; there are no equivalents of Balzac or Dickens who reached very far toward incorporating into their narratives the vast kaleidoscope of Paris and London. Whether it results from a deficiency in New York's literary culture or because of the peculiar difficulty of capturing the complexity of New York, the city has not had its Balzac. Whitman, who captured so much, relied upon his famous lists. Even he was unable to bring the many fascinations he found in the city into narrative form.

Where does one look for a unifying theme in the modern metropolis when fragmentation is practically its defining characteristic? The most important study of modern metropolitan culture is Carl E. Schorske's brilliant exploration of the beginnings of modernism in fin-de-siècle Vienna. Acknowledging the problem of fragmentation from the outset, he was able—with his vast and multidisciplinary learning—to move from one form of cultural expression to another, from architecture to pyschoanalysis, from literature to painting, from music to politics. His close examination of different fields reveals a common pattern: the dissolution of liberal politics and thus civic commitments. In field after field, politics is abandoned for the private, the personal, and especially the psychological. His *Fin-de-Siècle Vienna: Politics and Culture* (1980) thus finds unity in the disunity of Vienna, by specifying a kind of psychic and practical evacuation of the public realm.

Can one similarly approach the question of metropolitan culture in New York? I think not. The reason is the difference between New York and Vienna. High culture can speak for the general culture of the city in turn-of-the-century Vienna in a way it cannot in the New York of the same era. More obviously, and thankfully, New York did not experience the same kind of cultural and political catastrophe that played itself out in Vienna in the first third of the twentieth century. Both of these differences point to a livelier and more democratic public culture in New York. And this implies a different approach. For New York, then, I propose an alternative conception of metropolitan life and thus principle of synthesis. If in Vienna Schorske could locate the analytical center of his study in biographies and specific fields or disciplines, my starting point for New York will be what I call *public culture*. The inquiry thus becomes at once an inquiry into the making and meaning of public culture and the analysis of the public culture specific to New York.

Max Weber, the German social theorist, offers a starting point for me. He argued that the emergence of the modern city is distinguished by the market. According to him, the market "is the most impersonal form of practical life into which humans can enter with one another"; it is also, as Weber always understood, an arena of a characteristically modern form of power. The issue of power is crucial; much current celebration of the market omits this aspect, assuming all parties enter the market on equal terms. The market metaphor I have in mind is more complex. The qualities of the modern urban market are paradigmatic, I want to suggest, of broader qualities that I associate with the notion of public culture. The market and metropolitan culture more generally can be described as constituting a pattern of economic and cultural exchanges among strangers marked by subtle patterns of exclusion, distortion, and blockage that define these exchanges.

The central characteristic of the modern city is the ordinariness of the interaction of strangers in public. Whatever public and heroic qualities modern life possesses—and whatever brutalities and injustices plague it—come not from those periodic rituals of the early modern city but rather, as Baudelaire insisted, from the daily experience of city life. The market, so much less heroic in the traditional sense and apparently so formless and morally empty as a public phenomenon, symbolically represents—and on occasion creates—the public culture of modern cities.

Cities, I think it is fair to say, are ongoing contests over the possession and appropriation of terrains. From this observation, we may proceed to a conception of the making of public culture in terms of contested terrain. The topographical quality of this image appeals to me, since cities are distinguished from society generally by their peculiar conjuncture of spatial and social relationships. But I do not mean to restrict either the arena or the contest to matters only of physical territory. Whether the arena is the city's public space or its social institutions, the prize for the actors is relative influence, legitimacy, and security for the meanings they give to civic life. The result for the collectivity is public culture, which provides a frame for this continuing process.

In the market—as in the modern city generally—there is an "incomplete integration" of participants. People enter and withdraw from the market of public life without relinquishing other structural attachments. The values and local commitments brought to the central place of public culture affect the meanings and results associated with that contest. What we are talking about is a mechanism that connects, without destroying, mixed and homogeneous urban collectivities. Indeed, as the sociologist Hans Paul Bahrdt has argued, the cultural contribution of the market and the public life created in modern cities has been the development of modes of communication that form a bridge across the various social distances that exist in cities and will remain a part of city life.

Cities contain many private meanings; urban dwellers create and possess these meanings, many of which spring from their distinctively urban experiences. During the 1980s social historians were particularly anxious to investigate and bring to light these meanings. Often, however, such inquires were at the expense of a concern for the public realm as an object of study. There were many reasons for this shift in historiography. For some, study of the public realm evoked an old-fashioned political history that rarely noticed what and whom were excluded from the story. For students of women, blacks, native Americans, immigrants, and others excluded from significant involvement in the public realm, a history of public life seemed inherently exclusionary. Worse: it seemed to devalue the worth of the lives of such populations. Better to bring attention to the strength and dignity one finds in the contexts of family, ethnic neighborhood, and sisterhood. A final and more general reason for the historiographical withdrawal from the public realm was the influence of cultural anthropology. Historians strove to provide a deeper and, in Clifford Geertz's term, thicker description of the cultures of various social groups. To the extent that these explorations of the interior culture of groups succeeded, context and connections slipped into the background and were attenuated in the resulting histories.

Such inquiries do not in themselves constitute a cultural history of cities, though they are indispensible to such a history. The public culture of cities is the product of a set of relations between the worlds of private life and the larger terrain of the public. A cultural history of the modern city will build upon the interplay of the interior of cultures (the world of private life, the cultures of homogeneous groups) and the larger culture of public life (both political and cultural). What private concerns do individuals or groups bring to public life? How do the worlds of private life and the private concerns they nourish affect the larger world of public life? What aspects of public life intrude into and affect private life? The relations are reciprocal, and the line of public and private is always negotiable.

To examine each of these dimensions of life in isolation from the other misrepresents experience. To chronicle only the public dimension would seem a bit thin, while pursuing the interior of various urban cultures without connection to public culture risks not only fragmentation but insignificance.

This constant movement between local cultures and public culture, between the homogeneous sectors of the periphery and the heterogeneous and contested center, characterizes the modern urban experience. It might be said to correspond to what the anthropologist Victor Turner calls "liminality," but with a crucial difference. For Turner—and for the societies he has studied—liminality is a special condition, the periodic experience of being between structures and thus open to innovation. For a modern, metropolitan person this is not a special or periodic condition, but rather an ordinary one.

At the center, where public culture is made, there is always a "problem." It is a contest over what Heidegger called "the public interpretation of reality," and as such it is the product of a social drama in which there are winners and losers. Particular social groups, seeking power and recognition, "want to make their interpretation of the world universal." This thrust by the powerful to define for themselves *and for others* a public culture that looks very much like their own group values writ large presents the interpretive, analytical, and moral problem of the study of public culture.

The urban cultural history that I am here describing would seek to establish the various degrees to which identifiable groups participate and the terms of their participation in the public world. Unlike the older pluralism that stressed interaction in a somewhat narrower conception of public life, such a history would not assume that all relevant groups are represented in public. It would rather ask why some groups and some values are so much—or so little—represented in the historical construction of the public realm.

With such a multiplicity of mental structures represented and unrepresented, it is difficult simply to map the configuration of the field. Take mid–nineteenth-century New York. Intellectual and cultural life in the age of P. T. Barnum was a free-for-all. The multiplicity of learned traditions, the diverse institutional bases of learning, popularization, and vernacular cultures, make it no easy task to identify either elite or popular culture. A simple "high"-"low" scheme is utterly inadequate. The cultural life of the modern city, of New York City in particular, has been divided and subdivided along both horizontal and vertical axes—with no universally recognized principle of hierarchy or priority.

Conceive of a field "overpopulated" with voices, all striving to dominate meaning. The Russian critic M. M. Bakhtin is suggestive. Discussing the novel, which is, as Ian Watt and others have shown, intimately associated with the rise of modern urban society, Bakhtin offers an adaptable image of the dynamic and the transformations of city culture. "At any given moment of its historical existence," he writes, "language [read for my purposes public culture] is heteroglot from top to bottom: it represents the coexistence of socio-ideological contradictions between the present and the past, between differing epochs of the past, between different socio-ideological groups in the present, between tendencies, schools, cycles, and so forth, all given a bodily form. These 'languages' of heteroglossia intersect each other in a variety of ways, forming new socially typifying 'languages.'" When Bakhtin here and elsewhere insists upon resistance to monologue in art and life, he affirms, in effect, the historical configuration of metropolitan culture.

What one needs is a position from which to observe the movements of culture as they touch a single field—or fail to. The spectrum of movements considered must be broadly inclusive, ranging from commercial culture (that is to say culture sold for profit), to the informally organized and group-based expressive culture of various subordinate populations, to the more refined forms of culture insulated from the market, whether in museums or universities. All of these cultural activities are competing, not exactly fairly, for a legitimate place in the city and for a shared definition of public culture that can include them. A sense of urban cultural life as a contest over the establishment of civic meanings allows one to track the fortunes of participants as well as the changing shape of the ever shifting, never permanent battlefield resolutions of public culture itself.

Yet one must ask whether the multiplicity of urban discourses can share any common ground? The notion of interpretive communities developed by the literary critic Stanley Fish is relevant here. What if each social group or interpretive community in the city attributes radically different meanings to experiences, events, or texts? Does that preclude any possibility of even a partially shared public culture? Does fragmentation thus dissolve the public? Or can we believe in the possibility of certain shared and significant meanings? Without that, no public can emerge.

Because variant interpretations are possible, even likely, it does not follow that they will be mutually exclusive. It is difficult, even in our postmodern age, to believe in interpretation without limit. It would take a very expensive education, as the psychologist Jerome Bruner observes, to persuade one that no meanings find incarnation in a text, that commentary on *Paradise Lost* displaces the poem itself. It is the presence of incarnate meaning, not its absence, that gives significance as well as ultimate limits to indeterminate and plural readings of texts. One can, then, accept the reality of many urban subcultures (but not wholly autonomous cultures) without giving up the notion of a public culture. Put differently, specialized, even sectarian and deeply parochial communities of discourse can coexist with a more general and not trivial conversation.

It was such an assumption that was at the core of the urban ideas of Frederick Law Olmsted. Central and Prospect Parks in New York were supposed to give expression to the existence of a public made up of many different cultures. Addressing the American Social Science Association in 1870, Olmsted reported that in these parks "you may . . . often see vast numbers of persons brought closely together, poor and rich, young and old, Jew and Gentile. I have seen a hundred thousand thus congregated." He remarked upon their "evident glee in the prospect of coming together, all classes largely represented . . . each individual adding by his mere presence to the pleasure of all others." He assured his audience that he had looked "vainly among them for a single face completely unsympathetic with the prevailing expression of good nature and light-heartedness." Olmsted surely overstates the pleasure and social unity that his park brought to the city, but he has captured the way the public and the park worked.

Without ceasing to be what or who they were, without severing their lives from structures of culture smaller than the public culture of the city, these park users participated in the common experience of being a public in a public space. The people in the park represented the diverse, interclass, interethnic public, while remaining rooted in more limited and far more homogeneous worlds constrained by class, gender, ethnicity, and geography, among other determinates. The culture of New York City was made there, a fact noted by Henry James a generation later. In *The American Scene* (1907) he remarked upon the "alien" in Central Park, there in all his "singleness of expression," yet also sharing in a common "possession of the park."

Olmsted's parks were in fact designed to restructure and reform public culture. The movement with which his work is associated sought to exclude much of the dynamic of city life, particularly the commercial and competitive qualities of life in the city, while bringing citizens together in a kind of protected space—off the street, so to speak. Let me turn, therefore, to a different sort of example, one focused on the streets at the time Olmsted spoke. The streets in question are Broadway and Fourteenth Street; the focal point is Union Square.

In the third quarter of the nineteenth century Union Square became a very special kind of arena for public life. It was sponsored less by reform than by commerce and commercial culture. It was not the first such focal point along Broadway; for the previous generation public culture had been generated at City Hall Park; later it would be succeeded by Madison and Times Squares. These squares in their moments of high visibility in the city expressed the various components and overall configuration of the culture of New York.

During the 1860s and 1870s Union Square and Fourteenth Street was the central axis of the city's transportation system—where ferry, elevated, and streetcar lines interconnected—and the centerpoint of the city's always northward moving population, with 1864 marking the date when 50 percent of the city's population lived above Fourteenth Street.

Union Square presented New York culture at its most promiscuous. In using the word *promiscuous*, I am not referring to sexual abandon, though it is true that the city's major "red light" district was a brief walk from the Square. Rather, I am resorting to the word's primary meaning—the conjuncture of unrelated parts or individuals.

If one's only knowledge of the area was the opening pages of Edith Wharton's great New York novel set in this period, *The Age of Innocence* (1920), one would identify it simply as the center of elite New York culture and social life. Here was the Academy of Music, which, as she said, the elite of old New York cherished because of its "being small and inconvenient and thus keeping out the 'new people' whom New York was beginning to dread." For those who know well the geography of New York, this might seem to be a reference to the immigrant masses on the Lower East Side, who were just beginning to encroach on Fourteenth Street and Union Square. But, as the remainder of the novel reveals, the narrator and "social" New York were oblivious to the city's growing underclass. The reference is to the new millionaire class of robber barons establishing themselves in New York and who would soon return the compliment to the Academy of Music society by building the Metropolitan Opera House in the district that would later become Times Square.

Writing as a contemporary, Richard Watson Gilder, more venturesome than the elite society about which Wharton wrote, offers a more inclusive sense of the area, stressing its vitality and diversity. An editor of *Scribner's Monthly*, which under his editorship became in 1880 the prestigious *Century* magazine, Gilder worked in the Square. But the occasion of his commentary in his column in *Scribner's* was his move, after his marriage to the artist Helena deKay, to East Fifteenth Street. What he emphasizes is the Square as a place of amusement and recreation, of services and entertainments, not a place of work. "We are," he informed his readers

within two blocks of eight hotels, three concert halls, two public monuments, and one savings bank. We are within one door of the central square of the city; five minutes' walk of the great dry-goods stores; five minutes' walk from some of the best and some of the worst restaurants in the world. The most noted and noisy street in America is hardly a stone's throw from our front gate. I suppose I need not mention such minor convenience as butchers, bakers, and candlestick makers. . . .

Though a considerably broader evocation of the place and its culture than we find in Wharton, it is still partial, which is to say it is ideological. He leaves out other social classes except as providers of services to his own class. In fact, the Square was a major center for working-class consumption of popular culture. It was also the principal site for working-class parades for more than a half century following the Civil War. The historian's first task, then, is to penetrate the veil of ideology and establish the actual social diversity and multiple values contending on this public terrain.

The social geography of the area abutting the Square suggests its centering function. If immigrants flanked the Square on the southeast, to the west was exclusive Fifth Avenue. Just a block off the northeast perimeter was the city's most gracious residential block, Gramercy Park. The Gilder-deKay "studio" was the city's most important salon, where writers, theatre people, and artists met every week. It was here too that John La Farge, Augustus St. Gaudens, and other rebels from the National Academy of Design (which was a bit farther to the north at Twenty-third Street) met to organize the Society of American Artists, whose educational arm continues today as the Art Student's League. Next door to the Gilder home was the Century Club, where the gentry of the city gathered when they were not at the Union League Club, also on the Square.

All around the Square were restaurants, hotels, and luxury shops. There was, of course, Delmonico's. But there was also Moretti's restaurant, remembered by some as the place where Americans were introduced to spaghetti, macaroni, and Chianti. Among the shops serving the elite, the most notable were Tiffany's and Brentano's Literary Emporium. The new palaces of consumption, the department stores, clustered near the Square. Stewart's, Lord & Taylor, McCreery's, and Macy's drew enormous crowds of middle-class women to the area to shop, and working-class women to serve them or to pick up piecework. This significantly feminized the culture of the Square during the day.

If the area was the center of commercial culture, it was also a center for elite and official "not-for-profit" culture. Just north of the concentration of learned institutions at Astor Place and Washington Square (Astor Library, NYU, Union Theological Seminary, Cooper Union), Union Square was the first home of the Metropolitan Museum of Art. The New York Historical Society was just east of the Square on Second Avenue. Steinway Hall, just east of the Academy of Music, was the home of high-class entertainments, mostly classical concerts and the opera, and the home of Theodore Thomas's orchestra. The Steinways, moreover, made their great hall available free of charge for educational lectures. West of the Square, on Fifth Avenue, Chickering Hall offered a "jumble of events for many tastes." The home of the Mendelsohn Glee Club, directed by Edwin McDowell, it was also where Josephine Shaw Lowell called the first mass meeting to found the Consumers League, itself a cross-class organization, where "shop girl" and consumer met on different terms than in the nearby stores.

At night, of course, Union Square, dubbed the "Rialto" in 1874, was the city's first theatre district. Theatres ranged from Wallack's, a rather high-class comedy house, to Robinson Hall, on Sixteenth Street, whose bills of fare suggest its character: "The Turkish Bathers," "Female Models," "French Dancers," and "A Woman's Adventures in a Turkish Harem." Besides the theatres themselves, there was an array of theatre-support services and businesses. Many workers were employed by printers and theatrical publishers (and musical publishers, as this was the first home of Tin Pan Alley), agents, scenery and costume shops, photographers. There were also more indirect support services—boarding houses, cheap restaurants, and hotels.

During this period, Union Square had a remarkable concentration of genuinely popular entertainments. There was, for example, the Palace Gardens at Fourteenth Street and Sixth Avenue. Built in 1858 with an upper-class clientele in mind, it was immediately appropriated by housemaids and nurses during the day and whole working-class families in the evenings. Its entertainments were adapted to these patrons, including walks, fireworks, pagodas, mimes, and, for the children, magic, ventriloquism, and Indian dances. The Hippotheatron, across the street from the Academy of Music, was a rather peculiar, circular, corrugated iron structure that provided a home for equestrian shows, acrobatics, and pantomimes. Its three-tier price structure (25¢, 50¢, 75¢) suggests a mixed-class clientele. A bit farther east, next to Luchows, a German restaurant, was Huber's Dime Museum, the most famous of its kind. And, of course, there were many street entertainers, mostly musicians.

It was this remarkable mix of classes and sexes, work and play, high culture and popular culture, that defined this area as a public space. The first criterion of a genuinely public space is its accessibility, and it is clear that enough of New York felt free to enter the Square area to make the social experience there representative of the city's culture.

Within the Square's area, it was perhaps Tammany Hall that best represented the public culture of the city. Tammany was an example of a mixed-class, multiethnic, but not egalitarian, urban political institution. But Tammany was also a major cultural institution, and I want to make a point about its place in the culture of the Square. From time to time various musical and theatrical companies were housed there, but in 1881 theatrical history was made at Tammany when Tony Pastor opened his theatre there. Pastor is remembered because he recognized that the special interclass quality of public life created at Union Square and at Tammany Hall invited a new kind of theatre. Unable to draw more than working-class males and prostitutes to his earlier theatre on Broome Street and the Bowery, he realized that Fourteenth Street was safe enough and attractive enough to create a family theatre for the middle and working classes. Out of the social material of Union Square, he made an aesthetic innovation that represented the public life of the Square. All the ethnic and class categories present on the street were made objects of humor on the stage. He invented American vaudeville, an interclass popular entertainment that incorporated a good deal of working-class and immigrant culture, while insisting upon middle-class manners and morals.

One could extend this list of elements making up the promiscuous public culture of Union Square. But enough has been said to show the mix of classes and uses tugging at each other on this terrain, each participating in the definition of the public culture of the city, each taking home their own meanings.

All of these cultural transactions—and this is my main point—were shaped by the values and interests various populations brought to this public arena from local and homogeneous *gemeinschaftlich* worlds. Out of this interaction, groups found (or failed to find) a place in the culture of the city, while public culture found itself and broadcast itself. In this ever changing negotiation of culture one finds, I think, a frame for analyzing the content, form, and power relations in city culture.

This process, I would argue, is peculiar to the big city. It is a construction—at once projective, representative, and reflexive—that depends upon life in public spaces. Such life was most fully realized in the turn-of-the-century metropolis in Europe and in America. The culture of metropolitan life is largely the product of its spatial elaboration—the proximity and necessary contact of various competing narrative trajectories and hierarchies of representation.

This quality distinguishes the modern metropolis from small and earlier places. This is evident in Georg Simmel's famous essay, "The Metropolis and Mental Life." Any close reading of that essay, which was written in Berlin in 1902, impresses upon one the realization that for Simmel the novelty of metropolitan life was the *public* relation of the individual's subjective life to his or her collective culture. He does not argue that public life is the defining characteristic of metropolitan culture; he assumes it. The emphasis in the text is on the visual, the glance, the onrush of impression, surprise. All of this suggests that metropolitan life and culture is defined in the street, in public places, in theatres, in stores. Such are the sources of individual and collective identity in the metropolis. One might almost argue that if in the industrial city the key to social identity is to be found in the relations of production, in the modern metropolis it is to be found in the relations of elements of public culture.

But this is not to dismiss entirely the concerns of a Marxist perspective on city life. One must also track the making and remaking of the public spaces themselves, the places where public culture is inscribed. Here politics and money enter the story, often in their most crude and elemental forms. Too few students of urban culture realize the essential connection between urban history of the container and its cultural contents. They often take the public forms for granted, as something given, something that need only be read. But one must historicize the making of these physical places as much as the culture that is inscribed in their precincts.

If there is no text of the city for the convenient use of the historian, there is public space and the culture inscribed there. It is always changing, always feeding on new groups, always contested, always being absorbed into private life.

5

DEMOCRACY AND
CULTURAL AUTHORITY

As city life gets more complex, especially if democratic values are present, the question of cultural authority is subject to an increasingly multivalent contest. How in a democracy is cultural authority established? Democracy invites individual judgment. In fact, it demands it. Even if one accepts this premise in the realm of electoral politics, there is often hesitation in the domain of art and intellect. Are art, science, literature, and scholarship thus different? Should they be?

It may not be possible ever to resolve the tension between excellence and democracy, between qualitative values and the quantitative values inherent in the democratic idea. But New York has been an especially illuminating site for this particular public conversation. The question emerged first and forcefully in nineteenth-century New York City. By mid-century, the city was well on its way to becoming one of the major cities of the Atlantic world. New York contained the most diverse population of any of them. More important, nowhere were democratic values so loudly proclaimed than in Jacksonian New York, the crucible out of which Walt Whitman, democracy's poet, emerged.

That celebrated commentator on American democracy, Alexis de Tocqueville, directly addressed this question of cultural authority, and we might well begin with his typically acute reflections. When the aristocratic Tocqueville arrived in New York in 1831, the rhetoric of democracy was at its height. He spent his first six weeks in New York, and many of the questions and answers that shaped his analysis come from those initial impressions. He was immediately drawn to the question of authority in a democracy—whether in politics, morals, literature, or art.

We have become skeptical about the language of American democracy—and rightly so, given the exclusions we now recognize. But for the moment let us suspend that judgment. It is necessary in order to recognize how much more democratic New York City was in 1830, in practice as well as rhetoric, compared to other cities of the Atlantic world. Only then can we grasp how striking the democratic practices of New York were to the French aristocrat. They were far beyond anything anywhere else in the world. That democracy went well beyond the right to vote; it involved what might be called the expansion of the individual.

Tocqueville witnessed a pervasive and unprecedented commitment to individual judgment and a proliferation of choice, whether in commerce or in literature. The result was an utterly new sense of individual autonomy that Ralph Waldo Emerson would capture in his notion of self-reliance and that the extraordinary revivalist Charles G. Finney played upon in inviting huge crowds in his Broadway church to will their salvation. Of course, this sense of individual empowerment was heightened by the unacknowledged but real awareness of those in America denied freedom, a point recognized by Emerson and Finney but not by many of their readers and listeners.

How does intellectual authority work? Tocqueville wondered. On what grounds do opinions become authoritative? In the second chapter of the second volume of *Democracy in America*, he observed:

> There is no philosopher in the world so great but that he believes a million things on the faith of other people and accepts a great many more truths than he demonstrates. . . . A principle of authority must then always occur, under all circumstances, in some part or other of the moral and intellectual world. Its place is variable, but a place it necessarily has. . . . Thus the question is, not to know whether any intellectual authority exists in an age of democracy, but simply where it resides and by what standard it is to be measured.[1]

There is, Tocqueville suggests, a history to these assumptions about the locus of cultural authority. I want to lay out three phases in the history of cultural authority in nineteenth-century New York. Although I treat these phases as sequential, it is important to remember that they are also parallel. The earlier ones are never completely eclipsed by the later. One can say, however, that they successively defined the dominant values of the three periods.

The first of these periods is eighteenth century in its feel, but it extended well into the nineteenth century, at least among the city's patriciate. By the time Tocqueville arrived in New York, a newer pattern, a boisterous sense of boundlessness and confidence in one's own capacity to know, was increasingly evident. Historians often identify it with the rise of so-called Jacksonian democracy. Finally, beginning in the 1850s and accelerating with the Civil War there was a trend toward consolidation and the reassertion of discipline. The war and the specter of war was relevant to this change, but so was the concern to bring better order to the city—a concern that brought together the seemingly disparate initiatives to create Central Park, the Metropolitan Museum, the Metropolitan Police, and the Metropolitan Board of Health. A new elite, defined partly by wealth, of course, but also by their possession of knowledge and taste, sought control of cultural and other forms of authority.

In the first pattern, in what I will call patrician New York, cultural authority was dominated by general elites. Key individuals assumed positions of leadership and authority in all areas of life—from politics to art. No one better exemplified these leaders with general authority than did DeWitt Clinton, several times mayor of the city and the governor who promoted and carried through the building of the Erie Canal, called at the time "Clinton's Ditch."[2]

Had he done nothing else but orchestrate the building of the Erie Canal, the development that made New York the great emporium of the western hemisphere—just as he predicted it would—his place in history would be secure. But he also assumed a position as a cultural leader in the city. A bit pompous, he did not shy away from describing himself in print (using a fairly transparent pseudonym):

> Mr. Clinton, amidst his other great qualifications, is distinguished for a marked devotion to science:—few men have read more, and few men can claim more various and extensive knowledge. And the bounties of nature have been improved, by persevering and unintermitted industry. It was natural that such men should have high rank in literary institutions; and he was

accordingly elected first President of the Literary and Philosophical Society of New York.[3]

For whatever reason—modesty surely not one of them—he omitted other honors that had come his way. He was as well a founding member of the New York Historical Society, and he was president of the American Academy of Fine Arts.

What I wish to stress here, however, is his claim that individuals of learning (which then marked class as well as education) carried a general entitlement to fill roles of cultural authority. He had been as well educated as anyone of his generation; in fact, he was the first student to graduate from Columbia College (as Kings College became after the Revolution). Yet he was not a serious scholar, nor even a particularly keen student of art or science. He was often accused of resorting to conventional compendia of classical phrases to ornament his orations. It was his class and status that conferred on him positions of cultural and political authority. They came together in patrician New York. That was commonplace in the eighteenth century, and it was that claim to general leadership that would be fractured in the 1820s and 1830s.

This model of cultural authority came under attack by both scientists and artists. Clinton was a target for both attacks, but I will focus briefly on the attack from what would later be called the art world. In 1818, the *National Advocate*, an anti-Clintonian newspaper edited by Mordecai Noah, who would later be a leading New York Jacksonian, published a stinging attack on Clinton's plural officeholding in the city's many cultural organizations. Clinton had presumed that his standing as a political leader implied a right, even an obligation, to assume leadership in the cultural realm. But it was precisely that presumption that was challenged.

The authorship of the article is uncertain; it was either Noah himself or Gulian Verplanck, scion of old New York wealth, one of the city's leading writers, and an implacable political foe of Clinton. The key point of the attack was made in this way:

> One set of men govern and direct all the literary and scientific institutions in this city. . . . The gentlemen who are directors of the academy [of fine arts] are profound physicians, able lawyers, men of science and talents, but are

very poor judges of the value or merit of pictures, and, consequently, are not well calculated to advance the character of the Arts in this City.[4]

If, as I suspect, Verplanck was the author, he was not prepared to open up the question of authority to the masses. His hostility to Clinton, which knew no bounds, moved him to challenge a particular form of patrician authority over culture, but his move did not imply democracy. Indeed, it seemed to empower intellectuals like himself. Those who specialized in culture would become authoritative.

A few years later, in 1826, Samuel F. B. Morse would elaborate this position in surprisingly modern terms. His leadership in founding the National Academy of Design in 1826 was related to a new vision for the organization of culture. He explained his expectations in his founding statements for the Academy. His argument anticipated notions we have until quite recently taken for granted: that artists (or the art world more generally) ought to manage their own affairs.

The first exhibition catalogue of the National Academy of Design in 1826 declared that the members of the Academy "have no object in view but the advancement of the Arts and the benefit of the artists." Morse elaborated his point in characteristically felicitous prose: "The National Academy of the Arts of Design is founded on the commonsense principle, that every profession in a society knows what measures are necessary for its own improvement."[5]

Two important things are being done here. One has already been suggested. Morse is moving cultural authority out of the hands of a general elite to a specific profession. But he is also fighting on another front, anticipating the democratic future and worrying about the fate of art in a democracy. To give authority to a closed profession, as he did in the National Academy, encouraged, perhaps, a kind democracy within the fraternity of artists. But it was also a way of fending off an increasingly aggressive democracy already emerging at large as he wrote.

The pendulum had swung toward democracy. It was one of those adjustments that, as Tocqueville had recognized, come with history. The general authority—and I emphasize the notion of a *general* authority—of the established elite was challenged and seriously eroded. The self-sufficient individual, as good as anyone else, was empowered, and Morse feared this shift no less than the older patriciate he had challenged.

Tocqueville identified the emerging cultural assumptions of the era.

"Everyone," he wrote with some exaggeration, "attempts to be his own sufficient guide and makes it his boast to form his own opinions on all subjects."[6] The vice of Clinton thus repeated itself, but now the prerogative seemed to belong to everyone! For democrats it was happy news, while conservatives and artists were distressed.

James Fenimore Cooper, the novelist, was one of the distressed. Cooper, who was one of Morse's closest friends, wrote to a mutual friend, the sculptor Horatio Greenough: "You are in a country in which every man swaggers and talks; knowledge or no knowledge; brains or no brains; taste or no taste. They are all *ex nato* connoisseurs . . . and everyman's equal." Artists, he lamented, must expect their work to be "estimated by the same rules as they estimate pork, rum, and cotton."[7]

Commercial culture—suggested by Cooper's marketplace imagery— seemed to better fit the spirit of the time. The market presumes that each participant is autonomous, prepared and expected to make choices on his or her own authority. Not surprisingly, P. T. Barnum emerged as a cultural impresario at just this moment, and he invited the public to make their own judgments. Each individual, not a patriciate nor professionals, would be her or his own authority.

Barnum began with and respected the self-confidence of the self-consciously and aggressively democratic Americans. Let them judge for themselves, he said. We tend to think of him as someone who deceived the public, but in fact he did not lie. His advertising, as Neil Harris has explained, was clever rather than dishonest. It did not assert anything that was not true. Rather it invited inquiry. Some authorities, Barnum said, asserted that the "feejee mermaid" on display in his American Museum was real. Others said it was not, that it was a fraud. Come, he invited the public, judge for yourself. But pay your admission at the door.[8]

All ages, all classes, men and women were invited. They need not listen to the Clintons nor to the Morses. They need not listen to their social superiors nor anyone more learned than themselves. Knowledge was available equally to all; visual inspection was sufficient for one to come to a conclusion on one's own. This boisterous self-confidence that knowledge was immediately available—especially by means of visual inspection—was pervasive in the age of Jackson, and it made Barnum wealthy.

Barnum's American Museum was by our standards little more than an attic of curiosities, a promiscuous collection of all kinds of objects without any apparent logic of arrangement. Those categories that established a domain of the aesthetic later in the century—and which we have inherited, however controversially, in recent years—were not yet authoritative. At the theater, for example, a scene from Shakespeare might be followed by a juggler or a trained bear. Only later would New Yorkers dispatch one of Shakespeare's collaborators in such an evening's entertainment to the zoo and the other to the circus (also introduced to America by Barnum).

The idea that there were values other than commercial ones in works of art was not evident in Barnum's promotion of art and culture. His was an aesthetic deeply embedded in the world of everyday values, commerce in particular. Just as the market invited choices, Americans relished the dramatic expansion in the area of choice. If enslaved Africans in America and Native Americans were denied choices, the American majority revelled in the choices available to them—whether it was choosing truth in Barnum's museum, judging a work of art, or deciding to limit births. The historian Robert Wiebe has characterized the period as one defined by a revolution in choices.[9] Such an expansion of choice revealed the retreat of established authority.

Walt Whitman, who learned both from the streets of New York and from Emerson's rather elevated transcendentalism, inscribed the refusal of authority in the formal qualities and in the content of his great book, *Leaves of Grass*, first published in 1855. Indeed, he rejected the authority of critics by anonymously writing positive reviews of his own book! He challenged the established rules of those proper poets he called "genteel little creatures." In the process it might be said that he created modern American literature in an urban key. Never before or since has any writer—any American—been more hopeful that humans, ordinary New York humans, could at once have their own autonomous personhood and authority while being connected with others of the urban masses.

It is this combination of autonomy, individualism, and connection that is communicated so powerfully in his greatest poem, "Crossing Brooklyn Ferry." Whitman's individual was at once unique and at one with the all. He opened the 1867 edition of *Leaves of Grass* with these lines:

One's-Self I sing, a simple separate person,
Yet utter the word Democratic, the word En-Mass.

The confident, loud, and boisterous democratic American is celebrated in his long poem, "Song of Myself," first published in the 1855 edition.

> In all people I see myself, not more and not one barley-corn less,
> And the good or bad I say of myself I say of them.
> . . .
> I know I am august,
> I do not trouble my spirit to vindicate itself or be understood,
> I see that the elementary laws never apologize, . . .
> . . .
> Walt Whitman, a kosmos, of Manhattan the son,
> Turbulent, fleshy, sensual, eating, drinking, breeding,
> No sentimentalist, no stander above men and women or apart from them,
> No more modest than immodest.
> Unscrew the locks from the doors!
> Unscrew the doors themselves from their jambs!

Such was the democratic Whitman's attitude toward structures of authority external to the sovereign individual.

In the era of the Civil War, Reconstruction, and beyond, a resurgent New York elite sought to dampen these democratic spirits. Whitman, as is well known, lost his government clerkship because his supervisor had found a copy of *Leaves of Grass* in his desk and considered it obscene. Men like Frederick Law Olmsted, E. L. Godkin, and the founders of the Metropolitan Museum of Art embraced Culture, with a capital *C*, as a source of authority. For this "metropolitan gentry," an elevated and elevating notion of culture (along with the resources of class) conferred authority. To them authority ought naturally to adhere. Many urban improvements of the era testify to their success in acquiring and wielding this authority.[10] Unlike Clinton, they did not seek political power. Not quite experts, neither were they the same kind of general elite familiar to patrician New York. They derived their authority from their acquired culture, and they sought power in the cultural domain through cultural institutions.

Whitman was not oblivious to the problems urbanization and the war produced. Prompted by a biting critique of America penned by Thomas Carlyle, Whitman wrote in his "Democratic Vistas" that the city was becoming too materialistic, too corrupt, and he hoped that art might restore a healthy individualism and virtue. But he also worried about the notion of culture that the Union League Club elite was promoting; it threatened to remove authority from the individual and give it to a class.[11]

Culture as this class understood it was exclusive. It constituted a class and separated out the elite more than it unified the masses. With the word culture, Whitman warned, we are in close quarters with the enemy, but still he embraced a unifying notion of art. He wrote of and for the whole body of New Yorkers—Americans—and he unified them in his imagination. The dream of self-culture, of culture for everyone, persisted in the Gilded Age, but there was a shift that pushed it toward the margins.

A confident and aggressive new generation of leaders in New York were embracing culture for the very reason Whitman worried about it. They unself-consciously referred to themselves as "the best men," and they were confident that their opinions had a special claim on public attention. They sought to establish a metropolitan standard of cultural authority to guide the middle classes and others who mistakenly thought that their opinions were as good as anyone's.[12]

The problem, as E. L. Godkin, the founding editor of *The Nation*, put it, was that "a large body of persons has arisen," taught by common schools, newspapers, lyceum lectures, small colleges, magazines, and the like, "who firmly believe that they have reached in the matter of social, mental, and moral culture, all that is attainable or desirable by anybody, and who, therefore, tackle all the problems of the day." The result, he insisted, "is a kind of mental and moral chaos."[13]

Such was the context for the founding of the Metropolitan Museum of Art. It captured the category museum from Barnum and redefined it. The mental and moral chaos of Barnum's museum was banished; no longer would "feejee mermaids" share space with the old masters. Firm categories now would define what was and was not art—and to whom it fell legitimately to make these judgments. The Metropolitan Museum of Art was also intended to establish national standards as the cultural institutions of the capital cities of Europe did. (Hence the *metropolitan* in the name.) And in order to protect cultural institutions from the masses, they constituted themselves as a private body, not a public one. The Metropolitan Museum (and the nearly contemporary American Museum of Natural History) used the novel device of a nonprofit board of trustees to create a privately (and elite) controlled metropolitan institution. Or to put it differently, they created a private institution for the benefit of the public.

Here originated one the most characteristic institutions of American urban cultural life: the nonprofit sector. Although this form of cultural support, free of government interference, is often described as representative of our democratic, voluntarist institutions, it is important to recall that it was created to avoid the perceived vices of democratic governments. Ironically, it was only the intervention of the Tammany-controlled city government in the 1890s that forced the Metropolitan Museum to extend its hours so that working-class New Yorkers could visit it. It was then that a deal that continues was struck: the city offered the financially-strapped museum free maintenance of the building in exchange for greater accessibility to the public.

From the 1850s to the 1870s, it was hoped that some metropolitan institution like the Académie Française might ensure proper cultural authority. But none of these plans came to fruition. Gradually, Godkin and others of the elite turned to the idea of a great university, on the model of the University of Berlin, as a source of legitimate cultural authority. They pushed Columbia University to convert itself from a sleepy, inward-looking college to a university committed to research and the training of a civic elite, a transformation begun in the 1880s and achieved under the remarkable presidency of Seth Low.[14] Such a university would create professional authority based on science and scholarship. There was no room for either Barnum or Whitman in this world, and both were marginalized, with Whitman decamping to Camden, New Jersey, and Barnum to Bridgeport, Connecticut.

The logic of postwar cultural authority was reminiscent of Morse's ambition for the National Academy of Design, which flourished in the late nineteenth century. Yet it also anticipated the terms of cultural authority in our own time, the authority of experts. In the past decade or so the autonomy of art-world experts have been challenged, and not always from the right. The most notable controversy concerned a Richard Serra sculpture at the Federal Building downtown. The art-world experts defended it, but the General Services Administration listened to the opinion of those who worked in the building. They were not interested in its place in art history and theory; for them it seemed to be an insulting disruption of the building's public plaza.[15]

In conclusion, let me return to Tocqueville. He captured a key moment in the structure of cultural authority in New York and America. It was a moment that, for all of its exclusions, celebrated the capacity of the self-sufficient individual, and it sustained perhaps the most robust democratic cultural and political practices we have seen in New York. (Note that I say *robust*, not *inclusive*.)

But Tocqueville pointed to another important issue, one that has been my main theme. Cultural authority is the object of continual negotiation, even contest, among various social groups and understandings of culture. I have tried to evoke three phases in the history of cultural authority in nineteenth-century New York. Patrician, democratic, and professional authorities at once succeeded each other and contested each other through the nineteenth century. It was within this context that art was made and evaluated and collected in New York. And the contest continues.

6

METROPOLITANISM AND
THE SPIRIT OF INVENTION

There is a greater connection between the geography of metropolitan life and the creativity of city culture than we usually recognize. The tendency in studies of urban culture is to emphasize the center of the metropolis, but in fact the whole of a highly differentiated metropolitan region is important. There are important decentralized resources for the production of knowledge. The spirit of invention depends upon very complex habitats of knowledge, and innovation often depends upon connecting them. Thomas A. Edison's extraordinary career of invention in New York not only reveals his remarkable capacity to bring together the resources he needed, but it also offers an opportunity to examine a particularly important moment in the history of metropolitanism.

Between 1869, when Edison arrived in New York as a journeyman telegrapher and sometime inventor, and World War I—by which time he was world renowned, with his name attached to large corporate enterprises in many fields—New York was transformed. The dimensions of the transformation are captured in two views of New York, one from 1876, the other from 1906. (Figures 6 and 18)

The city in 1870 was still a mercantile city. The wharves loomed large in its economy and iconography. New York's economic elite had earned its wealth in commerce and real estate. Commodore Vanderbilt's first Grand Central Terminal had just been completed on Forty-second Street, but water

18. View of New York from Brooklyn, 1905. Courtesy of the Museum of the City of New York (Gift of A. C. Johnson, Print Archives—Views)

remained more important than rails, or any heavy industry. Otis elevators had been installed in the Haughwout Building on Broadway, the Equitable Life Assurance Building downtown, and the Fifth Avenue Hotel at Madison Square, but the city remained a five-story city.

New York's industrial sector was substantial, but it was in small units. Diversity and multitudinousness, not scale, characterized the manufacturing sector. As late as 1900, the average industrial establishment in New York employed only thirteen workers, compared to four times that number in Chicago.[1] What was true of Manhattan was true of the metropolis; in fact, even in 1956, two-thirds of the New York metropolitan region's manufacturing establishments had fewer than twenty employees.[2]

By 1910, New York was an administrative center; the New York corporate elite managed a national network of large factories located at a distance, usually near raw materials. Manhattan had also become, as it remains today, a center for specialized financial services. The industries that were located in New York produced mainly for direct consumption (food, clothing, construction) or they were industries highly responsive to changes in technologies of production or consumer taste (luxury goods, women's clothing, publishing, and early cinema).

Manhattan had emerged as the nation's marketing center. For business-men seeking a national market, it was considered "important that the selling end be located here [in Manhattan]."[3] Edison adopted this practice in 1881 when he established a Manhattan office to market the Edison Lighting System. He could invent in Menlo Park, New Jersey, but in order to sell his inventions, he set himself up in a brownstone mansion at 65 Fifth Avenue.

Skyscrapers are both the functional result of this transformation and a symbol of it. The emergence of the "skyline," identified as a distinctive archi-tectural formation in *Harper's Weekly* in 1897, coincides with the unification of the region by rail and telegraph and the consolidation of the boroughs into greater New York. (Figure 19)[4] The metropolis expanded outward and upward during this period, relying upon a dense railroad and communication network to facilitate local specialization over an extensive metropolitan econ-omy.[5] The small units remained, but the skyline marked not only growing Manhattan dominance but corporate ascendance too. Gradually, corporate values and Wall Street financial power reshaped the metropolitan economy and with it the conditions of innovation.

The roots of these changes ran deep into the city's past, but the earliest recognition of a new and distinctly modern New York came very soon after Edison's arrival. One can get a sense of this by comparing the different impressions of the city recorded by two scientists arriving in the 1870s. The physicist-inventor Michael Pupin, an immigrant from the Austro-Hungarian empire, arrived in 1874. He made no mention of skyscrapers. He was struck by the "multitude" of ships, the "great masses of people," and the "throb" of activity.[6] He might have made the same comments in 1850. Only two years later Thomas Huxley came to New York, on his way, as we have seen, to the inauguration ceremonies of the newly established Johns Hopkins University. Recall that from the bay he observed that the New York skyline was domi-nated by the Tribune Building and the just-completed Western Union Building. (Figure 20) "This is America," he remarked. "In the Old World the first things you see as you approach a city are steeples; here you see, first, cen-ters of intelligence."[7]

Edison had been given work space in the basement of the previous Western Union headquarters. But in the new building, designed by George Post, who would later design many of the city's most important commercial buildings including the Stock Exchange and the Produce Exchange, there

19. From "The Sky-line of Buildings Below
Chambers Street," by Fred Pansing.
© Collection of the New-York Historical Society

20. Western Union Building:
Broadway, Looking South
from Above Vesey Street
(undated, probably ca. 1876).
Courtesy of the Museum of
the City of New York (Print
Archives)

were no freelance inventors working in the basement. It represented the
beginnings of a new corporate culture, and in 1876 Western Union contract-
ed with Edison for research in his just-established Menlo Park laboratory.

I do not want to exaggerate the dimensions of this change during Edison's
era. In fact, my point is to emphasize the complex interplay of an older form
of metropolitanism and the emergent corporate form of a metropolis. As Jane
Jacobs argued in her quite brilliant book about economic innovation, *Cities
and the Wealth of Nations* (1984), a distinctively urban economy is made up of
innumerable small units, all of which rely upon other small businesses and
shops from which goods or services can be purchased. Each of these might
also serve as sources for analogical solutions to problems. Her argument
refers specifically to the way cities nourish the spirit of innovation in economic life and sustain continuing growth, but it is clear that she would be
willing to extend her analysis more generally as a theory of urban creativity.
She contrasts this vital economy of cities with national or international cor-
porate/bureaucratic economic organizations, which in their quest for self-
sufficiency and control become cumbersome and lose the entrepreneurial
spirit and capacity for invention that she so admires.[8]

One need not fully agree with her valuation of the two types of economic organization in order to appreciate the historical and analytical distinction she makes between urban and corporate/bureaucratic modes of organizing the metropolitan economy and social life.[9] Detroit and Route 128 outside of Boston are variants of the posturban corporate urban model she disdains. Following the argument of AnnaLee Saxenian, I would locate Silicon Valley closer to Edison's New York than to contemporary Route 128. Save for its centerlessness (San Jose, California, is as close to a center as one will find, if one can find the center of San Jose), she argues that Silicon Valley is a novel geography of invention and entrepreneurialism that replicates in a new way older forms of metropolitanism. The Valley, in her account, mixes corporate resources with small-scale entrepreneurial innovation. Lacking a strong civic sense coterminous with municipal boundaries, there is nonetheless a strong local identity that celebrates a particular cultural and entrepreneurial style. While large corporations and the national government programs play a role, the energy of small units remains vital. The complex pattern of interdependence and interaction that characterizes cities is shown by Saxenian to be amply present in Silicon Valley, where two great universities, major international corporations, and entrepreneurship flourish together.[10]

New York in the age of Edison had all of this—plus a center. What is important in New York at the turn of the century was the mix between centering and decentralization, large-scale/bureaucratic and small-scale and entrepreneurial, between shop-floor knowledge and academic knowledge. Each of these habitats of knowledge was sufficiently present to partially but not wholly define the context of innovation and invention. There was to be sure a tension between these intellectual and organizational styles or cultures. But it was a creative tension, and Edison's career reveals how fruitful it could be.

If the city and its metropolitan region were marked by an elaborate division of labor, which allowed for the "proliferation of small, interdependent producers," Edison chose well in establishing his first shop in Newark.[11] He may have been looking for lower rents than he could find in Manhattan—he later left Newark because of a conflict with his landlord. But it is more likely that he found in Newark a labor force of exceptional size, diversity, and skill, particularly in the trades most important to his work: iron and brass castings, hand and machine tools, precision metalworking, and chemicals. Edison, whose mode of thinking and working had been formed in the craft or shop culture of the world of telegraphers, preserved that kind of work environment in Newark and, later, Menlo Park.

In moving across space (or the Hudson River) he went backward in time to a still-vital world of mechanics in Newark, where three-fourths of the workforce were engaged in manufacturing, mostly in small shops and with expectations of owning their own shops.[12] But he reached for the future as well as the past: the great gift of the metropolis to Edison was the combination of an older work habitat in which he flourished and direct access to the capital and financial services, corporate leadership, and professional knowledge—especially in law and engineering—that was available in Manhattan. Edison understood this, remarking in his autobiographical notes that other cities "did not have the experts we had in New York to handle anything complicated."[13] Edison was not alone in exploiting the resources of the region. Between 1866 and 1886, 80 percent of the inventors with five or more telegraph-related patents resided in or within commuting distance of New York.[14]

Much of Edison's success was dependent upon Wall Street financing and corporate support services, especially legal expertise. After 1882, Edison and the Edison companies focused much of their work on litigation, defending patents. The availability of the extraordinary legal talent that had concentrated in New York by the end of the nineteenth century was crucial to Edison's success as a businessman and inventor.

When Edison moved his activities to Menlo Park in 1876, he brought his most valued Newark workers with him, and he maintained the shop culture they all shared. Over time, however, the balance of the older urban ways and newer corporate ones shifted toward the latter. Comparing pictures of his shop, a "plain wooden structure," described as "barn-like," with his later corporate laboratory at West Orange makes the change graphic.[15] (Figures 21 and 22) The Menlo Park laboratory was in fact a shop. It looked like a shop, and the work culture in it was that of a traditional, even preindustrial shop. The spirit was entrepreneurial; many of the mechanics later became quite wealthy as manufacturers, often by becoming Edison partners, manufactur-

21. Thomas Edison's "Invention Factory," 1880. Courtesy of the Edison Natural Historic Site

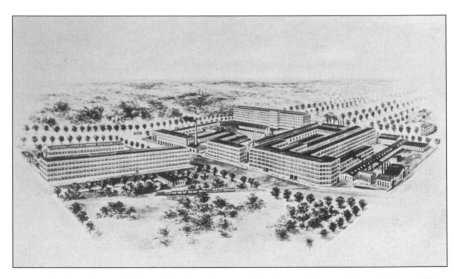

22. Bird's-Eye View of Edison Works, Orange, New Jersey. From *Office Appliances* (July, 1908). Courtesy of the Edison National Historical Site

ing one of his inventions. Charles Batchelor, his principal assistant, who became a wealthy partner, was a mechanic with a gift for imaginative experimentation.[16]

Edison worked with his mechanics. Anxious to maintain momentum on a project, he might keep them with him at the bench all night, but he would join with them in a festive break, sharing a midnight feast prepared for them by his wife, or he might horse around with them. His nearby house was not really apart from the shop and its workers, and he often he brought his children across to the shop. His leadership style, as André Millard has written, was like the "master" of a "machine shop."[17] If his house in Menlo Park was integrated with the lives of his workers and with the work of the shop, once the West Orange laboratory was established, Edison lived like a corporate executive in a named home, Glenmont, in the exclusive New Jersey planned community of Llewellyn Park. (Figure 23)

Although he understood the importance of the largely undifferentiated and free-flowing ways of shop culture in his design for West Orange, it could not be replicated in what was by the 1890s a corporate lab, funded by the Edison Companies as a central research facility with a managerial hierarchy and considerable specialization.[18] His attitudes toward labor moved from the spirit of shop-floor cooperation to managerial antagonism to unions.[19]

23. Glenmont: Edison's Home. Courtesy of the Edison National Historic Site

He described the lab at West Orange as "the best equipped and largest laboratory extant." That might well have been true, and he sought there a self-sufficiency that was corporate rather than urban.[20]

Edison flourished in a habitat where knowledge was developed out of discussion and doing.[21] His thought was also—and this is typical of nineteenth--century inventors and skilled workers—fundamentally visual in orientation.[22] Reading through the published volumes of the Edison Papers one is struck by the complete absence of mathematical or abstract formulations. Visual representation was for Edison a form of thinking. Only later, when he was working on the electric light, did he bring trained mathematicians into the Menlo Park lab, thus gaining direct access to the theoretical and abstract forms of knowledge produced in the city's universities.[23] He had earlier drawn upon mathematical expertise through less formal relationships with mathematicians and scientists at New York University, Stevens Institute of Technology, Princeton University, and the University of Pennsylvania, but he had not incorporated mathematicians into the laboratory itself.

But even then he and Batchelor discovered the crucially important carbon conductor for the electric light after the fashion of shop culture, simply trying a miscellany of carbonized substances until one worked.[24] He may have used university-based theory when he needed it, but he tended to rely upon his senses, especially his visual sense. He solved problems by drawing them or by making models. Models, immediately apprehended by visual inspection, provided a shop-floor alternative to theory.

There may have been something in the urban culture of metropolitan New York that promoted and rewarded visual understanding. Academic culture distrusted visual knowledge, favoring instead theorized knowledge not evident to the naked eye of the untrained. Modern metropolitan culture, outside of academic disciplines, I would argue, privileges sight. And no place more than New York, which seems to stimulate, educate, and recognize the eye and visual understanding more than most great cities.[25] In this context, it is worth recalling the argument of Brooke Hindle that the invention of the telegraph by New York's Samuel F. B. Morse depended upon his special capacity, as a trained artist, for visual understanding.[26]

At West Orange, where Edison moved in 1887, the number of employees with advanced scientific training increased, and mathematics became more of the workaday world of the laboratory, especially in the development of the dynamo.[27] There seems to have been some kind of fit between corporate industry and the way the emerging research university organized itself and produced knowledge. Hierarchical and seeking greater control over conditions of their own work, both tended to withdraw from the complexity of city culture and its ad hoc, informal procedures.[28]

Edison's technological gifts to New York partly established the city's distinctive modernity. No one better grasped and represented this new New York than the painter Joseph Stella. He was fascinated by New York's leap into a twentieth-century modernity. New York became the preeminent city of powerful technology and novel energy, most notably vertical height and electrical light. This city that so captured the imagination of American and European artists was in many ways Edison's city. The city they endlessly discussed, painted, and photographed he had helped make. He offered them more than new images of modernity; the city of skyscrapers and lights refigured the cultural possibilities of America, moving it from the periphery to the center. The new New York allowed artists to escape feelings of parochialism and marginality, for in painting New York they were representing America as modernity.[29]

Much of the change was represented by Coney Island. For example, when Marcel Duchamp—who had first come to New York in 1913 to display his controversial *Nude Descending a Staircase* at the Armory Show—returned in 1915, after the war had broken out in Europe, John Quinn, the lawyer and patron who was central to the show's organization, took him on an excursion to Coney Island.[30] In a way hard to grasp today, Coney Island, with its combination of technology and pleasure, somehow represented New York and New York's modernity. And Stella, soon upon his return to the United States from Paris, made it the subject of a painting.

In Paris Stella had discovered the French modernists and was fascinated by the fit between modernist aesthetics and modern urban life. Just before his departure, he had seen Robert Delaunay's *La Ville de Paris* (1912), which captured the modernity of the city in a single image of the Eiffel Tower. He tried in *Battle of Lights, Coney Island, Mardi Gras* (1913–14) to do the same for the American city. (Figure 24) Then he turned to the Brooklyn Bridge. But New York was to prove too complex to be represented by any one image or perspective; it required a multifaceted approach. In *New York Interpreted* (1920–22),

24. *The Battle of Lights, Coney Island, Mardi Gras,* 1913–14, by Joseph Stella. Courtesy of Yale University Art Gallery (Gift of Collection Socíeté Anonyme)

a series of five paintings now in the Newark Museum, he explored and brilliantly represented the essentials of the new New York, a city that had nourished Edison's inventiveness and was now in part a product of it. (Figure 25) Stella declared:

> Steel and electricity had created a new world. A new drama had surged from the unmerciful violation of darkness at night, by the violent blaze of electricity and a new polyphony was ringing all around with the scintillating, highly colored lights. The steel had leaped to hyperbolic altitudes and expanded to vast latitudes with the skyscrapers and with bridges made for the conjunction of worlds. A new architecture was created, a new perspective.[31]

The challenge for the "creative mind" at the turn of the century, Lewis Mumford observed, was "to face this New York of boundless misdirected energy and to capture a portion of that wasteful flow for his own purposes,

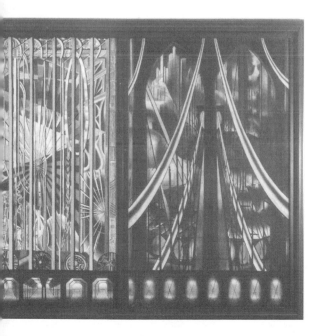

25. *The Voice of the City of New York Interpreted*, 1920–22, by Joseph Stella. Courtesy of the Newark Museum (Purchase 1937, Felix Fuld Bequest Fund)

using its force without accepting its habitual channels and its habitual destinations."[32] In fact, it was easier in New York to break out of conventional or traditional modes, simply because they were weaker. That is one of the keys to New York as a habitat for invention and innovation.

Henry James is often quoted on the weakness of tradition and institutions in New York and America. One recalls, of course, his famous listing of American absences in the preface to his biography of Hawthorne, published in 1879. James is always misunderstood on that point. The litany was not a condemnation of American culture. His point was that something novel was being created in America. He was insisting upon the need to probe more deeply into the opportunities of American culture. A suggestion of what James, the New Yorker—not the Bostonian so many try to make him—had in mind can be inferred from a private letter he wrote about the time of Edison's arrival in New York. He grasped creative opportunities inherent in the combination of the cultural energy described by Mumford and the institutional weakness he had observed. I quote from a letter of 1867:

> . . . [W]e young Americans are (without cant) men of the future. . . . I think that to be an American is an excellent preparation for culture. . . . [W]e can deal freely with forms of civilization not our own, can pick and choose and assimilate and in short (aesthetically etc.) claim our property wherever we find it. To have no national stamp has hitherto been a defect and a drawback, but I think it not unlikely that American writers may yet indicate that a vast intellectual fusion and synthesis of the various National tendencies of the world is the condition of more important achievements than any we have seen. . . . I expect nothing great during your lifetime or mine perhaps: but my instincts quite agree . . . in looking to see something original and beautiful disengage itself from our ceaseless fermentation and turmoil.[33]

James reaffirmed this understanding of cultural possibility in *The American Scene* (1907), with his observations on his return to New York in 1904 after many years abroad. Contrary to most accounts, which suggest an irredeemable ethnocentrism, he was drawn to the energy, passion, and invention of the café society of the Jewish Lower East Side. There, he thought, elements of the admittedly weak American tradition were being mixed with an ethnic particularism that might nourish cultural invention and a cosmopolitan greatness.[34]

The result was a cultural field that could be disorienting, but with the potential to nurture novelty and enable invention. In the language of con-temporary social science, New York was a liminal milieu, where established categories and distinctions blurred. As a result, creativity in New York was achieved in the interstices. One cannot, I think, overstate the importance of contest and mixing in New York, the mixing of levels and genres and aesthetic traditions. Just as Edison worked at the intersection of and blurred the boundaries of chemistry, physics, engineering, and capitalism, so a more gen-eral crossing of conventional barriers and definitions made New York the home of cultural innovation and modernity.

The center has never held firmly in New York; it has been continually undermined by the fragmentation of the elite and by manifold rebellions. New York provides a contrast to Boston or Paris, where established institu-tions were strong. If the habitats of knowledge in New York were sometimes diffuse and hard to bring into focus, the opposite was true in Boston and Paris. In Paris, the strength of centralized elite institutions prompted the invention of an avant-garde that in the name of innovation confronted estab-lished institutions and traditions.[35] Institutional solidity in Boston resulted in a culture of excellence that was deeply academic, seldom daring or rebellious, sometimes stolid, and often detached, genteel, and even mystical.[36]

New York was more welcoming of the new than was Boston, and the atmosphere was less confrontational than in Paris. But New York's virtues of vitality and openness bordering on the chaotic carried their own vices. There was always a danger. Standards were constantly at risk. Would the pursuit of profit or even the joy of invention for its own sake result in crudeness and superficiality? It was such a danger that proponents of high art and pure sci-ence sought to counter.

The challenge of anticommercialism, or an alternative to commercialism, is essential in a commercial culture. And one of the legacies of the metropolis in the age of Edison was the invention and flourishing of nonprofit institutions devoted to science, scholarship, and art—from the Metropolitan Museum of Art and the American Museum of Natural History, both founded in 1870, to the creation of graduate faculties at Columbia and New York universities in the 1880s, to the establishment of the New York Public Library in 1904, and the founding of the first generation of major American foundations devoted to the advancement of knowledge—Russell Sage, Carnegie, and Rockefeller.

New York has found it difficult, even if essential, to maintain these alternatives to commerce and to use them to establish a secure balance between the claim of aesthetic tradition and the greediness of commerce, between institutional inertia and anti-institutional self-indulgence, between genteel irrelevance and crude anti-intellectualism. When we seek to understand the conditions of creativity that enabled New York to become so closely identified with modernity in life and art, certainly commerce is fundamental. It fueled the materialist civilization that produced the physical transformation of life in Manhattan that so powerfully symbolized, for so many, "scenes of the world to come."[37]

Commerce is important in another way. Insofar as New York established itself as the center of culture, it was because the business of culture was located in the city. Whether one speaks of publishing and communications, of galleries and producers, it was the same entrepreneurial spirit that marked the Edison enterprises that characterized the culture more broadly. This marketplace absorbed innovation more readily than did the established institutions of Paris. The market diffuses conflict, whether economic or cultural, and this may account for the presence of many rebellions but few avant-gardes in New York, as compared to Paris.[38] But the market is worrisome, even as it supplies a field for diverse initiatives and rebellions of various sorts. Its absorptive powers can be costly: the commodification of art and dilution of its meaning.

The role of commerce in cultural transformation has been much examined by historians in recent years. The outline of the current interpretation was sketched out nearly twenty years ago by John Kasson, in a book about Coney Island. In the era of Victorian culture—what I would call the brownstone culture of New York—middle-class tastemakers and commercial cultural producers sustained the elite cultural ideals that were manifest in the support of museums, libraries, college curricula, and public art, like Central Park. But there was always a vigorous commercial culture that subverted the genteel ideals of brownstone culture, and it found legitimacy at Coney Island and Times Square. It also established itself in the spread of cabarets, movies, and popular music.[39] "Slowly at first," Kasson writes, "then quickly as the twentieth century advanced, the genteel middle-class cultural order crumbled. And the entrepreneur of mass culture, who had previously helped to solidify the authority of genteel values, discovered new opportunities outside of its confines."[40] Victorian gender roles and proprieties were undermined, and entertainment was transformed. Edison contributed his bit to this transformation of culture in one of his first movies, *Bathing Scene at Coney Island* (1896).

Gradually the new culture pioneered at Coney Island migrated to Times Square, which further sponsored a new tolerance of diversity and exploited the ambiguity of boundaries in the cultural realm, in life and in art. This new commercially generated culture was broadcast nationally from Times Square, at first through travelling theater companies, later through radio and the movies. Even after movie production moved to Hollywood, capital and talent remained in New York, and movie companies maintained Times Square headquarters.[41] The local vernacular that was invented in Times Square (such words as *scram, palooka, wisecrack,* and *pushover*) was nationalized by theater, radio, film, and Times Square writers like Damon Runyon and the lyrics of Irving Berlin.[42]

High art and more popular arts were less firmly separated in New York than in other American cities. The invention of modern dance by Martha Graham in New York, one of America's major contributions to international high art, built upon a variety of popular theater sources and the Delsarte women's physical-fitness program of the late nineteenth century.[43] The sources of jazz, another distinctive contribution of American culture to the high art of the twentieth century, were equally complex.

In New York, commerce helped to weaken the distinction between art and entertainment. Modernism absorbed popular art forms. But the influences went the other way as well. High art forms found their way into popular performance and imagery.[44] If George Balanchine drew upon the ordinary street life of Times Square in inventing his neoclassical ballets, he brought his sophisticated vocabulary of ballet to Broadway musicals of the 1930s and 1940s. And the Viennese-trained modernist architect, Joseph Urban, achieved a remarkable new form in bringing his European modernism to the design of the Roxy theater in Times Square.

Lawrence Levine has recently argued very aggressively that high culture and low were more sharply divided than ever in the period we are discussing.[45] He is surely wrong in respect to New York, and probably elsewhere. The career of James Gibbons Huneker, the critical advocate of international modernism in Gilded Age New York, explored a remarkably diverse musical culture and art world in New York. That very diversity both opened the way for modernism to emerge in New York and provided much of the material upon which it would build. In fact, the *Musical Courier*, where Huneker promoted modernism, had been founded as a trade magazine for manufacturers of pianos, organs, and sewing machines, an audience very close in class and culture to the men with whom Edison worked in Newark and Menlo Park.[46]

The musical culture of New York was inclusive, embracing, as Joseph Horowitz has recently demonstrated, all classes, immigrants and native born, men and women.[47] The very richness and range of that culture is the relevant context for the invention and commercial success of the phonograph. Perhaps a single musical institution or aesthetic dominated the musical culture of Chicago or Boston, but not New York's, where—like much else in the culture—opera and orchestras were a battleground over aesthetics. As the *Musical Courier* observed in 1903, "there is no civic pride" in New York; "the mixture of population prevents a consolidation of any one artistic direction."[48] Such fragmentation opened space for contemporary music, including American music and opera in English.[49] It enabled, perhaps encouraged, Antonín Dvořák, who wrote the *New World Symphony* in New York, to look toward African American music as the foundation of an American music.

I would not want anyone to infer from this last comment that some important cases of crossing racial barriers imply that New York was not marked, heavily marked, by racism.[50] Yet the crossovers were important and illustrative of the character of New York as a center for creativity. Much of the best writing, including Nella Larsen's *Passing* (1929), was about racial ambiguity. My point here, however, concerns a convergence of interests among modernist writers and artists, black and white.

Both groups were seeking to define a new, a modern American culture with room for people like themselves. That convergence was enabling in a fresh and important way. It invited rejection of past boundaries and restrictions and encouraged the mixing of aesthetic norms: genteel American culture, African American aesthetic traditions, and the modernist challenge became a terrain for invention, most notably in the poetry of Langston Hughes, the stories of Zora Neale Hurston, the murals of Aaron Douglas. White artists and intellectuals from downtown were interested in what was happening in the Harlem renaissance. So were Europeans. During the 1920s, while still in Europe, George Balanchine was becoming intrigued with the "jazzy and syncopated" rhythms he identified with New York, and that was one of the reasons he left Paris for New York in 1933.[51] A boundary that had isolated black culture was breached, if not removed, with positive consequences for creative endeavor on both sides of the boundary.

The domain of art was being redefined at the turn of the century, and the extension of the content of art had implications for formal innovations in composition, in both painting and literature. Theodore Dreiser, who had begun as a journalist, brought the subject matter of the daily press into fiction—and some of the cruder writing.[52] Similarly, John Sloan, the painter, earned his livelihood as a magazine illustrator, not selling his first painting until he was almost fifty. He brought daily-life episodes and ordinary people into high art. Like Edison, who had been a press telegrapher, Sloan used his familiarity with the world of the press and advertising to advance various artistic enterprises. He was thus able to make the exhibit of "the Eight" at the Macbeth Gallery in 1908, a cultural event that still echoes through the history of art and the city.[53]

"The Eight" also exemplify the fragmentation of the art world of New York, and the opportunities it offered. Between 1870 and 1917, the singular dominance of the National Academy of Design was challenged, not by a revolutionary avant-garde, as in Paris, but by the proliferation of commercial galleries, self-defined groups, and alternative schools. None of these were completely distinct; memberships in these groups overlapped. Several of "the Eight" were members of the Academy; most had recently shown in the Academy's annual exhibit.[54]

Let me return to Edison and move to a conclusion with a brief discussion of Edison and the cinema. The history of this Edison invention summarizes my themes—and highlights the paradox of successful innovation in New York. Early cinema, first of all, reveals the excellence of New York as a habitat for forms of business and art demanding a continuing conversation between commerce and creativity, technology and aesthetics, producer and consumer. The flow back and forth among commercial, technical, and aesthetic opportunities and decisions is almost seamless in the early movies.[55]

Cinema in its first decade also shows the transformation and movement of genres so common in New York. The early films have been characterized as a "visual newspaper," with news, cartoons, sports, travel, and human-interest stories.[56] One of the earliest films, as I have already indicated, sought to capture the new culture of Coney Island. After 1905, however, film moved away from this newspaper model to a storytelling mode seeking to define itself as "simple amusement," a shift that, after several intermediate steps, emerged as the so-called "classic" and corporate Hollywood style of the 1930s.[57]

The work of making movies at West Orange was very much in the tradition of the shop culture that had characterized Newark and Menlo Park. The studio building Edison constructed, dubbed "Black Maria," was more like a workshop than the rest of the laboratory complex. Among the Edison employees assigned to making movies, "work, pleasure, and socializing" were, in the phrase of film scholar Charles Musser, "interwoven." In fact, the first commercially successful Edison movie, *The Blacksmith Scene*, made in Black Maria in 1893, was developed and acted by Edison's mechanics as a group project.[58]

Edwin S. Porter, the first great American filmmaker, had been, like his employer, a telegraph operator and inventor. Committed to the values of the shop culture—and working in an informal, collaborative manner—he made commercially successful films for Edison, including two classics, *The Fireman* and *The Great Train Robbery*. But as the Edison company tilted more toward a corporate and hierarchical mode of organization, driven by the pursuit of profits and relying upon litigation in defense of Edison patents to achieve a monopoly, Porter became increasingly uncomfortable. By 1909, Porter, who represented an older metropolitan style of commerce and culture, was ready to quit, and Edison was prepared to fire him—and he did.

This little story encapsulates one of the key lessons of my whole account: let me call it the paradox of progress. The great gift of Edison's New York as a locale of invention and innovation was the diversity of habitats of knowledge and the possibilities of interaction among them. But the progress of invention seems to have facilitated a shift from urban complexity to corporate control. This shift threatened the complex interplay of urban and corporate/bureaucratic modes of living, thinking, and inventing. The challenge for culture-making as well as for profit-making is to devise ways of maintaining that richness of habitat—something that remains possible, Annalee Saxenian suggests, even in the new geographies that increasingly frame metropolitanism a century after Edison's New York.[59]

7

MODERNIST AESTHETICS
AND URBAN POLITICS

Urban modernity privileges the visual. Classic essays on the topic, whether one refers to Baudelaire's unsettling writings about Paris, Simmel's sociological analysis of Berlin in "The Metropolis and Mental Life," Carl Schorske's historical evocation of fin-de-siècle Vienna, or Richard Sennett's essayistic explorations of contemporary New York, utilize a scopic approach to frame their representations of specifically modern urban culture.[1] Not surprisingly, artistic modernism, at least in painting and photography, has been closely associated with the city—and vice versa.

With these commonplaces reiterated, I want to examine a phase of artistic modernism in New York City in roughly the first third of the twentieth century. Not too long ago, there was thought to be a single logic to artistic modernism in New York: the development of abstract painting and sculpture, from the introduction of Postimpressionist art into New York by Alfred Stieglitz at his 291 Gallery and a couple of years later in the famous Armory Show of 1913 to the international "triumph" of Abstract Expressionism in the 1940s.[2] But that story has now been complicated, partly by curatorial judgments that elevated Edward Hopper, for example, to the status of major modernist, and partly by recent scholarship.[3] It is now becoming common to delineate a realist or representational as well as an abstract modernism in the history of painting and photography in New York City. At least two additional major modernisms centered in the city deserve note, though they will not be addressed here. One I would call Duchampian conceptualism, with his ready-mades, and it points toward New York minimalism.[4] The other is an African American modernist tradition in painting, beginning with the painters of the Harlem Renaissance and continuing. It partly tracks the other modernisms, but it is clearly distinguishable—not only for its content, but also in terms of genres and styles.

Here, however, I will examine two bodies of early modern New York painting and photography, one representational, the other abstract, treating each—to adapt a phrase of Raymond Williams—as a "structure of perception" that aims to frame the meaning of modernity in New York City.[5] There is a politics embedded in each of these two strategies, and I propose to identify that politics not only in the realm of aesthetics, but also in the conventional political ideologies and movements of the city in the twentieth century. In associating art and politics here, I mean to suggest that aesthetics, by giving powerful form to our structures of perception, helps to shape, reinforce, and reshape structures of power. One of the services of history and of the humanities in general is to highlight and continually reexamine these historical constructions of perception and power.

The structures of perception that we shall be defining here bear a partial resemblance to a brief commentary on New York in Michel de Certeau's book, *The Practice of Everyday Life*. In a chapter titled "Walking in the City," Certeau explores his subjective relationship to the physical and visual force of the modern city, which he describes elsewhere as "a sort of *epic* of the eye." Recounting a visit to the observation deck of the World Trade Center, he speaks of the pleasure, even erotic ecstasy, of seeing the city "whole" from above.

In fact, here and elsewhere, his references to a totalizing vision and a panoptic perspective bring little insight to the notion of the whole. But he does say quite a bit, perhaps unconsciously, about perspective, and in particular about being able to look down upon parts of the city. One becomes Icarus, flying high, transfigured by the elevation "into a voyeur." The voyeur observes at a distance. Position "transforms the bewitching world by which one was 'possessed' into a text that lies before one's eyes. It allows one to read it, to be a Solar eye." Here is realized "the lust to be a viewpoint and nothing more." Posed against this Olympian site of clarity available to the "voyeur-god," is the darker, grimier city of the masses who lack the self-awareness and understanding that comes with height and enlightenment. "The ordinary practitioners of the city live 'down below,' below the threshold" of such empowering visibility. Down there are the "walkers" who write the urban text, but, claims Certeau, "without being able to read it." To enter this world is to become enmeshed in the story, in "the networks of these moving, intersecting writings [that] compose a manifold story that has neither author nor spectator."[6]

Certeau explicitly identifies the first structure of urban perception with the modern planner, and I will do the same in what follows. But his second characterization invites challenge. Even as he wishes to rescue the ordinary lives of the city, Certeau, like the planner, grants them too little. There are authors to the stories, and spectators as well. The narratives, however, inevitably remain obscure; one will know there is a story, but not be sure of its origins or its trajectory. What Certeau, like the planners, omits is the historicity of the city. The two structures of perception to be examined here also constitute two attitudes toward history: one largely denying or freezing history into a perpetual urban present; the other insisting that the city itself is historical, perhaps even a sum of microhistories. The ordinary people of New York are continually and partly making their own and the city's history.

Although Certeau does not say it directly, he implies, quite correctly, that twentieth-century planning converts the city into an abstraction, often articulated in either geometric or quantitative terms. What he does not say, but could say, is that history resists abstraction, and insofar as one understands urban places as the precipitate (social, narrative, physical) of lived experience over time, the historical city represents a contrast to that of the planners.

Modern painting and literature in turn-of-the-century New York moved out of doors and explored a novel kind of urban life and form. The modernity of New York was a sudden, even a startling, discovery. The illustrator John Pennell remarked at the time that "the new New York has come, come in my life time. I have seen it come. . . ." Like other artists of his generation, he sought to possess this moment in his art. "I have," he reflected, "loved it, and drawn it, and I shall go on drawing it till the end, it is mine, it was made for me."[7]

Magazine illustrators had long been interested in the city, and popular literature often narrated the urban scene, as in Horatio Alger's *Ragged Dick* (1867). Higher forms of literature, most notably the novels of Edith Wharton and Henry James, kept the action mostly indoors. But Theodore Dreiser, who had worked as a newspaper reporter, brought the themes and the style of the press into the novel. The boundary between the enclosed city of brownstone culture and the more public city life that characterized popular writing was blurred. The same shift occurred in painting as one moves, for example, from John Singer Sargent's studio to William Glackens's and Maurice Prendergast's paintings of the out-of-doors.[8]

If both versions of New York modernism that I will discuss were deeply indebted to the process of discovering and representing the city, I want to emphasize that writers and artists discovered and represented two very different cities. One is a City of Ambition, what Dreiser in *Sister Carrie* characterized as a "walled city" or a "sea of whales."[9] The other city, not often described in the canonical works of American literature, is a City of Making Do. It is focused on daily life, on neighborhoods, local streets, and families. One finds accounts of this New York in stories and novels written by immigrants, especially women, like Anna Yezierska's stories. But some WASP writers, like Hutchins Hapgood in *The Spirit of the Ghetto* (1912) and even the canonical Henry James in his remarkable report on New York in *The American Scene* (1907), were drawn to the more "authentic" life of the Lower East Side.[10] The imagery of this city is that of ethnic enclaves and neighborhoods, of local entertainments and small businesses. Certainly this world too is a milieu of ambition, but this ambition is complicated by external constraints and, often, internal doubts. Here the aim is more to prevail than to triumph.

The two traditions (or faces) of artistic modernism to be considered here can be most conveniently identified as the work of distinct circles of self-consciously modern artists in early twentieth-century New York. It is even more convenient to identify each with a particular figure: Alfred Stieglitz for one group, and John Sloan for the other.[11] Both were deeply interested in the city, and they were equally fascinated by the aesthetic implications of its representation.

The different kinds of literary representations that I have outlined parallel the distinction I want to make in respect to pictorial representations in art and photography. To some extent, it is a contrast between "realism" and "abstraction," but that is not quite correct. One might also call it a difference between content and form, or politics and aesthetics. But neither is this formulation really accurate. I cannot think of a better way of stating the difference than this: Steiglitz and his circle were particularly interested in the formal qualities of the city, in its geometry. The city for them is largely physical, something to see: it represents novel and interesting forms. The most interesting forms, moreover, seem to be associated with the architecture of modern, corporate power. Sloan too is drawn to the physical qualities of the city, but for him and his circle they are never so important as the human activities and connections for which they provide a stage. Formal opportunities are often exploited with great effect, but the emphasis is elsewhere, on human stories. Both groups are drawn to the romance of the modern city, but the nature of the romance is radically different for each: warm, soft, and slightly nostalgic for Sloan; cool, hard-edged, and futuristic for Stieglitz.

Pictorial space is handled differently by the two groups of artists. Among the Sloan group there is an invitation to enter the picture, an invitation not apparent in the work of the Stieglitz group. Put differently, not only is there more pictorial depth in the work of Sloan, but one can imagine oneself being in these spaces—and their optical character, not their thematic content, is the reason. The inviting depth we find in these pictures recalls a comment by Clement Greenberg, when he compared the relative flatness or "silting in," as he called it, in the work of the Impressionists with Cezanne's restoration of depth or "stereometric" space.[12]

Alfred Stieglitz identified the "City of Ambition" with the skyscraper—the Singer Building, to be precise—in a photograph of that title, made in 1910. (Figure 26) It is a powerful image; the skyline represents the desire that gives content to ambition. Stieglitz inscribed the print he gave to Paul Haviland with a phrase that implied the endlessness of this desire: "Does it tower into the skies? Beyond them?" he wrote.[13]

Not only is it difficult to imagine oneself into this pictorial space, but two questions emerge when one moves from its aesthetic qualities to its social history context: 1) What historical narrative connects this city with the lived experience of the viewer? 2) How does one enter this city? Even with the shadowy ferry slip visible in the foreground, it is difficult to find a practical route into the walled city. The City of Ambition is nearly always viewed from the outside; it is hard to enter, whether from the Jersey towns from which Stieglitz photographed the Singer Building or from Sloan's New York neighborhoods. Perhaps no one said it better in one sentence than did Norman Podhoretz a generation later. He opened his autobiography, *Making It*, with

26. *City of Ambition*, 1910, by Alfred Stieglitz. Courtesy of the J. Paul Getty Museum, Los Angeles. © Estate of Georgia O'Keeffe

the observation that "one of the longest journeys in the world is the journey from Brooklyn to Manhattan—or at least from certain neighborhoods in Brooklyn to certain parts of Manhattan."[14]

In some ways, Stieglitz's picture could represent the search for the gate into the walled city of Dreiser's *Sister Carrie*, or, perhaps even more precisely, the city Dreiser described in his autobiographical work, *The Color of a Great City*, when he wrote:

> If you were to . . . see the picture it presents to the incoming eye, you would assume it was all that it seemed. Glory for those who enter its walls seeking glory. . . . The sad part of it is, however, that the island and its beauty are, to a certain extent, a snare. Its seeming loveliness, which promises so much to the innocent eye, is not always easy of realization.[15]

Whatever the similarities of their fascinations with the city, Stieglitz understood the challenge of New York very differently than did Dreiser. The early chapters of *Sister Carrie* establish Carrie Meeber's trajectory and indicate the resources available to her as she enters into the life of the American metropolis. Dreiser warns that New York is no easy triumph, promising success to no one, neither the ambitious nor the virtuous, and the story becomes a dialogue between the talents and aspirations of Carrie and the city as the terrain of her ambition. Stieglitz offers a very different representation of the meaning and possibility of ambition. That representation is aesthetically powerful, but there is no sense of trajectory or history. He has created an icon that silences such stories as Carrie's.

The denial of history, of narrative, is typical of the urban representations of Stieglitz and his circle. Compare it, for example, with Aaron Douglas's later sequence of paintings that constituted *Aspects of Negro Life* (1934), painted for the Countee Cullen Branch of the New York Public Library. He too understands, especially in a preliminary sketch, the power of the skyscraper, but it does not stand alone for him. Murals as a genre are narratives, and Douglas offers the history of an epic folk movement, the story of the African American quest for freedom and equal opportunity. Describing the final panel, *Song of the Towers* (Figure 27), which presents the city as a destination of promise, Douglas wrote:

> A great migration away from the clutching hand of serfdom in the South to the urban and industrial life in America, began during the First World War. And with it was born a new will to creative self-expression which quickly grew in the New Negro movement of the 'twenties.[16]

Vertis Hayes, in *The Pursuit of Happiness*, a mural done in the 1930s for the nurses' residence of the Harlem Hospital, offers a similar narrative and iconography of African American aspiration.

The romance of the modern city for modernists of the Stieglitz stripe is represented by an aesthetic of distance. When Sloan and his circle got closer and put their feet on the ground, the romance changed. Instead of a distant, glistening modernity, one becomes aware of the oldness, the layers, and the mixing that characterizes the metropolis.

Few visions of the City of Ambition include people. If they do, they are often dwarfed by huge structures representing the power of modern technol-

27. *Aspects of Negro Life: Song of the Towers*, 1934, by Aaron Douglas. Oil on Canvas, 9' x 9'. Courtesy of the Schomburg Center for Research in Black Culture, Art and Artifacts Division, the New York Public Library, Astor, Lenox, and Tilden Foundation

ogy. By contrast, the closer view of the ordinary city portrayed by Sloan and his ilk stresses common city people doing the things they ordinarily do. More often than not, the people represented are working class—or not far from working class. New York has today become such a racially and class divided city that it takes some effort to recall the essentially working and lower-middle-class character of the city in the first half of the twentieth century. Save for a few photographs in the first decade of the century, Stieglitz did not explore that city, but Sloan and his circle identified with and represented it.

In Sloan's painting, *The City From Greenwich Village*, there is some suggestion of the larger City of Ambition, but the point of view, the unmistakable location of the creator of the image, is that of a local, neighborhood observer. (Figure 28) We are drawn to Sixth Avenue at West Third Street in Greenwich Village, not to Wall Street in the distance. One is reminded of Jean-Paul

28. *The City from Greenwich Village*, 1922, by John Sloan. Photograph © 2002 Board of Trustees, National Gallery of Art Washington, D.C. (Gift of Helen Farr Sloan)

Sartre's comments on New York in the 1940s. He was struck by the grid and especially the avenues. The streets running without end and stressing free movement were, he wrote, symbols of energy and ambition. In Paris, by contrast, small streets and neighborhoods surrounded residents, providing enclosure and security. In this respect, Greenwich Village was like Paris. Yet Frenchmen, from Le Corbusier (who celebrated New York's grid and despised Greenwich Village) to Sartre, were looking for a different kind of modernity, and simply failed to recognize that such archaism was part of the modernity of New York, just as it was of Paris.

It was this New York that Sloan painted. Even when he portrayed people in an entertainment district, as in *Movies* (1913), he did not emphasize midtown glamour. (Figure 29) There is a feel at once of an outing and of local comfort and context. Nor did he establish much distance between institutionalized forms of entertainment or culture and the common humanity of life in the city.

The men and women he painted might work in various parts of the city. Yet

29. *Movies*, 1913, by John Sloan. Oil on canvas (19 ⅞ x 21 in.). Courtesy of Toledo Museum of Art, Toledo, Ohio (Museum Purchase Fund)

his focus on them was not at work, but at home in their neighborhoods. In *Six O'Clock Winter* he portrays the elevated and the crowds of working New Yorkers streaming home from work and animating the local streets. The city's modern economic institutions and places of work have little presence in this image of the city; the emphasis is on the humanity of those who work, wherever they work, and who, more importantly, live in ordinary neighborhoods. When Sloan painted New Yorkers at work, it was more likely to be, as in *Women's Work* (1912) (Figure 30), which shows a woman hanging out the laundry, a routine domestic task, or the low-paid workers in his *Scrubwomen, Astor Library* (1910–1911). While there is in this picture a hint of class exploitation, there is equally a sense of personal connection between the women in the picture that suggests a certain blending of work and sociability. In a painting of *McSorley's Bar* (1912), today still a popular bar on the borderland between Greenwich Village and the Lower East Side that only in the 1970s allowed women to enter—men find security and friendship at work. (Figure 31)

30. *Women's Work*, 1912, by John Sloan. © The Cleveland Museum of Art, 2002 (Gift of Miss Amelia Elizabeth White, 1964)

Perhaps Sloan's *Three AM* (1909) (Figure 32) is fittingly paired with *McSorley's Bar*. Here two women return home from an evening out; again it is security, friendship, pleasure—not glamour—that he emphasizes. There are presumed narratives in Sloan's vignettes. Not the whole story, of course. The whole story is never known in the city, yet one knows that there is a story.

Knowing that Sloan was a socialist, one might argue that the representation of both work and culture in his paintings was a critique of modern, hierarchical, bureaucratic structures of power and cultural categories, but that is not clear. Nor is it clear that Stieglitz's fascination with the skyscraper, the symbol of modern economic power, stood for a political commitment. In fact, Stieglitz always identified himself as a radical in politics as well as in art. Yet there were rather different political implications that adhered to each of these structures of urban perception.

31. *McSorley's Bar*, 1912, by John Sloan. Photograph © 2001, The Detroit Institute of Arts (Founders Society Purchase, General Membership Fund)

32. *Three AM*, 1909, by John Sloan. Courtesy of Philadelphia Museum of Art (Given by Mrs. Cyrus McCormick)

At Madison Square, as we have seen, Stieglitz was drawn, almost irre-sistibly, he later recalled, to the Flatiron Building. (Figure 11) He turned that prow-like skyscraper form into an icon that represented, at least to him, the progress of American culture.[17] While Stieglitz looked up at the Flatiron, Sloan surveyed the park itself, noting the people who regularly populated it. His *Nursemaids, Madison Square* (1907) (Figure 33) focused on working-class women, giving them pride of place over the structural forms so fascinating to Stieglitz and many other modernist photographers.[18]

The increasingly rationalized city, the capital of capital as New York was becoming, depended upon a highly skilled but tightly managed labor force. The people who were that city, according to Waldo Frank, a modernist writer and friend of Stieglitz, were mostly ground down, living a routinized and spiritually impoverished life. His critique of capitalism is thus so thorough that it effectively erased the people for whom he would speak. "Our centers of civilization," he wrote, "are cities not so much of men and women as of buildings."[19] That city is recognizable in the work of the circle that formed around Stieglitz. Charles Sheeler's *New York Buildings* (1920) offers a city of

33. *Nursemaids, Madison Square*, 1907, by John Sloan. Courtesy of Sheldon Memorial Art Gallery, University of Nebraska, Lincoln (F. M. Hall Collection)

34. *New York Buildings*, 1920, by Charles Sheeler. Pencil drawing on ivory wove paper (50.5 x 33 cm) © The Art Institute of Chicago. All rights reserved

its title, without people. (Figure 34) Paul Strand's celebrated and ambiguous *Wall Street* (1915) is difficult to read as social commentary, either directly from the print or on the basis of Strand's later comments. (Figure 35) Making matters yet more complex, the tone (and thus the emotional feel) differs in the two most famous prints. Still, whatever its precise political intent (if any) and meaning, the picture surely tends to diminish the working people rushing past the J. P. Morgan banking house.[20]

But Sloan and the others in the group called the Eight documented an utterly different relation of people, buildings, and street. George Luks's evocation of *Hester Street* (1905), for example, portrayed working people's lives with color and vitality, even if they lived within recognized limits enforced by social conditions.[21] (Figure 36) Likewise, in George Bellows's famous paint-

35. *Wall Street*, 1915, by Paul Strand. © 1971, Aperture Foundation, Inc., Paul Strand Archive

36. *Hester Street*, 1905, by George Benjamin Luks. Courtesy Brooklyn Museum of Art (Dick S. Ramsey Fund)

37. *Cliff Dwellers*, 1913, by George Bellows. Los Angeles County Museum of Art, Los Angeles County Fund. Photograph © 2002 Museum Associates

ing of the *Cliff Dwellers* (1913), the immigrant working classes are distinctly not ground down to drabness. (Figure 37)

When Bellows focused on an architectural object, as in *The Bridge, Blackwell's Island* (1909), he presented as well the texture, people, and ordinariness of the general cityscape. (Figure 38) The bridge is not monumental or awesome. Nor is it utterly separated from the artist or the spectator. The people on the right-hand border of the painting catch the eye of the viewer, thus humanizing the scene. Much the same can be said of his painting *New York* (1911), with the people and street activity in the foreground of the city's large commercial buildings.[22]

If Sloan and his circle focused on the spunky, pugnacious people who carried on in spite of the odds of New York life, modernists emphasized physical forms and a vital but cool energy. For both groups, the city represented escape from the constraints of traditional notions of order, whether social or visual. But the Stieglitz group was more drawn to the visual novelty than to

38. *The Bridge, Blackwell's Island*, 1909, by George Bellows. Courtesy of Toledo Museum of Art, Toledo, Ohio (Gift of Edward Drummond Libbey)

the social lives of the new city, and in this they learned from and agreed with the European avant-garde temporarily living in New York.

Marcel Duchamp, on arriving in the New York in 1913, declared that "New York is itself a work of art, a complete work of art." Europe, he thought, was finished; the future was the dynamic city of skyscrapers. This view was shared by Francis Picabia, also just arrived for the Armory Show. "New York," he famously declared in 1913, "is the cubist city, the futurist city. It expresses in its architecture, its life, its spirit, the modern thought."[23] Their interest, however, was not in documentation of form, but rather in evoking the heights, the kinetic energy, and the emotional power of the city, a theme that would especially interest John Marin of the Stieglitz group. Others in the group were fascinated by the perspective of height but were drawn as well to study the precise forms, angles, massing, and shadows of the recently formulated and emergent skyscraper aesthetic.

The painters associated with the 291 Gallery, those in the Stieglitz circle, understood themselves as forming the first American avant-garde. Still, their perceptions and representations of the city bore greater similarity to those of the Europeans than to those of "the Eight." They sought to represent the energy, the barely contained chaos of the city, or—at the opposite extreme— the formal qualities of the city's buildings, often stressing the precisionist geometry of the modern skyscraper and other urban technologies.

There are differences among the pictures made by this group, of course, but they have much in common. They portray a city of power, whether that power is represented by turbulent energy, as in John Marin's watercolors, or cool energy, as in the paintings and photographs of Charles Sheeler. It is almost always an image of the city from a distance, one that diminishes people. These paintings are all versions of Stieglitz's *City of Ambition* photograph.

In a remarkable series of drawings and watercolors, John Marin, who had studied architecture in his youth, captured New York's dynamism in his explorations of the city's physical forms. He was obviously influenced by Cubism, but he was especially affected by the direct experience of the city's newness and energy upon his return from Paris. Its jagged skyline came to life in his images. The tall buildings that made up a panoramic wall jostled against each other: one could say that they even danced with each other. His was an unmistakably physical and kinetic city. Commenting on his paintings of the Woolworth Building in 1913, he explained: "I see great forces at work; great movements; the large buildings and the small buildings, the warring of the great and small."[24]

These mobile buildings are portrayed in his many versions of the Woolworth Building and in the remarkably kinetic *Movement, Fifth Avenue.* (Figure 39) His paintings before World War I tend to bring together street and buildings in a kind of symbosis of energy. Only occasionally, as in his later *Related to St. Paul's, New York* (1928), did he explore the relation between historical fixity and modern energy and transformation. Or put differently, in this work he addressed the meaning of monuments in modern cities.[25]

Contrary to the usual association of the Stieglitz group with Greenwich Village bohemianism, I would argue that the artists associated with the 291 Gallery, located above Madison Square, faced north, toward midtown. Few of that group lived in the Village. In the 1920s, for example, Stieglitz and Georgia O'Keeffe lived in midtown; Marin, who lived in the New Jersey suburbs, was

39. *Movement: Fifth Avenue*, 1912, by John Marin (water color, with traces of black crayon, over charcoal, on off-white watercolor paper, 42.8 x 34.8 cm). Alfred Stieglitz collection.

always a visitor in the city. The Sloan group, by contrast, lived mostly in the "extended" Village.[26] Each group depicted its own neighborhood.

Sloan painted a Village made up of working-class immigrants, mostly Italian, and the newcomers to the adventure of bohemianism. Stieglitz and O'Keeffe, who moved to the Shelton Hotel in 1925, photographed and painted the prosperous world of midtown that was particularly fascinating to them for its geometry. Georgia O'Keeffe's *Shelton with Sun Spots* (1926) (Figure 40), with the sharply etched skyscraper forms energized by a giant sunspot on the building at the picture's center, stands somewhere between Marin's kinetic and playful evocation of the city and the much less mobile urban aesthetic of Charles Sheeler, toward which she moved. Her more famous *Radiator Building, Night* (1927) wonderfully enlivens the skyscraper forms with the fantasies prompted by the city night light and colors. But in *City Night* (1926) (Figure 41) and *New York Street* (1926) the colors are muted and the feel of the city is more somber. Her exploration of the massive forms of New York urbanity owes much to Sheeler, but the buildings—overlarge, somewhat intimidating—are not so cool as Sheeler's. Rather, there is an aura of mystery close to the evocation of the skyscraper city found in Hugh Ferriss's *Metropolis of Tomorrow*, published in 1925. O'Keeffe's city anticipates the modernism that would become associated with Le Corbusier, though without the open space.

I have emphasized the external perspective of the City of Ambition artists. Yet these uptown bohemians had entered Dreiser's "walled city." Stieglitz and O'Keeffe resided at the Shelton Hotel, near Rockefeller Center. From that roost in the middle of New York's commercial wealth they recorded the city. In the late 1920s and early 1930s Stieglitz made a remarkable run of photographs from their windows in the Shelton, particularly of Rockefeller Center, both its construction and its finished form, as in *From the Shelton, Looking West* (1933), wherein he explores the line and shadow in that spectacular skyscraper complex. (Figure 42) Several of O'Keeffe's paintings depicted the city as seen from their hotel window. All of them were confidently inside Dreiser's "walled city," including *East River from the 30th Story of the Shelton Hotel* (1928) (Figure 43), that turns away from the commercial center to show the dull industry-scape of Queens, from whence came some of the men and women who were captured in Sloan's *Movies* and *White Way* (1926).

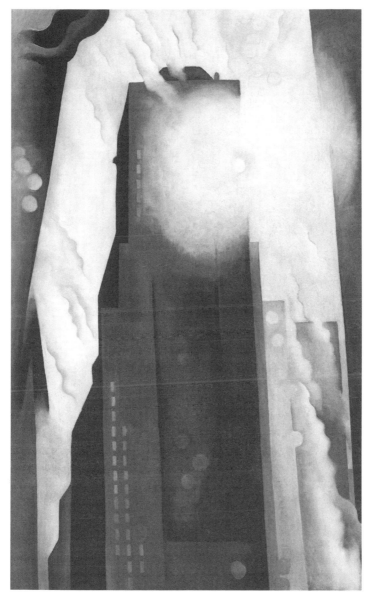

40. *Shelton with Sun Spots*, 1926, by Georgia O'Keeffe (oil on canvas, 123.2 x 76.8 cm). Gift of Leigh B. Block. © The Art Institute of Chicago. All rights reserved

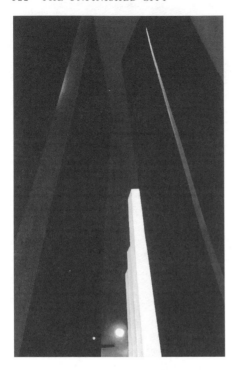

41. *City Night*, 1926, by
Georgia O'Keeffe. Courtesy of the
Minneapolis Institute of Arts (Gift of
Regis Corporation, W. John Driscoll,
the Beim Corporation, and others)

Whether looking in, looking out, or exploring the city within the walls
from within those walls, the view offered by Stieglitz and O'Keeffe in the
1920s was always distanced by the position from which the two of them
viewed the city. If Sloan and his circle were on street level, mixing with the
urban populace that was their subject, O'Keeffe and Stieglitz almost always
assumed a perch well above the ground, cut off by that elevation from the
human life below. "New York," Stieglitz commented in a letter to Sherwood
Anderson in 1925, "is madder than ever. The pace is ever increasing. But
Georgia and I somehow don't seem to be of New York—nor of anywhere. We
live high up in the Shelton. . . . All is so quiet except the wind—& the trem-
bling shaking hulk of steel in which we live. It's a wonderful place."[27] Others
in the circle seem to have shared this sense of distance, whether Edward
Steichen in his *Sunday Night on 40th Street* (1925) or Sheeler in his *New York*

42. *From the Shelton*, 1933, by Alfred Stieglitz. Courtesy of the J. Paul Getty Museum, Los Angeles. © Estate of Georgia O'Keeffe

43. *East River from the 30th Story of the Shelton Hotel*, 1928, by Georgia O'Keeffe. Courtesy of New Britain Museum of American Art, Connecticut (Stephen B. Lawrence Fund). Photograh by E. Irving Blomstrann

Buildings. The city thus presented is a frozen city without history. At one point Dreiser may have described this city too:

> It was silent, the city of my dreams, marble and serene, due perhaps to the fact that in reality I knew nothing of crowds, poverty . . . It was an amazing city, so far-flung, so beautiful, so dead.[28]

The Stieglitz group was interested in form and order. There is no attempt to penetrate the human qualities of the city, and little concern with evoking human sympathy or dignity. They display a detached playfulness about urban form and power, reiterating a contemporary literary stance that articulated a new urban "sophistication," first in the magazine *Vanity Fair* and then, beginning in 1926, in *The New Yorker* magazine. Theirs is a new kind of urbanity: detached yet affectionate; anonymous but not alienated; exploring or curious but not penetrating or engaging. This sensibility establishes an attitude toward urban phenomena, but it does not engage it.

Another major difference between the Sloan circle's city and that of the Stieglitz circle is the absence of domestic environments portrayed by the latter group, who focus on offices, symbols of power, money, and ambition. They display little interest in the intimate locales of security and identity. Indeed, Stieglitz and O'Keeffe did not have a home; they lived in a hotel. Nor do they show men at work. Lewis Hine (not a member of either group but a contemporary) celebrated the skyscraper by photographing the workers who constructed the Empire State Building.[29] Not the Stieglitz circle. For them the city is a place of visual delight, not a place of working, living, and laughing; nor a place of homes, families, or neighborhoods. Neither is the city a place of active public life, of people enjoying the streets, or using them for formal rituals of self-representation. One looks in vain among the Stieglitz group for a

44. *Parade Along Seventh Avenue*, ca. 1925, by James VanDerZee. © Donna Mussenden VanDerZee

photograph at all like James VanDerZee's mid-1920s street-level *Parade on Seventh Avenue*, taken from near his Harlem studio and so humanly complex with its combination of everyday life and festive ritual. (Figure 44)

I have emphasized the separation of these two traditions of urban representation—and one could further track that difference in the contrasting work of the near-contemporary photographers Paul Strand and Walker Evans. But later, in the 1930s, the two modes of urban representation meet in fascinating ways in the photography of Berenice Abbott. Between 1935 and 1937, she photographed the city, and in 1939 a selection of these photographs were published under the title *Changing New York*.[30] Few have done better than Abbott in capturing the aesthetic possibilities of the city's tall buildings. Her brilliantly conceived and rigorously cropped vertical image, *Exchange Place* (1935), is a powerful delination of the form of verticality and of the feeling of closure in the forest of lower Manhattan skyscrapers. (Figure 45) But in *Changing New York* her purposes were different. Abbott's city is dynamic, historical, defined in narrative terms.[31] By the order she gave the pictures in the book, she achieved both a narrative of change and a conversation between the New York of Stieglitz and that of Sloan, between a newer and urbane New York and an older and more common New York.

Abbott paired a photograph of Broadway meeting the Battery from the air with one of the firehouse on the Battery; on the east side, near South Street, she paired the Manhattan Bridge tower with a nearby rope store; a downtown tower, portrayed in what she called a "city arabesque," is contrasted with a local shop in the nearby Lower East Side. Most compelling of all to me—perhaps because it shows where I live and work—is her photograph of Washington Square. (Figure 46) Here she captures the narrative of urban transformation that is her theme in a single picture of considerable formal interest. The caption to this picture makes the point: "Behind the arch the old houses of Washington Square North so far have resisted demolition; but the skyscraper apartment at No. 1 Fifth Avenue symbolizes the fate the old square may look forward to."[32]

During the 1930s others represented the city in ways quite like Abbott. The Great Depression produced in all writers and artists a deeper interest in the "people" and in social issues.[33] This is obvious in the murals of the era, as we

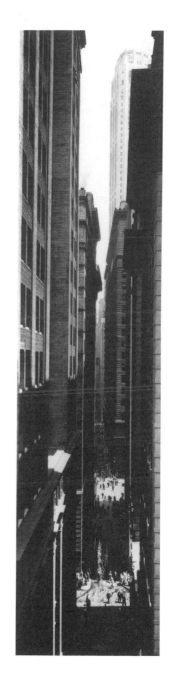

45. *Exchange Place*, ca. 1935, by Berenice Abbott.
Courtesy of the Museum of the City of New York

46. *Washington Square, Looking North*, April 6, 1936, by Berenice Abbott. Courtesy of the Museum of the City of New York (Federal Arts Project)

have already noted with those of Douglas and Hayes. But more striking, partly because it is surprising, is the shift in the work of John Marin, who changed his focus to human figures, seeing in them something of the drama of urban life. The lifelike structures that had earlier represented the drama of the city were moved back in the 1920s, and he examined the street. In his *Mid-Manhattan*, painted in 1932, he goes farther yet. It is a cultural comment on the City of Ambition. (Figure 47) The city of towering ambition is not working: in the foreground of the city of skyscrapers are the residents of a Hooverville.[34]

At the outset, I promised to establish the political importance of these different representations of urban modernity. I would argue that these alternative

47. *Mid-Manhattan, I,* 1932, by John Marin. Courtesy of Des Moines Art Center (Nathan Emory Coffin Collection). Photo credit: Ray Andrews, Des Moines

structures of urban perception in fact define the twentieth-century politics of urban development. They inscribe social and geographical divisions that have been the focus of urban politics since the emergence of the modern geography of cities that established the contest between the center ("downtown") and the periphery, that separates work and home, and that always threatens to separate people further yet by race, class, gender, and ethnicity.

There is a significant and surprisingly direct translation of artistic visions of the city into public policy, and this in part for aesthetic reasons. The midtown vision of the city offered by Stieglitz, O'Keeffe, Sheeler, and Ferriss resonated with the midtown financial elite who supported the Regional Plan of New York, published in six fat volumes between 1929 and 1931.[35] This privately financed plan aimed to enhance those qualities of the city that had fascinated the Stieglitz group—a Manhattan of grand ambition: devoted to high-rent uses of business administration, luxury housing, and luxury retail. It was a plan, as the young Lewis Mumford pointed out in a stinging critique, designed to develop the center, to serve the elite who lived there and made their money there.[36] All other uses—working-class housing, cheap retail, and industrial jobs—were relegated to the fringes.

Those who fashioned the Regional Plan pioneered new analytical techniques. It is a vast compendium of impressive statistics about the economy, about housing, about jobs, about traffic, about communication, and more. Their city was in part a statistical city—a city of aggregate figures on needs and services. But it was, for that very reason, a city devoid of the particularities and textures of places and the peoples who lived in those places. To read the Regional Plan is to discover a city whose social meaning is numerical, whose visual representation is geometrical.

When it presented its own urban vision, the Regional Plan Association drew directly upon the City of Ambition aesthetic I have described. They hired Hugh Ferriss to give visual representation to their ideas. In his book, *Metropolis of Tomorrow* (1925), the City of Ambition is represented as pure form and atmosphere.[37] No image more powerfully represents the seemingly unreachable City of Ambition than his *Lure of the City*. (Figure 48) Ferriss was fascinated by form, and it was he who developed the handbook of skyscraper forms allowable under the 1916 New York City zoning law. His beautiful drawings reduced the city to a geography of skyscraper forms. The aesthetic power of the visual parts of the plan that he contributed, especially those in

48. *Lure of the City*, by Hugh Ferriss. From *Metropolis of Tomorrow*, by Hugh Ferriss, 1925. Courtesy of Avery Architectual and Fine Arts Library, Columbia University, New York

volume two, *Building the City*, surely enhanced its appeal and advanced its prospects of implementation. And it was largely implemented. It has been argued, and plausibly so, that it was this city that Robert Moses created between 1933 and 1964—a city of highways and towers, of offices rather than factories, of professionals rather than workers, of Lincoln Center at the expense of the sort of local, neighborhood cultural vitality chronicled by Sloan and his circle.[38]

Did the vision of the city represented in the work of Sloan's circle find political expression? One need look no farther than *The Death and Life of Great American Cities* by Jane Jacobs.[39] Marshall Berman has praised her book for "perfectly expressing" an urban modernism "close to home, close to the surface and immediacy" of the lives of "modern men and women."[40] Jacobs, who forged her ideas in opposition to Moses, begins her book with a discussion of the street, emphasizing the particularity and texture of local street life in her neighborhood, only a few blocks west of where John Sloan lived and painted. She rarely addressed social units much bigger than the neighbor-hood. She articulated and gave powerful literary form to what was apparent-ly a widely felt concern; the city planners and architects at whom she had aimed her arrows absorbed her ideas with alacrity, substantially altering urban policy.

Most of us, I think, are probably drawn to both of these New Yorks, and we may hope that art will—as it did in the 1930s—again provide us with com-plex and aesthetically compelling representations of a city that offers its citi-zens both the romance of skyscraper ambition and the romance of local neighborhoods, the power of utilitarianism and the humanity of sympathy.[41]

The divided image and experience of the city is not unique to New York; one finds the same conditions in Paris, Rio de Janiero, Mexico City, and else-where. Such is the condition of metropolitan modernity, as it has been for nearly a century now. The neighborhood and the center (the *CBD* in plan-ning jargon) are *both* products of modernity, both distinctively characteristic of the specifically modern city. Art has often, as I have argued here, repre-sented and reinforced these divisions, which have in turn been a focal point for our politics. Yet it is to art as well as politics, again, to which we might look for new structures of urban perception, ones that may bring these aspects of urban life into a mutually enriching relationship.

8

THE ARTS AND

THE WORLD OF INTELLECT

One of the legacies of the 1930s is a conception of the New York intellectual as a literary-political commentator. Certainly, there has been an important tradition of such intellectuals. But they do not represent the whole story. To focus exclusively on them seriously reduces the richness of the world of intellect, for it misses the historical engagement of New York intellectuals with the visual and aural arts. To forget or overlook this tradition is to lose connection with one of the distinctive qualities of the city's intellectual culture that goes back to the nineteenth century.

The traditional and perhaps special relation of the word and image in New York is represented in *Kindred Spirits* (1849), a painting by Asher Durand that today hangs on the third floor of the New York Public Library. Commissioned by Jonathan Sturges, merchant and patron, it was a gift to William Cullen Bryant, the poet and newspaper editor. It was a gesture of appreciation for Bryant's eulogy of the painter Thomas Cole, their mutual friend. Durand locates the two men in the densely wooded Catskills. They are in conversation, and the painting thus celebrates the friendship of the two men and their association with American nature. This friendship between writer and painter was not at all unique. In fact, the circle of writers and artists around Cole and Bryant (and Morse) established the Sketch Club, which in 1846 became the prestigious Century Association. Even a minimal list of notable New York intellectuals engaged with the visual, from Bryant,

Walt Whitman, Frederick Law Olmsted, and William Crary Brownell in the nineteenth century to Lewis Mumford, Clement Greenberg, Ada Louise Huxtable, Susan Sontag, and Richard Sennett in the twentieth century are difficult to overlook. We recognize them, but we do not realize that they imply a richer and broader definition of the city's intellectual culture.

Irving Howe, who was formed as an intellectual within the political and literary group associated with the *Partisan Review*, discovered in 1971 that there were notable artists and critics previously beyond his ken. Writing in *Harper's* magazine, he explained that at Lincoln Center, where the New York City Ballet had moved a few years before, he "blundered onto a great artistic enterprise." He recognized the "genius" of George Balanchine, the founding choreographer of the company. Self-consciously a literary man, one who "enjoys Wallace Stevens," Howe approached the City Ballet as an amateur. In time, however, he turned for further instruction to the dance writings of Edwin Denby, encountering thereby a "great critic," whom, he declared, ought to be as well known as Edmund Wilson, the very incarnation of the ambition of the *Partisan Review* intellectuals.[1] Even as the literary culture to which Howe was so devoted was being nudged aside by the increasing visualization of culture, he was generous in his acknowledgment of the power of the art form and its critics. His previous isolation from the world of dance was not unique; it signified a division in intellectual New York that has been perpetuated by historians as well memoirists.

The political and literary intellectuals associated with the *Partisan Review* are so well remembered that they obscure what I will call the "other 1930s" and its legacy. An adequate memory of the dimensions of the world of intellect in New York in the middle third of the twentieth century needs to rediscover and incorporate those intellectuals who engaged the city's visual and aural culture. Dance, which combines both the visual and the aural, provides an entrée to this issue, and it will provide the guiding thread for my account. My objective is not a comprehensive reinterpretation; rather I seek only to raise to visibility a lost dimension of the culture of the metropolis.

Memory, whether personal or collective, is seldom straightforwardly false, but it often gets the proportions wrong. Such is the case in this instance; our memory mistakes a part for the whole. The rubric "New York Intellectuals" has been construed too restrictively. There is no doubt that among the city's intellectuals the *Partisan Review* group was important; they played a crucial role in challenging Stalinism in American intellectual life, in defining a particular liberal political ideology, and in sustaining the movement of literary modernism during the Cold War era. There were, however, other New York intellectuals working in a different key, exploring the worlds of music and the visual arts. These other intellectuals were not oblivious to politics, having worked in the Works Progress Administration (WPA) arts projects. They collaborated, for example, with the great documentary director Pare Lorentz, when he made his classic thirties political films, *The Plow That Broke the Plains* and *The River*. But their attitude or their relation to politics was different, less exclusive, less tightly focused.

Virgil Thomson, one of the leaders of the second group of intellectuals, observed that between the 1930s and 1940s there was a shift in the sensibility of intellectuals in New York from politics (ideology) to art (aesthetics). He is right to see this in chronological terms, but the change was uneven, never complete, and the division persisted well into the 1960s. So I adapt and expand Thomson's fine phrasing to describe two contemporary orientations. One group, as he put it, argued "esthetics with intelligence and politics with passion," while the other, with whom he allied himself, discussed "esthetics with passion and politics with intelligence."[2]

Intellectual historians have failed to grasp the variety of artistic and critical work that characterized the 1940s, partly because concerns of the Cold War era gave precedence to certain ideological themes and political trends. Scholars have pored over political magazines that discussed art, but they have overlooked arts magazines that were often politically alert. The attention given to *The Partisan Review*, *The New Republic*, and *The Nation* is legitimate, but it has been too exclusive. The world of the arts disappears in this selection, particularly if, as is usually the case, one leaves out the back of *The Nation*, where in the 1940s, literary editor Margaret Marshall had brought together a remarkable and eclectic collection of cultural critics, including James Agee on film, B. H. Haggin on music and dance, Clement Greenberg on art, and Diana Trilling on literature.

New York's stature as a capital of culture during the past half century has not been sustained solely by the contributions of its intellectuals to political ideology. Such cultural achievement that can be identified with the city specifically has been as often, if not more often, associated with remarkable creativity and critical discourse in the fields of painting, sculpture, photography, architecture, music, and dance. Historical entry to these worlds is to be gained through magazines only infrequently consulted by general historians. Intellectuals writing about the aesthetics and politics of a metropolitan democratic culture can be found in several places, including *Modern Music* (1924–46), *New Theatre* (1933–37), *Dance Index* (1942–49), and *View* (1942–46).

Edited by Minna Lederman, *Modern Music* was devoted to the advancement of modern music and critical writing about it. The magazine's range was broad, covering dance and set design, and its visual material was of high quality. The first issue, for example, carried drawings by Picasso. Lederman published Virgil Thomson, Roger Sessions, Aaron Copland, and Elliot Carter, helping them to become writers as well as composers. They wrote both technical articles and more reflective ones that probed the relations of culture, society, and nationalism. Lincoln Kirstein was provided with space to write about dance and musical theatre, while Edwin Denby, the extraordinary dance critic, credited Lederman with forming him into a serious critic. *Dance Index* was edited and funded by Kirstein. It was monographic in spirit, but visually brilliant, with covers designed by Joseph Cornell. It was a dance compendium, literally a collection of western dance history and traditions, both classic and folkloric, including American popular dance forms. It documented and thereby created a dance heritage upon which Americans could build. *Dance Index* carried a remarkable article by Lederman on Stravinsky and the theatre as well as two important ones by Balanchine: "The Dance Elements in Stravinsky's Music" and "Notes on Choreography," in which Balanchine summarized his choreographic principles. Music, dance, and drama were covered by *New Theatre*, which was a self-consciously radical magazine, exploring the relation of art to politics. It carried articles from a wide variety of intellectuals—from Lincoln Kirstein, Robert Edmond Jones, and Paul Robeson to quite obscure coterie and pseudonymous writers.

The most wide-ranging and important of these magazines lost to conventional intellectual history was *View*, founded and edited by Charles Henri Ford, with the close collaboration of Parker Tyler, who wrote widely on film and art. Less portentous and more playful with ideas, politics, and aesthetics than the *Partisan Review*, *View* addressed many of the same issues as the more famous magazine. Some writers identified with the *Partisan Review* were regular contributors to *View*, including Harold Rosenberg, Lionel Abel, Paul Goodman, and Meyer Schapiro, among others. But the focus on the arts was clear, with writers and artists not likely to be encountered in the *Partisan Review*: Henry Miller, Paul Bowles, Alexander Calder, Max Ernst, Georgia O'Keefe, e.e. cummings, William Carlos Williams, Marianne Moore, and Joseph Cornell (on the actress Hedy Lamarr). Lincoln Kirstein translated Jean-Paul Sartre's "The Nationalization of Literature" in 1946, and in the same issue Lionel Abel wrote an article with a title reminiscent of our own time, "Georges Bataille and the Repetitions of Nietzsche." The work of the neoromantic artist Pavel Tchelitchew was probably overrepresented—he and Ford, the editor, were lovers, and Parker Tyler was later to write his biography. But Tchelitchew is an important, if mostly forgotten, figure in the art world I am describing. For example, it was Tchelitchew who introduced Kirstein to Balanchine, and he later designed sets for Balanchine's early American ballets. He also brought Joseph Cornell into the world of ballet, a domain of sexual fantasy that became an obsession for Cornell.[3]

The early issues of *View* took direct aim at the *Partisan Review*. In the first issue the editors of *View* accused the rival magazine of being still in the Stalinist camp, and in the second number it attacked Clement Greenberg, closely associated with *Partisan Review*, for misunderstanding and disdaining surrealism, which Greenberg, declining instruction, later called a "spurious kind of modern art."[4] Greenberg had earlier offended by characterizing the neoromantic paintings of Tchelitchew shown at the Museum of Modern Art (MOMA) in 1942 as having set "a new high in vulgarity," and this no doubt invited response from the editors of *View*.[5]

Many of the contributors to *View*, but not those of the *Partisan Review*, were part of the circle of intellectuals with fairly direct ties to Lincoln Kirstein and the city's ballet world. There were, of course, a few intellectuals who moved between the different groups, most notably W. H. Auden, who was closely involved with Edmund Wilson and the *Partisan Review*, yet a longtime friend of Kirstein and an admirer of Balanchine. In 1939, Auden worked with Benjamin Britten to develop a libretto for Balanchine's Ballet Caravan, even though he always considered the ballet a "minor art."[6] James Agee, who had been Kirstein's roommate at Harvard and who shared Kirstein's interest in the photography of Walker Evans, was another. Willem de Kooning seems to have crossed nearly every group boundary there was in New York in the 1940s and 1950s. It was thus fitting that he remarked in 1951 that "there is no style of painting now . . . I don't need a movement."[7] Later, in the 1960s, one must add Susan Sontag to this list of crossovers. The poet Frank O'Hara who, like his friend de Kooning, touched most of the city's intellectual affinity groups in the 1950s and early 1960s, felt strongly that the interesting people in New York "were in the art world, not at the *Partisan Review*."[8]

The *Partisan Review* group formed a fairly well-bounded intellectual circle; the sociologist Daniel Bell, one of the central figures in the group, even used a family metaphor to develop a formal genealogy, with "elders," "younger brothers," "second generation," again with younger brothers, and with "gentile cousins" identified for each generation.[9] Mapping the art-world intellectuals is more difficult. There was no single focus or position to be argued to the world. The best approach to them is to look for overlapping networks and linkages, rather than for bounded families or circles.

The originating networks date back to the 1910s and 1920s. There were, on the one hand, a series of interconnected salons that traced their lineage to prewar groups. On the other hand there were two student organizations at Harvard, both largely the work of Lincoln Kirstein: the Harvard Society for Contemporary Art and the literary magazine *Hound and Horn* (1927–34). By the 1930s, these networks, never firmly bounded, became intertwined.

The moveable salons emerged in the aftermath of the Armory Show in 1913, and Marcel Duchamp, who came to New York for the show and who remained to live intermittently in the city throughout his life, was an important shadow and often real presence in these salons. This network of modernists had three principal meeting places: the Upper East Side home of Walter and Louise Arensberg; Muriel Draper's meetings in a loft over a garage on East Fortieth Street; and the elegant Stettheimer residence at Alwyn Court, near Carnegie Hall, where the painter Florine Stettheimer, her mother, and her sisters lived. The Stettheimer salon continued into the 1930s, but the Arensberg and Draper gatherings were replaced by Constance and Kirk Askew's East Sixty-first Street salon. During the 1940s, Julien Levy's Gallery, which specialized in surrealist and neoromantic art, was a major link in the art-world networks. Levy's artists included Joseph Cornell, Max Ernst, and Pavel Tchelitchew, and it also promoted photographers, giving Walker Evans, George Platt Lynes, and Henri Cartier-Bresson their first New York shows.[10]

Muriel Draper's salon, characterized by Kirstein as "the High Bohemia of Manhattan," included Gurdjieff, Langston Hughes, Edmund Wilson, Gilbert Seldes, Paul Robeson, and Carl Van Vechten. It was at Draper's, while still a Harvard student, that Kirstein met Van Vechten, from whom he learned, as he put it, the "idiosyncratic authority of elegance." From Van Vechten too Kirstein learned about Harlem, and he began to think about it more as "an arrondissement of Paris than a battleground of Greater New York," a place of "high low-life" that evoked for him Josephine Baker.[11] For Kirstein, who took seriously the moral legacy of his first name, African Americans were visible, part of the city, and in the first outline he drafted for a school of ballet he proposed that half of the students be African American.[12]

Many of the regulars of the Stettheimer salon can be seen miniaturized in situ in the magnificent dollhouse made by Ettie Stettheimer, now in the Museum of the City of New York. The group included a number of painters and critics—Marsden Hartley, Charles Demuth, Duchamp, Albert Gleizes, Jo Davidson, Gaston Lachaise, Elie Nadelman, Van Vechten, and Henry McBride. By the mid-1930s, it also included Pavel Tchelitchew, Charles Henri Ford, Parker Tyler, Kirk Askew, Glenway Westcott, Monroe Wheeler, and Virgil Thomson.

The Askew salon had a wider range of participants, but it also included Florine Stettheimer, Muriel Draper, Kirstein, and, of course, Van Vechten, who after 1930 had become a serious photographer, particularly making portraits. Aaron Copland was a regular, as were John Houseman and Agnes de Mille. It was quite common for the Askew salon to adjourn to Harlem, and at least two African Americans, Taylor Gordon and Edna Philips, were regulars. Virgil Thomson and John Houseman were particularly interested in racially integrating artistic life in New York. As is well known, Thomson and Houseman recruited an African American cast for *Four Saints in Three Acts*. This remarkable collaboration, with the libretto by Gertrude Stein, music by Virgil Thomson, direction by John Houseman, choreography by Frederick Ashton, and sets by Florine Stettheimer, cast African Americans in roles that were not race-typed. Later, Houseman and Thomson tried (without success) to stage a *Medea* following a translation by Countee Cullen, with African American Rose McClendon in the lead. During the New Deal, with Orson Welles, they famously staged a *Negro Macbeth* set in Haiti, and Houseman, under WPA auspices, organized the Negro Theatre in Harlem.[13]

These artists and intellectuals were notably ready to engage the whole panoply of the arts, looking to collaboration at the personal level and the enrichment of particular art forms by mixing at the aesthetic level. Inter-arts collaboration of this sort found little opportunity in Balanchine's work. Yet he appealed to their equally strong commitment to the visualization of culture. Dance is, of course, at once an art of the eye and of the ear, but Balanchine rethought the presentation of dance. He extruded the distractions of elaborate sets and costumes, and he isolated the dancing body, thereby capturing the eye for the examination of the body in motion. Thus purified but not reduced, his ballets, made of fast and wonderfully complicated movements, aided by brilliant lighting strategies, multiplied visual complexity. His ambition, one that appealed to these visually acute intellectuals, was to achieve by a purification of the field, but not the movement, an actual enhancement of the experience of the eye, enabling it to *see* music.

The Harvard Society for Contemporary Art and *Hound and Horn* brought together a group of talented Harvard students, only one of whom was a native New Yorker. Kirstein, the son of a Boston department-store magnate, was the leader, but he was joined by Virgil Thomson from Kansas City, later to become a composer and critic; Philip Johnson, from Cleveland and later to become an architect and critic; Edward Warburg, whose family home on Fifth Avenue is now the Jewish Museum, became an early financial angel for the ballet enterprise; Kirk Askew, like Thomson from Kansas City, who later became a New York art dealer, and A. Everett "Chick" Austin, who went on to become director of the Wadsworth Atheneum, where *Four Saints* premiered and where Balanchine had his first, if brief, American base. Alfred H. Barr, a graduate student at Harvard, shared their commitment to modern art and in some ways, along with Paul Sachs of Harvard's Fogg Museum, guided them. After he became the first director of the Museum of Modern Art in New York, the Museum became a base in the city for them.

While still in their twenties, these men had already accomplished much. *Hound and Horn* was a recognized venue for modernist literature, and the Harvard Society for Contemporary Art mounted a series of exhibits that prefigured—perhaps not surprisingly, given the personnel—the exhibition program of MOMA. All of them, save Austin, who was ensconced in Hartford, came to New York. Kirstein probably spoke for them all when he reminisced: "I wanted to repudiate Harvard. I wanted to repudiate Boston. I wanted to make myself a New Yorker or much more of a cosmopolitan."[14] In 1931, when MOMA established an "advisory committee" chaired by Nelson Rockefeller, the members included Warburg, Johnson, and Kirstein. A year later, Johnson collaborated with Henry-Russell Hitchcock in creating at MOMA a show that named the "International Style," and which was perhaps the most influential architecture exhibition ever mounted.[15] Remarkable resources were available to these talented and wealthy young men. When Kirstein met Balanchine (in the London home of Askew), he turned to Warburg for the financial means to promise Balanchine both a company and a school in America. Austin was able to promise a home for both in Hartford, at the Wadsworth Atheneum. Later, Nelson Rockefeller arranged a Latin American tour that provided the occasion for Balanchine to create two of his greatest plotless ballets, *Concerto Barocco* and *Ballet Imperial* (both 1941), the latter since reworked as the *Tchaikovsky Concerto No. 2.*

After World War II, this uptown bohemia became more difficult to place, but partly as a result the City Ballet may have become more of a focal point. Certainly, MOMA was no longer the clubhouse for this or any other group. Though Kirstein's ties to the museum were close through the 1940s, by the end of the decade he would turn against abstract art and MOMA's modernist agenda, accusing the movement and museum of corrupting art. Stettheimer died in 1946, and the Askew salon ended. There was both a growth and a diffusion in the increasingly multi-nodal avant-garde, scattered through the city in a number of smaller networks. But nights at City Center, where City Ballet was institutionalized at last, provided invaluable occasions, fleeting but repeated, when the arts networks could momentarily be one, visible, material. Thus the informal network of uptown bohemians held together, sustaining both very personal ties and a certain aesthetic sensibility.

At the same time this community was extended to a number of arts networks downtown. When John Cage came to New York, MOMA not only provided an orientation to the art world for him, but it provided a performance space for him and for Merce Cunningham, among others, thus linking uptown music and ballet with the experimental groups downtown.[16] In 1951, Frank O'Hara began working at MOMA, thus linking the downtown New York School poets with the world of MOMA and the ballet he regularly attended, often with his Harvard roommate Edward Gorey. De Kooning and Joseph Cornell were also becoming close during this period, thus linking the world of ballet, Julien Levy's surrealist gallery, and the downtown Abstract Expressionists, who owed more than is usually acknowledged to the surrealists.[17]

Uptown now had entrée to the fairly tough crowd of the Cedar Tavern. De Kooning, who was already personally very close to his Chelsea neighbor and dance critic Edwin Denby (often, like Gorey, O'Hara's companion to the ballet), was a regular at the Five Spot Cafe, a place for jazz at Cooper Square, not far from Cedar Tavern. The Five Spot, which was a base for Charles Mingus and Thelonius Monk, connected de Kooning to the interracial literary, musical, and theatrical world of LeRoi Jones, who in turn could often be found at the heavy drinking, often violent, evenings at the Cedar Tavern.

Jones further extended the network to the emerging Beat scene, which found a focus in *Yugen*, a poetry magazine he edited in the Village with Hettie Cohen, his wife. The spirit of *Yugen* was captured on the title page of the first issue: "*Yugen* means elegance, beauty, grace, transcendence of these things, and also nothing at all." It was a rebel magazine, a point expressed by Diane di Prima in her short poem, "For Pound, Cocteau & Picasso," also in the first number:

> So you sit
> robes and all
> you old ones
> and having broken every rule
> they ever made
> you now preach Order
> ain't you the cool ones.

Yugen was at the center of an arts community, and one that was distinctively interracial. The world Jones created and that of the Five Spot Cafe was, in Dan Wakefield's recollection, marked by a "bebop kind of occasional, hopeful harmony."[18] Before it was shattered in the early 1960s, an unravelling represented by LeRoi Jones's reincarnation as Amiri Baraka and by his move from downtown to Harlem, it was possible for Norman Mailer to feel a "marvelous sense of optimism," saying that "blacks and whites were moving toward one another" in this downtown art world.[19] Even uptown, in 1957 Balanchine had made a striking interracial gesture in casting Arthur Mitchell and Diana Adams in the remarkable pas de deux of his plotless masterpiece, *Agon*. With a stark set and minimal costumes that offered no distraction, who could miss the obvious fact that the ballet was raising the issue of race and sex. *Time* magazine noticed, calling attention to "a languorous, sensual pas de deux exquisitely danced by Virginia-born Diana Adams and Arthur Mitchell, a talented Negro member of the company."[20]

Jones published all the Beats in *Yugen*—and Frank O'Hara, whose aesthetics were closer to the conceptualism of Cage and Jasper Johns than to the Beats, as well. O'Hara, motivated, as was often the case, by a combination of "sexual attraction, politics, and friendship," strongly supported Jones, and he introduced him to other people and places in the art world, including Kirstein and Balanchine.[21] "With Frank O'Hara," Jones recalled, "one spun and darted through the New York art scene, meeting Balanchine or Merce Cunningham or John Cage, or de Kooning, or Larry Rivers."[22]

Although those in the overlapping arts networks I have described had serious political interest, mostly on the left, they identified with aesthetic, not political commitments. What were the intellectual and aesthetic affinities that held this loose, complex, and crosshatched art-world network together? It may be that we can clarify the allegiances at the center by investigating a contested border. I have already alluded to the tension that put the surrealists and neoromantics on one side of the border and the Abstract Expressionists—and especially their explicator, Clement Greenberg—on the other. Although I will focus on Greenberg and his ideas here, it is a broad and important division. With the exceptions of de Kooning, O'Hara, and perhaps Franz Kline, there was very little traffic between the Abstract Expressionists and the other domains of the visual art world of the 1940s and early 1950s.

In fact, the territory of modern art in New York in that period was highly pluralized, more so than received history suggests.[23] But all was not peace and harmony. Clement Greenberg—and those for whom he spoke, with or without authorization—presumed to know the inherent logic of painting, and he was anxious to protect what he called the "mainstream" of western art from contamination. A brilliant and combative art critic for *The Nation* and a some-time editor of the *Partisan Review*, Greenberg demanded purity and autono-my for modern art. Contamination was a constant worry (no doubt a legacy of the sometimes crude intrusions of politics in the 1930s), but so was any notion of a big-tent art world, something other New York arts intellectuals generally welcomed. Because they mixed media, opera and ballet could never be major art forms, however much one might enjoy them. Not only were sur-realism and neoromanticism a wrong turn in art, but for Greenberg the whole idea of MOMA, which mixed a variety of media (film, photography, architecture, design, including commercially produced products, and, briefly, dance, theatre arts, and music, as well as painting and sculpture), seemed to misunderstand the nature of art.

Beginning with his famous *Partisan Review* article on "Avant Garde and Kitsch" in 1939, he sought to protect high art from the contamination of commerce.[24] In "Towards a Newer Laocoon," published six months later, he insisted that there has been "a confusion of the arts" and that "purism is the terminus of a salutary reaction against the mistakes of painting and sculpture in the past several centuries which were due to such a confusion." To the avant-garde, he believed, had fallen the task of escaping from transgressive ideas and ideology that have contaminated art. He happily reported that the New York avant-garde had "achieved a purity and a radical delimitation of fields of activity for which there is no previous example in the history of cul-ture." The arts, he assured his readers, "lie safe now, each within its 'legiti-mate' boundaries, and free trade has been replaced by autarchy."[25]

Greenberg—who like others in the *Partisan Review* circle relished polemic—possessed remarkable dialectical skills. He always assumed ultimate values were at stake, and he dominated critical discourse. Lincoln Kirstein, who was never afraid of controversy, challenged Greenberg, though fairly ineffectually, in his famous attack on modern art.[26] But my point is not to recount and weigh a debate. Rather I aim to illustrate the existence of two versions of modernism: one singular, autonomous, and seeking purity within the discipline of a single field; the other polymorphic, less worried about con-tamination, even absorptive.

Irving Howe, who survived the ideological wars of his youth but later wor-ried about the politics and culture of the 1960s, was, even with the 1960s on his mind, less anxious about mixing than was Greenberg. He displayed greater sympathy and understanding of the virtues, rather than the dangers, of absorption, at least as he witnessed it in the work of Balanchine. Howe observed that Balanchine effectively incorporated jazz, social dancing, like waltz steps, Busby Berkeley's Hollywood style, and vernacular movements like walking in the street. For Balanchine and his audience, none of these assimilations threatened to undermine ballet. In Balanchine's hands and imagination, such alien materials enhanced rather than degraded art, for he insisted that they become ballet.[27]

In a different but related way, the extraordinary visual imagination of Cornell quite openly worked with ordinary materials and images, transforming "the quotidian and the overlooked into beguiling mysteries."[28] Certainly, when de Kooning painted Marilyn Monroe, he was, contra Greenberg, allowing the substantive concerns of the larger culture, even in popular form, onto his canvas, no less than Andy Warhol later did. But he too made powerful art of it. De Kooning, Cornell, Balanchine, and those intellectuals who followed their work were confident of the sufficiency of art's powers, and they were, therefore, quite comfortable with free trade.

So far my account of the intellectuals who were in the audience at City Center has emphasized the sociological. I have tracked lines of association, and argued that they liked being in a big tent pledged to an inter-arts perspective, including the ballet, the movies, surrealism, neoromanticism, Beat and New York School poetry, among other art forms and movements. They were not worried about boundaries, or at least not greatly so, and following Duchamp they were not anxious to separate art and life too definitively.

But there was in fact more substantive content, recognized today as a politics, embedded in their aesthetic commitments, and it animated much of the art. Of all unlikely people, Greenberg quite sympathetically noticed this preoccupation and drew public attention to it. The world of ballet, he insisted, was bringing a vital private matter, gender and sexuality, into the domain of public consideration. Writing in 1945, the only time, at least to my knowledge, that he wrote about dance, he complained that Anthony Tudor's *Dim Luster* was apparently too realistic in its address of contemporary sexuality and was for that inappropriate reason dropped from the Ballet Theatre repertoire. If ballet was in his view a bastardized art form, it nonetheless, perhaps even for this reason, had important cultural work to do. It might valuably explore troubled sexual relations, examining the possibilities and impossibilities of modern romance and sex.[29] He notices, rightly and with great insight, that in Tudor's ballet "a homosexual pattern is shown imposing itself on a heterosexual situation."[30]

One cannot miss the centrality of sexuality to the art, criticism, and lifestyles of the intellectuals who found work and pleasure with the arts of the eye and ear during this period. Sexuality, or, better, a complex relation to sexuality, was at the center of Duchamp's art, from his photograph of himself as Rrose Sélavy to his famous *Large Glass* and many of his ready-mades.[31] Stettheimer was forgotten, not worth discussing, in the 1950s, precisely because her paintings, in the words of Elisabeth Sussman, "reveal a sexually ambiguous fantasy of the human body." But of course this is the reason for her reappearance in the 1980s and 1990s.[32] *View* had it right when it linked Stettheimer and Cornell in a special issue on "Americana Fantastica" (1943), for Cornell, like Stettheimer, was, in the words of his biographer, "a pioneer of sexual ambiguity."[33]

There was, of course, more to the art of Duchamp, Stettheimer, and Cornell, and not everyone I have named engaged in this public discourse of sexuality. Still, it is fair, I think, to offer this broad characterization of a diverse group of intellectuals. The blurring of boundaries between life and art, the mixing of art forms, and the focus on gender and sexuality point so clearly toward our own time as to invite further reflection. I am not sure whether anything is to be made of my serendipitous discovery that Cornell, Warhol, and the philosopher Ludwig Wittgenstein were all fascinated by the movie star Carmen Miranda. But surely it is revealing that Warhol and Jasper Johns were, in the early 1960s, among the first artists to rediscover Stettheimer.[34] Nor is it surprising that Charles Henri Ford and Parker Tyler, the latter of whom was Stettheimer's biographer, showed an early interest in Warhol.[35] And it is by this point almost predictable that in 1962, the year it was created, Philip Johnson purchased and donated to MOMA Warhol's *Gold Marilyn Monroe*.[36] In the 1980s, Frank O'Hara received official recognition in New York, winning equal public billing with Walt Whitman when the Battery Park City Authority inscribed lines from one of his city poems on the fence along the seawall in lower Manhattan. Cornell not only anticipated Pop Art, but he became friendly with Warhol, who in the 1960s visited him in Queens.[37]

In pointing out these connections—and I could offer more—I do not mean to assert some kind of hidden but surely false continuity. I urge only a recognition that the other intellectuals of the 1940s may bear a closer, if still complicated, relation to our own time than the more celebrated "New York Intellectuals." Without pushing too far, I would also suggest that there were historical versions of modernism that were closer to current sensibilities than many postmodernists allow. But still one must acknowledge, even insist, that meanings and significance have changed with the passage of time. Not only postmodern, but all appropriations and reappropriations distort. Elisabeth Sussman, for example, points out that in Stettheimer's own time her work was "an epitome of modernist sophistication," but today it is recognized for pre-saging "the subjective, narrative, sexual, and decorative tendencies that are at the core of postmodernist art at the end of the century."[38]

The networks I have been describing largely dissolved in the 1960s. The dance historian Sally Banes has argued that 1963 was a year of transition and transformation in the New York art world, and certainly, if we can add a year to either side, it well dates the end of the world I have been describing.[39] But with that ending, there are roots too, for there were important anticipations of the culture we now call postmodern.

To begin with the larger global events that marked the moment as noted by Banes, we can observe that during the period 1962–64 the United States and the Soviet Union almost started a nuclear war (Cuban missile crisis) even as they signed the nuclear test-ban treaty. Involvement in Vietnam began to deepen, and very soon, especially as it got entangled with cultural conflicts, including the wrenching conflict at Columbia in 1968, it fractured the intellectual community into old and new left, to say nothing of invigorating a right in New York that came to power as neoconservatism in the Reagan years. Others yet responded by withdrawing from political engagement. In 1963, Martin Luther King went to Washington seeking aid for the poor and proffering a dream of justice and integration. But other African Americans were already discouraged by continued white resistance and acquiescence in injustice. Listening to Malcolm X, many turned to various forms of political and cultural nationalism. LeRoi Jones, a key figure of the arts networks, became Amiri Baraka and he moved to Harlem. Black Power and the Black Arts movement both marked and furthered the division in the city and its intellectual networks. In a stupid (intentional?) accident, Frank O'Hara, who from his curatorial position at MOMA (and in seemingly endless rounds of parties) had connected so many people, died. *Partisan Review*, so closely identified with the intellectual life of New York, would soon move from the city to suburban New Jersey, subsidized by Rutgers University. More and more intellectuals became academics, incorporated into a national system of universities. The world of the New York intellectuals was coming apart. It was the end of an era.

Yet there were interesting connections. Rejecting the purity prescribed by Greenberg, multimedia happenings defined the agenda of a new avant-garde. What we today call *performance art* found a particularly welcoming home in New York, and came to define the city's avant-garde.[40] In 1963, Red Grooms founded Ruckus Productions as a "multimedia performance company," and the new minimalist dances at Judson Church in the Village sought literally to *embody* contemporary, democratic, metropolitan culture.[41] The art world was transformed, but the past lingered on. In the early 1960s, Duchamp still lived in the Village, Denby watched the Judson performances with interest, and Warhol went to Judson Church with Charles Henri Ford.[42]

There is, of course, much more to be examined. Yet I think some important conclusions flow from this exploratory inquiry. It is fair to propose, I think, that the Cold War and the function of the *Partisan Review* intellectuals in nourishing liberal anticommunism foregrounded them in our collective memory. But as 1989, to say nothing of 1947, recedes into the past, the *Partisan Review* intellectuals seem less central, if still important, while the cultural issues raised by the other New York intellectuals have become more resonant. With the relations between modernism and postmodernism more of a shout than a conversation, a closer examination of this history will surely complicate that debate and enrich it with a firmer historical grounding. A more diligent history will reveal the strategic exaggerations that make understanding of what is and is not new in postmodernism so difficult to achieve. Only if we incorporate the eye and ear of intellectuals into our account of the cultural history of the past half century can we begin to adequately describe where we have come from, where we are, and what we are to make of it.

9

THE UNIVERSITY

AND THE CITY

In 1978, the *New Yorker* magazine's famous "Talk of the Town" column carried an interview with Joshua Lederberg. The Stanford University geneticist and Nobel Laureate had just assumed the presidency of Rockefeller University, a distinguished center of scientific research and graduate training. He was asked how it felt after many years in suburban California to return to New York, the city of his youth. What he said was a mixture of nostalgia and insight into the nature of cities, universities, and creativity.

New York played a special role in my scientific career. It was, and is, a communication network. New York is a super-university. Evolutionists will tell you that you get the most rapid diversification of species where you have an archipelago—where you have islands that are not totally isolated from one another but have sufficient isolation so that each can develop its distinctive flavor and sufficient communication so that there is some gene flow between them. That's how I would characterize the intellectual environment of the city. . . . [1]

Of the many interesting aspects of this statement, I want here to pull out two. One is the theory of cultural innovation proposed; the other, of course, is the association of this process with a semi-cloistered heterogeneity that he finds in both the university and the city. The city and the university seem to share a common sociology, or—in a language a biologist would probably prefer—ecology.

In 1963, soon after Lederberg settled in at Stanford and received his Nobel Prize, Clark Kerr, who presided over the University of California a few miles away in Berkeley, published his famous book, *The Uses of the University*. In that book he characterized the "multiversity" as "a city of infinite variety." More recently, the architectural historian Paul Turner of Stanford University, in *Campus*, his history of American college and university architecture, likewise assimilated the university to the city. And more distantly, farther removed in time and quite far from suburban California, Goethe described a great city in terms that made it the functional equivalent of a university. "Conceive a city like Paris," he told Johann Peter Eckermann in 1827, "where the highest talents of a great kingdom are all assembled in a single spot, and by daily intercourse, strife, and emulation, mutually instruct and advance each other; where the best works, both of nature and art are open to daily inspection."[2]

Are the city and the university analogical social institutions? Is it plausible to assimilate the one to the other? Or to see the one in the other? Were one to adopt some conventional sociological indices often used for comparative work, the result might well sustain that notion. Over the course of the past few centuries cities and universities have shared some key formal sociological characteristics: secularity, tolerance, specialization, concentration, diversity. Yet the city and the university are surely different human creations.

I strongly believe in a university *of*, not simply *in*, the city. But that hope does not imply that it ought to be or can be the same thing as a city. When Lederberg walked onto the becalmed and tree-filled campus of Rockefeller University, he surely felt its quality as an enclave, its difference from the kinetic energy and commotion of nearby midtown Manhattan.

Why do the analysts from the suburban San Francisco Bay area detect so little difference, if any, between city and university? Is the university in fact increasingly like the suburbs? And is it a commentary on academic culture that the distinguishing qualities of city, suburb, and university are blurred? I worry that there may be a long-term tendency toward making the university more like the suburbs than like the city, or even a part of the city.

There has always been in the history of the modern university, especially in the United States, an impulse toward withdrawal from the city, seeking less social complexity. Is there a real and, to my mind, worrisome affinity of universities with the purified, safe, and calm life of idealized suburbs? Both the university and the suburb are privileged locales with the feel of wealth and the security of self-containment, and they are chararacterized by diversity of the most benign sort. Indeed, Daniel Coit Gilman, the founding president of The Johns Hopkins University in 1876, the first modern research university in the United States, proposed the same advantages for universities (in contrast to cities) as real estate developers offered to would-be suburbanites. The purpose of the university, he argued in the 1890s, is to create a community of scholars insulated from the "turmoil" of the city and free of the "distractions of modern civilization."[3]

There is a great danger in this suburbanization of the intellect. Both vitality and relevance are at risk. The semi-cloistered heterogeneity praised by Lederberg is threatened by a compartmentalization marked by firmer and less permeable boundaries. One cannot but fear scholasticism and self-referentiality. This worry is not mine alone, nor is it so recent as we might think. In his *Essay on the History of Civil Society*, written in the middle of the eighteenth century, Adam Ferguson, the Scottish philosopher who even before Adam Smith grasped the promise and dangers of division of labor, wrote: "Men at a distance from the objects of useful knowledge, untouched by the motives that animate an active and vigorous mind produce only the jargon of a technical language, and accumulate the impertinence of academic forms."[4] Ferguson's fear has found repeated articulation in our own time.[5]

Ferguson, Adam Smith, David Hume, and others in the Scottish Enlightenment discovered that a university in the city might provide a guard against academic enclosure. That is because the city and the university favor and make different kinds of culture, or knowledge, and each benefits from the countervailing influence of the other. The university is best at producing abstract, highly focused, rigorous and internally consistent forms of knowledge, while the city is more likely to produce descriptive, concrete, but also less tightly focused and more immediately useful knowledge, whether this is generated by businessmen, journalists, or professional practitioners. The academy risks scholasticism, but the culture of the city is vulnerable to the charge of superficiality and crude pragmatism.

The obvious point, of course, is that one need not be forced to choose the vices of either of these cultures of intellectual life. And part of the interest in inquiring into the similarities, differences, and interrelations of the city and the university is to better devise ways of obtaining their respective virtues. But even here we must be careful: neither is completely bounded or monolithic. What is interesting about each of these institutions, the city and the university, is the incredible plurality they both contain. There is in each a complex combination of intellectual cultures and social purposes (or interests), some more autonomous than others.

If the university and the city cannot be treated as analogues, they do complement each other. But partnering is difficult for universities. Part of the ideology of the research university, and one of the reasons it has been so strongly supported, has been its claim to be the custodian and producer of authoritative knowledge in all domains. That claim is being challenged today from multiple perspectives—by stingy governments, by postmodern critics from within, and by an increasingly powerful and global commercial culture carried by mass media and the revolution in information technologies. The result has been a significant reallocation of resources, and it is possible that we have only seen the beginning of this shift.

To some degree this has been made possible, at least in the United States, by the revival of a virulent and ugly anti-intellectual pseudopopulism. But there are also important changes in what I'll call the infrastructure of knowledge production that enable this reorientation. In the realms of general social theory and public policy analysis, the well-financed political right has created a network of privately funded think tanks in the United States. With this structure in place, conservative politicians have cut off funding for the universities, which they believe (more or less correctly) provide a resource base for liberal intellectuals who do not have the private resources available to the right.

But the impulse to shift support of intellect from universities to other sites is not always so crudely ideological in its genesis or aims. Various specialized interest groups—finding academic knowledge inadequate and persuading donors of this point of view—have created institutions that are at once devoted to research and advocacy. I refer to Human Rights Watch, Save the Children, various groups working on behalf of the homeless or the environment, the International Rescue Committee, and many others. New York City is the home of hundreds of such groups, and they represent a growing influence in our intellectual and cultural life. These developments have important implications: just when the notion of a "knowledge society" and the economic and political value of knowledge is being widely accepted, the university is losing its putative monopoly on knowledge.

Let us consider for a moment some of the urban-style intellectual milieus that pose either an alternative to the university or a complementary partner. I have in mind, for example, the extraordinarily creative milieu sustained by the small and competitive businesses that populate Silicon Valley in California. Or the "Silicon Alley" emerging in lower Manhattan. Both of these patterns recall the New York metropolis in the age of Thomas Edison, and they rather nicely conform to the vision of urban creativity that Jane Jacobs offered in *Cities and the Wealth of Nations* (1984).

Silicon Valley has been portrayed as a vital, open, egalitarian, and dialogic intellectual culture that would surprise most academics as much as it might appeal to the more venturesome among us. While the Silicon Valley example is more scientific in its activities, focusing mainly on hardware, Manhattan's Silicon Alley is an incredibly dense interdisciplinary world of writers, artists, and computer freaks, making multimedia CDs and other interactive media creations, some commercial products, some art—which in this post–Andy Warhol era are sometimes difficult to distinguish.

Fascinating research recently reported by an international team of sociologists in *The New Production of Knowledge* (1994) shows much is going on outside the universities and outside traditional disciplines in opportunistic and transdisciplinary social and economic settings.[6] And the intellectual style is different from that associated with the university. The production of knowledge is much more closely connected to its use than is the case of university-based knowledge. That closeness, as in the case of Edison, may be a source of both vitality and invention.

Such statements may evoke corporate science and technology laboratories. But part of the burden of the report is to insist that such alternative settings are becoming increasingly important in the humanities and social sciences as well. The researchers point out: "Such knowledge is intended to be useful to someone whether in industry or government, or society more generally, and this imperative is present from the beginning. Knowledge is always produced under an aspect of continuous negotiation and it will not be produced unless and until the interests of the various actors are included."[7] Truth-making becomes more participatory and dialogic, much after the fashion of John Dewey's pragmatism, though without in any way relying on Dewey's or any other formal philosophy—and without Dewey's explicit democratic commitments.

In these alternative settings the very process of making knowledge is coterminous with the diffusion of knowledge, thus dissolving the old categorical distinction between production and popularization. By thus bringing scholarship and scholars closer to the place and purposes of use, it is quite likely that they will become more sensitive to the broader implications of particular knowledges. The humanities once claimed this domain, the realm of values and ethics.[8] But increasingly scholars form their research and even teaching questions within the scholarly literature, not from our quotidian existence. When was the last time you sought counsel on an ethical question from the *Journal of Philosophy*?

To the extent that traditional academic disciplines have withdrawn from the public culture in their pursuit of purity and autonomy (philosophy has probably gone the farthest in this direction in the United States), society has been inventing (or recovering) alternative and often metropolitan-based sources of knowledge.[9]

Does this mean that the university is soon to go the way of the dinosaur? No. Does it mean that it must renegotiate its relation to the city and the city's many and diverse habitats of knowledge, much as the universities did to revitalize themselves in early modern Europe, especially at Leiden and Edinburgh?[10] I hope so.

Such a move is especially welcome at this moment. Given the contemporary rejection of grand theory—of all-encompassing meta-narratives that might unify the intellectual project of academe—there is an invitation to move toward more localized knowledges and more particularized audiences for academic work. In a university environment—isolated from the particularities of local life, of public controversy, and of institutional power—such a development has in the United States led to "a slide into the aestheticized localized discourse, exemplified most famously by Heidegger."[11] The challenge facing advanced thought and contemporary theory in the human sciences, as critic Edward Said observed, is to bridge the gap between the academy and the conditions (and politics) of everyday life.[12] The way to go, it seems to me, is to work toward a pattern of purposive academic knowledge that is honed in the world of power and complexity that is the metropolitan environment. To that end, universities would do well to conceive knowledge, society, and politics in Deweyan terms.[13]

University scholars must grasp that their disciplines are not ends but means. The logic of professional development may be in tension with that obvious fact. The professionalizing project is one of achieving autonomy and self-legitimization, which points toward self-referential enclosure. Of course, service is a part of the professional ethos, but too often it becomes a bit abstract: all knowledge is good, so we are serving society by the creation of knowledge, *any* knowledge. But it is astonishing how few social scientists (outside of professional schools) at New York's two great research universities, NYU and Columbia, are studying the issues on everyone's minds—the delivery of health care, poverty and inequality, race relations, education, urban politics, the parties and the electoral system, the environment, and others one could name.

As they open themselves to the local world in which they live, my colleagues might find some enormously interesting domains of research and teaching. They may also discover that there are a variety of clusters of scholars, writers, and activists outside of the academy who are developing quite valuable bodies of research on these issues.

A century ago, John Dewey, the greatest twentieth-century American philosopher, discovered just this when he joined the faculty of the University of Chicago. Outside of the university he also came to know Jane Addams and her colleagues at Hull House. It was they who were doing the most important social thinking in Chicago during the 1890s. Others in Chicago had similar experiences, and the result was a mutually beneficial collaboration of philosophers, social scientists, and activists.

Let me say more about John Dewey and the relation of academic knowledge to public purpose. Dewey was strongly committed to the rigorous scholarship of the academy, even to esoteric knowledge, and his own work included a vast number of articles on technical philosophy, published in the *Journal of Philosophy*. Yet he worried about the isolation of trained intellect from our common life, even more so after he moved to New York in 1904.

These issues are treated in *Experience and Nature*, a great summary book, published in 1929, when he was seventy years old. He argued that the scholar must begin with the ordinary life experiences he or she shares with others. The special contribution of scholarship is its access to a refined and severe method of thought informed by special knowledges. The scholar must not, however, claim any special privilege or power on the basis of that knowledge. He or she must engage in dialogue as a whole person, sharing his or her insights with other people in a variety of settings, not simply the classroom or the learned journal.

In evaluating the worth of a scholar's participation in such dialogues, Dewey proposed the following test. Does the scholar's special knowledge, when "referred back to ordinary life-experiences . . . render them more significant, more luminous to us, and make our dealings with them more fruitful? Or does it terminate in rendering the things of ordinary experience more opaque?"[14]

Metropolitan academics ought not work so hard at keeping the city at bay: it is a source of energy, of wonderfully complex intellectual problems, and of nonacademic intellectuals who have much to offer. What is needed is not the old university expert model, but a newer approach that facilitates continuing two-way conversations between the various academic groupings on the campus and the appropriate constituencies in the metropolis. The sociologist Mary Lindenstein Walshok is right to argue that "universities will not integrate the experiences and expertise of individuals and institutions outside of the academy without a deeper appreciation of the invaluable resources they represent."[15]

One must understand that such interactions imply different ways of thinking about the creation of knowledge. Such work will be less self-contained. Rather it will be a matter of drawing upon "diverse sources of expertise and multiple forms of knowledge," some of which is best communicated in face-to-face exchanges that are more characteristic of metropolitan culture than in the academy, where the more usual form of communication is through articles and books.[16]

This vision of the future recalls a key moment in the past, when the research universities were new. In turn-of-the-century New York, Thomas Edison exploited a remarkable variety of decentralized habitats of knowledge, including that of academic knowledge, to create much that defines the modernity of the world we live in—from electric light, to cinema, to recorded music. In bringing such diverse knowledges together, he established an intellectual style that privileged no one habitat of knowledge or type of knowledge but rather brought them together in creative ways. It was possible only in the metropolis, something he fully recognized. Academic enclosure would have been fatal to his work, as would have been isolation from university expertise.[17]

Seth Low, successively mayor of Brooklyn in the 1880s, president of Columbia in the 1890s, and mayor of the newly consolidated greater New York after the turn of the century, grasped the place of the university in the metropolis better than any university president before or since.[18] Between 1889 and 1901, the years of his presidency, Columbia was transformed from a struggling college with only a handful of students into Columbia University, one of the twentieth century's most distinguished research universities.

Scion of a wealthy mercantile family, Low respected academic research, but his commitment to it was not exclusive. He did not presume that other modes of making knowledge lost legitimacy. He could not imagine a metropolitan university that could be—or would want to be—self-contained. Nor did he envision a university dispensing expert knowledge to a receiving city. He thought that the city offered as many lessons for the university as the university did for the city. Recognizing the different but complementary qualities of academic and civic culture, he believed that dialogue offered the possibility of mutual education. He established important institutional collaborations with various learned societies, from the New York Botanical Garden and the New York Academy of Sciences, to the American Museum of Natural History and the Metropolitan Museum of Art, to Union Theological Seminary and the Jewish Theological Seminary. But he went beyond these elite institutions to settlement houses in lower Manhattan and to organized labor. Declining to claim the privilege of authoritative knowledge, he was willing to enter into dialogue, even debate, with various groups that viewed the world from different perspectives.

With his own funds, he established the nation's first chair in sociology, "to take advantage, so far as possible, of the special opportunities for sociological study incident to our location in the City of New York." Such an academic initiative, of course, may not be entirely benign. It could result in labelling social groups as "problems," thus denying the worth of working-class and immigrant self-perceptions and, by implication, politics. Looking at the emerging social sciences as a whole, one might well stress this point, but Low's approach was different. At the same time as he supported the new academic discipline, he invited workers to offer to the academy their *own* views of social conditions. He would be glad to "have it known to the workingmen of America," he announced, that "at Columbia College . . . the disposition exists to teach the truth . . . without fear or favor, and *we ask their aid to enable us to see the truth as it appears to them*." Such a university, even as it enabled the "profoundest scholars" to pursue "research in all directions of study," would be a part of the city, absorbing "that which is characteristic in the life of the city in which it does its work."[19]

It was a noble vision. Yet Low underestimated the centrifugal forces of academic professionalism and overestimated the essential unity of knowledge. Under Low's chosen successor, Nicholas Murray Butler, president from 1901 to 1948, Columbia liberated the disciplines to develop in increasing isolation from the city. Columbia's professional disciplines, like those developing within the modern research universities in general, looked increasingly to the nation, even the world—not the city—as its context.

The modern academic disciplines were born in alliance with the rising nation-state, not the city. Wilhelm von Humboldt's university was a product of the court, not the city of Berlin, and the modern disciplines that developed in the course of the nineteenth century in Germany were adjuncts of the German state, nourishing its science and culture as a national project.[20] To greater or lesser degrees university development elsewhere followed this model, and for its first century the modern university and nation have been more closely linked than the university and the city. Today, however, there is a question of whether the nation is secure enough to host either science or scholarship. Can it justify and sustain a university system based on such national premises? Might the metropolis or metropolitan region supersede or at least complement the nation as the sustaining milieu for the modern research university in its second century?

In the course of the past half century, it has been possible for universities to chose rather freely whether to identify with locality or nation. Harvard University, which was a distinctly and deliberately regional university before

World War II, became a national university in the decades following the war. While Columbia continued to associate itself with the nation, New York University tied its fortunes, with great success, to the city. A less obvious comparison is Stanford and Princeton. In the period since World War II, these two institutions raised themselves from rather ordinary standing to positions of distinction as research universities. But they took very different paths. Princeton proposed to serve the nation, and it looked to Washington, not to its region, as a source of the resources that would enable it to raise its profile. Stanford, by contrast, turned to its immediate region, and was willing to associate itself with the practical and commercial concerns of such recent graduates as David Packard. The result was a vital symbiosis of university and local surround, which resulted in Silicon Valley and the elevation of Stanford to the first rank of universities in the United States.[21]

But what do I mean by a university of the city? As my opening remarks should have indicated, to be *of the city* is not to be assimilated to the city. The university has its distinctive culture to be brought into dialogue with the city; it ought not become impossible to differentiate it from the city. Perhaps an architectural example (or more precisely an urban design example) will provide a clear image of what I have in mind. Some years ago I was invited to an international conference in Barcelona on "The Metropolis and the University." It was co-sponsored by the municipality and the university. After two days of papers, the hidden agenda of the conference (at least hidden from me) became clear, in the course of a reception hosted by Pasqual Maragall, the mayor of Barcelona. The conference, it turned out, was part of the university's scheme to persuade him to give the university some buildings across the street from its main entrance.

To me, it seemed an odd and unnecessary strategy. Coming from a culture in which universities have historically been separate from or uneasy with cities, Barcelona seemed to have nothing to learn from the experience of the United States. Yet it did. The university building was walled, as many Mediterranean public buildings are, with a central courtyard providing access to the various parts of the university. The university leaders wanted to open the university out to the city, to make it, they said, like New York University, located as it is on the various streets converging on Washington Square Park at the foot of Fifth Avenue in Manhattan. Was the contrast they made apt? Was a walled university not engaged with the city? Would breaching the street make for a better relationship, symbolically and in real terms, between the university and the city? Or was the whole thing simply about space and real estate?

The urban issues involved were even more complicated than these comments reveal. It was soon apparent that the university leaders in Barcelona did not understand the importance of the park in New York. The street the Barcelonians wished to span was a very busy thoroughfare, an important boulevard. Were the university to come out from its walled enclosure, it was in danger of being lost in the traffic. New York University, by contrast, has the park, which establishes a place and slows down the traffic, both vehicular and pedestrian. In this fact of urban design we find a representation of a very nuanced relation of the city and the university: the metropolitan university is of the city, but it does not dissolve into the city. It is physically and intellectually at one with the city, yet a distinct place. To more effectively represent the interrelations of the university and the city, NYU has more recently hung large flags from all the university buildings in the neighborhood of the Square. These flags effectively mark the place of the university without isolating it.

And that distinctive place may provide the best space available in metropolitan regions for the enactment of a public culture. Coffee bars are everywhere, but the coffeehouse—which traces its origins to and is implicated in the birth of the public sphere in the eighteenth century—is no more, not even in its more recent and somewhat bohemian café form.[22] Metropolitan universities enable the work of the contemporary public sphere; they offer the possibility of creating a dialogue across the differences that largely define metropolitan life in our time.

The metropolis, according to theologian Paul Tillich, offers both centralization and the inclusion of diversity. "A metropolis," he observed a generation ago, "is a center city. It is likewise an including city." It is the home both of "the stranger" and of the "critical spirit."[23] In our own time there has been a profound diminution of the spaces characterized by difference and dialogue. There is difference without dialogue, and dialogue without difference, a mark of the suburbanization of metropolitan life and of the triumph of commercial mass culture.

The most important gift of the university to its metropolis is the creation of such a space. If Los Angeles anticipates the metropolitan future, then the challenge facing city culture is clear there. The absence of a public space and public culture in Los Angeles is notorious. Most discussion of the riots following the Rodney King trial there noted the absence of a public culture capable of sustaining a serious political discourse that incorporated the subcultures of difference. Without such a public sphere, according to some, a social explosion was inevitable.

Yet in the aftermath of the tragedy many noticed that there in fact was an inclusive place for very important, if obviously insufficient, political talk. At UCLA, a great urban public university, in its classes and public fora, there existed an opportunity for serious talk across difference. During that period I was in Los Angeles and was regularly on the UCLA campus, and I heard constant political discussions. The faculty I knew there then felt that these issues infused many class discussions, at least in the humanities and social sciences. Almost on a daily basis, whether in the classroom, the lunch room, or the steps in front of buildings, a metropolitan university provides such a place for a diverse society to form itself into a public culture, even if only as a temporary creation.

The metropolitan university becomes a rare, incomplete, but essential site for democratic debate and deliberation. Guided by a commitment to the very protocols that defined the public sphere in its seventeenth- and eighteenth-century emergence in scientific societies and coffeehouses, the metropolitan university provides the center, the engagement with strangers, and the work of inclusion of which Tillich spoke.[24] To effectively enact this role, the university—at least in its metropolitan form—must resist its internal tendency toward suburbanization. It must strive for ever greater inclusion in its student body—indeed even for inclusion of a larger community of teachers, students, and staff, although such work will not, in and of itself, constitute the world of difference that is the promise of the city. But by committing itself to the urban values of public life, the university does provide essential resistance to suburban values and to mass commercial culture. Such a metropolitan university does not become the city, but it enriches the city and becomes enriched by it.

The creation of a public culture in self-consciously metropolitan (as opposed to national) universities speaks directly to the issue of multiculturalism, a notion that seeks to describe our increasingly pluralized world. Cities all over the world are now receiving immigrants from a greater variety of origins than ever before in history, and one must understand the complex patterns of cultural dialogues and transformations implied. These developments make necessary talk about new cultures built from the materials brought by immigrants and from previously suppressed groups. But such talk is very threatening in the context of *national* identities.[25] Yet if we think of cities, of metropolises, instead of nations, as the key units of society and culture, the prospect of diversity is less threatening. Cities have always had this quality, and they have always continually redefined their culture through the work of inclusion. They have always been more successful at this work than have nations. Nations are falsely thought to be unitary and homogeneous, but cities have always been understood to be diverse, local, having their own distinctive mixes.

By reorienting academic culture from the nation to the metropolis, and from national cultures to the metropolitan cultures in which universities are deeply implicated, one might acquire important new resources for the making of the pluralized public culture that must be constructed in the coming generation—not only in the United States, but in every open, democratic society.

With these comments I have opened the city out to the world; let me conclude then with a brief comment upon a more literal worldliness of the university. The current fascination with globalization seems radically to devalue the nation. There has been a diminution of the nation-state to be sure, but obituaries of the nation-state are premature. I would not want to be associated with them. Nonetheless, the present moment seems to restore cities and their regions to some of the advantage they had in the early modern period, before the consolidation of modern nation-states.[26]

The world economy and culture, it seems, is increasingly organized by a network of international cities. The qualities of the emerging global culture have a considerable resemblance to the eighteenth-century cosmopolitan republic of letters, an ideal and mode of practice inherited by the modern university. Today's cosmopolitanism, however, extends more deeply into the social body. The pluralized culture of the university resembles the complex life of contemporary immigrant neighborhoods, where residents live at once in local urban neighborhoods and diasporic networks. Teachers and students in a university, much like the new metropolitans, live at once in the past and the present, in a local place and a trans-local culture of international scholarship. They must constantly bring together in fruitful ways the past and present, the local and the trans-local.

The challenge for us as contemporary metropolitans (and cosmopolitans) is to locate ourselves—both in time and in relation to the places of local knowledges—in such a global perspective. The modern urban university is particularly well suited, by structure and culture, to provide the place and the model for such cultural redefinition. No other institution remains institutionally so historical, so persistent even as it transforms itself, and no other institution has such rich connections at once to a local intellectual, political, and social milieu and to a global network of ideas, structures, and powers. If, as I have been suggesting, universities have much to learn from the practical life of cities, cities too, as they enter into a new cultural and spatial organization of metropolitan experience, have much to learn from the practical life of universities.

PART III

POLITICS

10

CITIES AND

AMERICAN POLITICAL CULTURE

"The United States was born in the country and has moved to the city." Thus Richard Hofstadter observed in the opening sentence of *The Age of Reform* (1955), his Pulitzer Prize–winning examination of American political culture. He believed that the political and cultural values that historically defined America were rooted in rural life, not in the city. For him this was a problem, and he argued that our political culture must urbanize with our population.

The Age of Reform identifies itself with a distinctly urban sensibility. Highly critical of the narrow parochialism and moralism that Hofstadter associated with agrarian and small-town America, the book celebrates urban, pragmatic, and cosmopolitan values. Hofstadter was representative of a number of mid-century American intellectuals, mostly from New York, who identified with the metropolitan ideals and sought to find room for cities and their people in American history and culture.

More than a decade earlier, Alfred Kazin, a friend of Hofstadter's, had published *On Native Grounds*, an urban interpretation of American literature. Both men brought to their respective studies an urban sensibility nourished by the liberal and cosmopolitan atmosphere of New York in the New Deal era. Various New Deal projects revealed a fascination with the diverse peoples who represented America, something manifested in the WPA state-guide series. Popular culture had absorbed much of this sensibility—evident in the war movies of the 1940s. It was still novel in the 1950s, however, for a professional historian to associate the best in our political tradition so unambiguously with the life, values, and people of our big cities. The historiographical legacy of Frederick Jackson Turner's "frontier thesis" was thus challenged. Indeed, in a note to the American edition of his book *Victorian Cities* (1965), the British historian Asa Briggs welcomed Hofstadter's political history as an innovative work of urban history. It is hard to imagine any political history before Hofstadter's being thus assimilated to urban history.

Today it is so easy to assume the rightness of Hofstadter's urban and cosmopolitan perception that we may forget how thoroughly and for how long the city has been doubtfully American. Whether cities were American has been quite uncertain in American history and historiography. Recovering the feel of the anti-urbanism that marks our political history is essential, therefore, to understand the history of American politics, cities, and the ways historians have written about American political culture.

In 1789, Dr. David Ramsay of Charleston—then one of the new nation's five major cities—published the first history of the American Revolution. Addressing his fellow Americans, Ramsay counselled them:

> Your towns will probably e're long be engulphed in luxury and effeminacy. If your liberties and future prospects depended upon them, your career of liberty would probably be short; but a great majority of your country must and will be yeomanry, who have no other dependence than on Almighty God for his usual blessing on their daily labour. From the great excess of the number of such independent farmers in these States, over and above all other classes of inhabitants, the long continuance of your liberties may be reasonably presumed.[1]

That cities were not the real America was not Ramsay's idiosyncratic assumption. More prominent Americans held the same belief: George Washington warned that "the tumultuous populace of large cities are ever to be dreaded," and Alexander Hamilton, in his celebrated report on manufacturing, endorsed husbandry as "a state most favourable to the freedom and independence of the human mind."[2]

We have here something more than a bias or an aesthetic preference. Agrarianism of this sort is a political theory. It asserts that the good citizens who make possible a good state live in the country. In his *Notes on the State of Virginia*, Thomas Jefferson unequivocally praised farmers for their political virtues: "those who labor the earth are the chosen people of God" and are the repository of "substantial and genuine virtue." In contrast, according to Jefferson, "the mobs of great cities add just so much to the support of pure government, as sores do to the strength of the human body." Jefferson clearly deemed rural virtue essential to the success of the new government. Farmers, being virtuous, could be trusted to:

> . . . reserve to themselves a wholesome control over their public affairs and a degree of freedom, which in the hands of the Canaille of the cities of Europe, would be instantly perverted to the demolition and destruction of everything public and private.[3]

In a similar vein, John Adams noted that:

> In the present state of society and manners in America, with a people living chiefly by agriculture, in small numbers, sprinkled over large tracts of land, they are not subject to those panics and transports, those contagions of madness and folly, which are seen in countries where large numbers live in small places, in daily fear of perishing from want.[4]

The demographics of the early republic allowed Jefferson and Adams to espouse these notions. In 1790, the population of the United States was about five million people; there were only 183,000 Americans living in the six cities with populations over 10,000 persons. These six cities, moreover, were seaports, mere specks on the edge of an immense continent. If the existence of one million slaves (20 percent of the population) did not undermine Jefferson's rhetoric of equality and freedom in the Declaration of Independence, surely a mere 183,000 city residents would not counter the assumption of a rural nation.

That Thomas Jefferson excluded cities from his interpretation of America may not be surprising, but so did that consummate eighteenth-century urbanite Benjamin Franklin. "Forming an opinion of our People and their Manners by what is seen among the Inhabitants of the Seaports," he observed, "is judging from an improper Sample." He insisted that "the Country possesses all the Virtues, that tend to private Happiness and public Prosperity." When a British writer criticized America, Franklin responded that the critic had erred by basing his judgment on life in the towns, which are, he explained, "not much regarded by the Country; they are hardly considered an Essential part of the States."[5] In 1803, Jefferson as president echoed the same sentiments, excluding cities from the political community of the new United States. "The great mass of our people are agricultural," he wrote. "The commercial cities, though by command of the newspapers . . . make a great deal of noise, have little effect in the direction of the government."[6]

Two months later Jefferson purchased Louisiana from France in order to perpetuate to the "thousandth generation" the agrarian character of America. He did so despite his doubts—as a strict constructionist of the Constitution—whether he possessed constitutional authority to make such a purchase. But his grand agrarian vision of the United States made his legal reservations seem small and perhaps not pertinent.

Americans moved west in the nineteenth century, as Jefferson had hoped they would, but they also moved into cities, both east and west. By 1860, there were more than five million urban dwellers. Nine cities had populations in excess of 100,000, while New York surpassed the one million mark. No nation urbanized faster than the United States in the nineteenth century. While the total population tripled between 1820 and 1860, the urban population increased ten times.

The logic of agrarian virtue and the demographics of urbanization were on a collision course. Was progress dooming the democratic experiment? Landscape painter Thomas Cole, who was a part of the New York art world but who gained fame as the preeminent artist of the Hudson River School with his Catskill region landscapes, captured this paradox of progress in *The Course of Empire*. This series of five large and compelling allegorical paintings, now in the New York Historical Society, were commissioned by New York merchant and patron Luman Reed in 1836. In a letter to Reed, Cole described his intentions:

A series of pictures might be painted that should illustrate the history of a natural scene, as well as be an epitome of Man—showing the natural changes of landscape, and those effected by man in his progress from barbarism to civilization—to luxury—to the vicious state, or state of destruction—and to the state of ruin and desolation.

The first panel portrays a wilderness, the second a pastoral scene with a Greek temple—Jefferson's ideal political landscape. Continued progress brings what Cole called "The Consummation of Empire": a "great city" in the "fullness of prosperity." Nature, which dominates the first two panels, is nearly obliterated in the third. With the ascendance of urban artificiality, the "scene of destruction" in the fourth panel is predictable. The last depicts "the funeral knell of departed greatness."[7] (Figures 49, 50, 51, 52, and 53)

Cole was a painter, not a political theorist or even a sophisticated com-

49. *The Course of Empire: The Savage State*, 1836, by Thomas Cole. © Collection of the New-York Historical Society

50. *The Course of Empire: The Arcadian or Pastoral*, 1836, by Thomas Cole. © Collection of the New-York Historical Society

51. *The Course of Empire: The Consummation of Empire*, 1836, by Thomas Cole. © Collection of the New-York Historical Society

52. *The Course of Empire: Destruction*, 1836, by Thomas Cole. © Collection of the New-York Historical Society

53. *The Course of Empire: Desolation*, 1836, by Thomas Cole. © Collection of the New-York Historical Society

mentator on society and politics. Partly for that reason, his painting reflects thinking common to the world in which he lived, including New York City, where patrons, lithograph publishers, critics, and fellow painters sustained his career as an artist. The novelist James Fenimore Cooper, who treated the same themes in a more subtle way in his novels, thought the immense popularity of the series well earned. He considered it "the work of the highest genius this country has ever produced."[8]

Alexis de Tocqueville, by contrast, was one of the nineteenth century's most sophisticated students of society and politics, and perhaps the closest and most perceptive analyst of the United States. Yet he articulated some of the same warnings about the threat cities posed to democracy in America. In 1835, a year before Cole painted *The Course of Empire*, the first volume of Tocqueville's great book, *Democracy in America*, appeared. He did not discuss cities extensively, but he revealed a strong concern about them. He recognized their rapid growth, but that seemed to be a cause for worry rather than celebration. These cities posed a challenge for the historic meaning of America and the practice of democracy. In a chapter entitled "Principle Causes which Tend to Maintain the Democratic Republic in the United States," he focused his attention on cities and their implications for the future of the American democracy.

He framed his discussion within the rubric of "the peculiar and accidental situation in which Providence has placed the Americans." Three such circumstances, he thought, favored democracy. First, there were the gifts of the natural environment of America. Settling an "empty" country with vast resources and no hostile "neighbors" was an advantage. His vision of emptiness—a common one during the first two centuries of European settlement—effectively erased the Indians, for the convenience of the Europeans. Second, he remarked on the good fortune of the original settlers who brought with them British political traditions. With the third circumstance, he directed attention to the issue of a metropolis. "America has no great capital city, whose direct or indirect influence is felt over the whole extent of the country." The absence of a large, dominant, and centralizing city—an American Paris—was, Tocqueville thought, a singular blessing. He hoped none would develop, but like Cole he recognized its inevitability. In a long and remarkable footnote, he reflected:

The United States has no metropolis, but it already contains several very large cities. . . . The lower ranks which inhabit these cities constitute a rabble even more formidable than the populace of European towns. They consist of freed blacks . . . who are condemned by the laws and by public opinion to a hereditary state of misery and degradation. They also contain a multitude of Europeans who have been driven to the shores of the New World by their misfortunes or their misconduct. . . . As inhabitants of a country where they have no civil rights, they are ready to turn all the passions which agitate the community to their own advantage; thus, within the last few months [1834], serious riots have broken out in Philadelphia and New York. Disturbances of this kind are unknown to the rest of the country, which is not alarmed by them, because the population of cities has hitherto exercised neither power nor influence over the rural districts.

Nevertheless, I look upon the size of certain American cities, and especially on the nature of their population, as a real danger which threatens the future security of the democratic republics of the New World, and I venture to predict that they will perish from this circumstance, unless the government succeeds in creating an armed force which, while it remains under the control of the majority of the nation, will be independent of the town population and able to repress its excesses.[9]

Apparently without a moment's hesitation, Tocqueville here explicitly disenfranchised the supposedly inferior population of cities. Moreover, his perceptions were widely shared—indeed common sense—among the urban elites with whom he associated during his stay in the United States. Writing in 1840, Philip Hone, a former mayor of New York City, noted that "scenes of violence, disorder, and riot have taught us in this city that universal suffrage will not do for large communities." Why? Hone mistrusted the kinds of people living in cities, especially the "heterogeneous mass of vile humanity" constituting the poor.[10] Tocqueville's idea found more tangible, institutional expression with the creation of the Metropolitan Police force in 1857. Control over the forces was taken away from the untrustworthy democracy in New York City and lodged in Albany, with the state in effect placing the city's police under upstate rural and small-town jurisdiction.[11]

This suspicion of urban suffrage was not momentary; it is a subtheme of

New York's history. After the Civil War, E. L. Godkin, the founding editor of *The Nation* magazine, proposed disenfranchising the urban working classes, insisting that democracy did not require mass suffrage. The workers and immigrants of the cities and the still slowly growing northern urban African American communities worried urban elites. In 1876, a commission appointed by Governor Samuel J. Tilden seriously considered and proposed to the voters of New York a plan for excluding the poor and working-class citizens of the city from the suffrage. The scheme was rejected by the voters, amidst a rich discussion of democracy. Yet such an action was considered well within the domain of reasonable policies.[12]

There are, to be sure, many more discomfiting statements about cities and democracy one could cite. But I trust my point is clear: there is a substantial tradition of anti-urbanism in American cultural and political life. And, more surprisingly, many of those speaking for this point of view were themselves urban.[13] More specifically, denying the Americanness of the city, especially the big city with its social differentiation and cultural heterogeneity, is a long-standing American habit. A fear of differences has supported the idea that cities are un-American, even though, of course, their accommodation of difference might make them the epitome of America.

Yet there have been different voices. During the 1790s, Samuel Miller was an active Jeffersonian and a member of a small but notable intellectual circle in New York City. In 1801, he published *Brief Retrospect of the Eighteenth Century*, the first work of intellectual history written by an American. Later Miller moved to Princeton to become a professor of theology at Princeton Theological Seminary. With this move he disowned some of the secular, Enlightenment radicalism of his youth in New York City, but he continued to consider cities central to the moral and political advancement of nations. In 1820, when he had been living in Princeton for several years, he argued that "a large city . . . forms as it were, the heart, the most vital portion of the state or country to which it belongs. . . . A happy impulse given here [in the city], will vibrate, and be beneficially felt to the remotest bounds of the social body."[14] For Miller and his successors in the urban tradition, cities represented a constructive challenge for American democracy. Increasingly the fate of the cities became identified with that of the nation.

The novelist James Fenimore Cooper, whose Leatherstocking novels celebrated Natty Bumppo and depicted the American drama of the penetration of civilization into the wilderness, might be expected to hold deep reservations about the city. And he did for much of his life, but by mid-century he had shifted toward an embrace of the city. He recognized the city's importance as a vital focal point in American life. In fact, he was writing an affectionate history of Manhattan when he died in 1851. In that unfinished work, he wrote:

> It has long been a subject of investigation among moralists, whether the existence of towns like those of London, Paris, and New York, etc. is or is not favorable to the development of the human character.

Cooper dismissed the supposed "superior innocence and virtue of a rural population." He observed that while there are "incentives to wrong-doing in the crowded population of a capital town . . . there are many incentives to refinement, public virtue, and even piety, that are not to be met with elsewhere."[15]

After the Civil War, worries about the cities remained, but, much after the fashion of Cooper, there was less celebration of the redemptive character of rural life. In fact, after the Civil War, which had pitted the more urban North against the slaveholding agrarians of the South, Jefferson's reputation fell under a dark shadow. The agrarianism and anti-urbanism that he had advocated came increasingly under attack. Ebenezer Platt Rogers, a New York minister, declared Jefferson wrong in having called cities sores on the body politic. He agreed there were many "forces that are potent for evil" in cities, but "there is a great deal [said] of the superior virtue of a rural population, which is not warranted by facts. And there is a great deal that is good and great and glorious about large cities."[16]

Even more striking was a nascent pro-urban position that linked democracy and reform. Americans, Leonard Kip wrote in 1870, were coming to a new understanding of cities. "Of late years," he observed, "it seems as though we [are] beginning to learn a new lesson upon the subject [and] are beginning to slowly understand what of itself ought rather to have been accepted from the first, . . . that uncleanliness, inordinate disproportion of crime, and a dingy absence of beauty, are not of themselves necessary concomitants of city life, but are rather mere unholy parasites which long neglect has allowed to cluster around it; and that it is possible, with good management, to retain the advantages afforded by large massing of population, and not necessarily assume its disadvantages also."[17]

Few nineteenth-century Americans thought more deeply about the city and few did more to redeem its democratic possibilities than did Frederick Law Olmsted. Remembered for designing Central Park, Olmsted was also a major social thinker. Olmsted and Charles Loring Brace, a childhood friend and the founder of the Children's Aid Society, which still operates in New York, long pondered the challenges of urban life. For them the city was more than a problem; it was a starting point for national political and social reform. Olmsted, whose books on the American South during the 1850s helped to define the ideology of the newly founded Republican Party, considered the city—not the rural South, with its slaves—to hold the promise of American democracy. "Our country," he reflected, "has entered upon a stage of progress in which its welfare is to depend on the convenience, safety, order and economy of life in our cities. It cannot gain in virtue, wisdom, comfort, except as they also advance."[18] Indeed, soon after Brace and Olmsted arrived in New York, Olmsted had written to his friend, asking him to "throw your light on the paths in Politics and Social Improvement . . . [for] there's a great *work* [that] wants doing in this our generation, Charleylet's off jacket and go about it."[19]

Unlike his contemporary Baron Haussmann in Paris, Olmsted's urban vision was not wholly architectural and infrastructural. Indeed, many commentators have misunderstood Olmsted and labelled him antiurban. Was not his great accomplishment, Central Park, green, not urban? Was not the park a nostalgic refusal to accept the modern city? In fact, Olmsted—and for that matter Brace—were more complex than that. They sought to enrich human experience by bringing into dynamic relation landscape and cityscape, informal and formal, spontaneity and order, familial and institutional arrangements. But in each case it was in the interest of advancing "urban civilization," making it possible to proceed toward an urban modernity that they identified with democratic life.

Olmsted, like Lewis Mumford many years later, envisioned cities and regions, nature and artifice, as providing a terrain for a fuller humanity.[20] Central Park became a symbol as well as a practical device for this distinct

54. *The Architect's Dream*, 1840, by Thomas Cole (oil on canvas, 53 x 84⅟₁₆ in.). Courtesy of the Toledo Museum of Art, Toledo, Ohio (purchased with funds from the Florence Scott Libbey Bequest in memory of her father, Maurice A. Scott)

version of urbanism. The counterpoint of nature and city—and I distinguish counterpoint from the blurring of city and suburb that increasingly characterizes the formless cities of our own time—was one of the most important cultural revisions of the mid-century.

In fact, the painter Thomas Cole created the first important artistic expression of this new understanding well before Olmsted. Apparently hoping, like other Americans, to find a way out of the cycle of destruction he had portrayed in *The Course of Empire*, Cole reconfigured the relation of country and city a few years later in *The Architect's Dream* (1840). (Figure 54) Rather than elaborating an inevitable sequence, in this painting he fashioned country and city in a dialogue or contemporary relation. The painting was commissioned with the request that it exemplify a variety of architectural styles, and that is one of its fascinations. My concern, however, is not with the styles but with the way he organized the canvas. He divided it roughly diagonally, with nature and a

Gothic church on the left side, and a grand white city on the right. Here country or nature and city are held in a dynamic and mutually enriching tension. The historical inevitability of the earlier series of paintings has here been replaced by the political possibility of finding a fitting balance. Such was the opportunity that Olmsted grasped, and he devoted his career as America's first professional urban planner and city designer to doing that work.

Brace, who was the most important nineteenth-century proto–social worker, followed a similar logic. When he arrived in New York as a young ministerial student, "delinquent" children were placed in asylums, where, it was thought, the regularity of institutional life would make up for family failures. While Brace shared many of the prejudices of other child savers about immigrants, their children, and notions of delinquency, he rejected their methods of reforming children. He felt that the artificial institutional environment of the asylums failed to prepare children for participation in a democratic society. He created the Children's Aid Society in 1853 to place such children in farm families, where a more "natural" experience would better prepare them for adult futures. He also created industrial schools in the city to provide education for working and working-class children who found the rigidity of the public schools difficult to abide. He introduced "Object Teaching," which he believed was a more natural way of teaching and learning.[21]

The point is not that Brace or Olmsted had the solution; in retrospect there is much in their work to which we would object on the grounds of a fuller notion of urban democracy. My concern with them is to provide concrete examples of the particular form of urbanism that made it easier to assimilate the city into the idea of America. Whatever its limits as a social and cultural revolution, the mid-century strategy, which extends into the twentieth century, has marked American urbanism. It infuses all of the work of Lewis Mumford, perhaps the most important twentieth-century American commentator on cities. And it provided the nub of the bitter controversy between Mumford and Jane Jacobs, the next most significant American urban thinker. She vigorously attacked Mumford and this halfway urbanism in her *Death and Life of Great American Cities* (1961).

If Jefferson, Franklin, and Tocqueville had repudiated the city in their expectations for the American experiment, Olmsted and many of his generation found space for cities within the national mythos, indeed associating them with progressive civilization. Two distinctively American policy traditions emerged from their activism.

The first became what we now call the nonprofit sector. Tocqueville had been struck by the pervasiveness of voluntary associations in American life. Olmsted, Brace, and other elite reformers turned to such associations and enhanced their power. Brace's work for children was done through a private charity, the Children's Aid Society, not under government auspices, and a later generation would use this form to establish settlement houses. Often, however, the seemingly democratic language of voluntarism was used to mask elite avoidance of democracy. The fear of the masses did not entirely disappear. Olmsted and Godkin, for example, were allies in establishing nongovernmental institutions, particularly in the cultural domain, partly to avoid control by a democratic electorate they did not trust. Among the most important nineteenth-century examples are the Metropolitan Museum of Art, the American Museum of Natural History, and New York's great research universities. Still, whatever one thinks of the variegated landscape of nongovernmental organizations in American life, they are a product of the challenge of the city.

The second tradition turned to the government. The liberal interventionism that was elaborated in the New Deal had its origins in the opposition of urban activists to laissez-faire. Indeed, between the failure of the Populist movement in the 1890s and the Civil Rights movement, all major social movements to extend democracy have had urban roots and ideals.

I would argue that the New Deal was the translation of a new kind of urban activism, especially that of New York, into national politics. The years between the two World Wars were the great age of the city, which found representation both in the movies and the White House. Urban understandings of the complexity of social life and the possibility of using government for human betterment flourished. Moreover, the New Deal—and Hollywood movies—gave standing to urban workers and immigrants as genuine Americans, though too often at the expense of African Americans.[22]

Since World War II, the suburban movement of economic activity has undermined the interwar metropolis. In 1990, the 45 percent of Americans living in the suburbs significantly outnumbered city dwellers. Even more important, 95 percent of the 120 million suburbanites were white, while the population of center cities was becoming increasingly nonwhite. The emergence in the 1980s and 1990s of African American and Latino mayors in our cities reflected less a realization of urban democracy than the white middle-class abandonment of cities.

As we shall see in a later chapter, there is some reason to believe that suburbs since 1990 have become more diverse and may well continue in that direction, which might help unify city-suburb metropolitan regions. But it is difficult to predict. While the presidential election of 2000 will go down in the history books for the voting irregularities in Florida and the extraordinary intervention of the Supreme Court, from an urban perspective one cannot but be struck by the geography of the vote. The least urban parts of the country, those cities with the fewest immigrants, and those with the least commitment to cosmopolitanism tended to vote most heavily for George W. Bush, who spoke to their antimetropolitan fears.

The first nine months of the Bush presidency has been explicitly antiurban, culminating with his extended August vacation in Crawford, Texas, where, he explained, he had returned to the real America. Yet one of the striking results of the terrorist attack on New York's World Trade Center on September 11, 2001, is the seeming acceptance of New York as America, not only by President Bush but apparently by Americans in every section of the country.

Perhaps the tragic events of September will mark a turning point in the history of cities and the national political culture. One hopes so, for urban neglect is now of long standing. Lyndon B. Johnson was the last president to consider cities and their people an essential part of America. No president since Johnson has raised his voice or used his political weight in behalf of the population of American cities. No president but Johnson has ever insisted that life in the cities is the index of the quality of our national life. And no president since Johnson has been willing to invest in cities and empower the people who live in them. In 1964, addressing an audience at the University of Michigan, Johnson concisely summarized his position in a single sentence reminiscent of Olmsted: "Our society will never be great until our cities are great."

Lyndon Johnson failed America terribly. His monumental folly in Vietnam sacrificed thousands of Americans (and Vietnamese). It tore our society apart. Vietnam, however, also cost us the strongest spokesman for urban justice ever to reside in the White House. This president from rural Texas not only identified the cities with the nation and responded to the obvious social needs of their residents, but he recognized the political aspirations of city dwellers—the poor and dispossessed as well as the middle classes. Demanding "maximum feasible participation" in social programs, he massively shifted political and economic resources in their direction. We can only hope that someone will yet reclaim Johnson's grasp of our domestic needs and the democratic promise of our cities. Contrary to the assertions of pundits on the left and the right, urban liberalism did not fail. It did not succeed, but neither did it fail. Johnson and his successors deserted it.

The inequalities of our cities cannot be traced to urban liberalism. The responsibility resides with the neoliberal and neoconservative embrace of the nineteenth-century laissez-faire vision that cities had challenged a century ago.[23] These philosophies of governmental irresponsibility have callously narrowed the terms of public obligation. Can cities again press a claim for inclusion and democracy, as they did a hundred years ago? Are cities American? Yes and no. Cities and their populations have never been completely excluded from the promise of American life, but neither have they yet been wholly accepted.

11

NEW YORK AS A
CENTER OF DIFFERENCE

Culture and politics in New York are based on premises not quite shared by the nation generally. When other Americans speak of New York as being different, something other than America, they often have in mind its size, density, big buildings, and harried lifestyles. But they seem also to have in mind a special quality of the city's culture and politics, perhaps associated with its ethnic makeup. Such perceptions, however imprecise, have a ring of truth. For Americans, in contrast to foreign observers and visitors, the remarkable social compound that is New York does not fit easily the dominant notions of the meaning of America.

The most influential myths of America, those that have been incorporated into the culture, are very much identified with the regions of their origin: Puritan New England and Jeffersonian Virginia. Often American history—and the meaning of America—has been framed as a political and cultural dialectic between Virginia and Massachusetts, Cavalier and Yankee.[1] In fact, neither region is nearly so representative of America as are the more difficult-to-characterize middle colonies. Yet in spite of the narrowness and purity of the Puritan dream of "a city upon a hill" and of agrarian Jeffersonianism, these myths have come to be associated with the essential America, evoking the virtues of the small town and the agricultural frontier.

It is puzzling but true that the outlook associated with New York's cosmopolitan experience has been unable to establish itself as an American standard.

The other two myths—or, to use a more current terminology, these other two representations of the American ideal—have managed to deflect, if not completely obliterate, the alternative cosmopolitan understanding of the promise of American life that since the eighteenth century has been an abiding (if not always controlling) theme of cultural discourse in New York City.

Scholars a generation ago devoted themselves, perhaps too much, to the study of the communitarian myth of the American town and the agrarian myth of the American frontier.[2] It is worth returning to the point of those scholars, for the myths persist despite their debunking. Our acceptance of these myths—whether passively or, as in the case of campaigning politicians, aggressively and cynically—has been consequential, limiting the ability of Americans to grasp the complexity of cutural and political issues.

When we examine these myths we can better see what makes New York City uncomfortable with America and America uncomfortable with, even fearful of, New York City.[3] The New York experience and the outlook associated with that experience posit a political and cultural life based upon difference, while the myth of rural and small-town America excludes difference from politics and culture. Of course, on the ground, there is more difference in even the smallest towns in America than myth and habits of thought acknowledge. But the exclusionary structures of perception—whether habitual or self-conscious—concern me here, for they are limiting. Such exclusion impoverishes civic life and invites injustice. It thins public culture and weakens democracy.

Can one really bracket Puritanism and Jeffersonianism? Everything about them, it seems, is different: one religious, the other secular; one hierarchical, the other egalitarian; one town-oriented, the other rural; one reminiscent of the medieval worldview, the other drawing upon the Enlightenment. More differences could be enumerated, but I want to point out a crucial similarity: *both reject the idea of difference.* Neither can give positive cultural or political value to heterogeneity or conflict. Each in its own way is xenophobic, and that distances both of them from the conditions of modern life, especially as represented by the historic cosmopolitanism of New York and, increasingly, other cities in the United States.

Few phrases reverberate more deeply through American history than John

Winthrop's proclamation in 1630 that the Massachusetts Bay Colony would be as "a Citty Upon a Hill." "We must," Winthrop urged his party as they sighted the land that would become Boston, "be knitt together in this worke as one man." Never has the ideal of community been more forcefully stated in America. The Puritans envisioned a single moral community, one that acknowledged no distinction between private and public values. "Liberty," Winthrop explained in his famous "Little Speech" in 1645, permits "that only which is good, just, honest"—something to be determined by the consensus of the community.[4]

Contrary to much American mythmaking, neither individualism nor democracy was nourished in the New England town. Its significance, Michael Zuckerman has argued, is rather that it nourished "a broadly diffused desire for consensual communalism as the operative premise of group life in America."[5] You had a place in a Puritan village or town only if your values coincided with those of your neighbors. Rather than incorporating difference, Puritan town leaders were quick to offer strangers the "liberty to keep away from us."

The myth of consensus and sameness was sustained in the towns by a peculiar pattern of "democratic" practice. Votes were, of course, taken in town meetings, but the minutes of those meetings rarely offered evidence of split votes, thus making a single opinion the only recorded history. The idea of concord and sameness underlay religion as well. When Jonathan Edwards described heaven for his congregation, it was the New England town ideal made eternal. Heaven, he explained, is a place "where you shall be united in the same interest, and shall be of one mind and one heart and one soul forever."[6]

Although the social basis for such a consensus had been undermined by the beginning of the nineteenth century, enough remained to sustain belief in it for many Americans. The ideal of a covenanted community persisted, as Page Smith has demonstrated, especially in the midwest.[7]

Even in the seventeenth century there was more diversity than these ideals of a unified town could accommodate, and so they had to address the issue. Their solution anticipates the classic age of the American suburb. You cannot stay in our town, but you are free to establish your own town with your own people and beliefs. This sort of pluralism, defended (unsuccessfully) before the Supreme Court as recently as 1982 (seeking to justify school-library censorship in suburban Long Island) is a pluralism of many supposedly consensual communities.[8] Today in gated communities and "New Urban" towns a similar dream of living surrounded by sameness, with all differences kept at a distance, persists.

The dark side of the New England communal ideal is intolerance, as many a seventeenth-century Quaker or woman suspected of witchcraft learned. Otherness is a problem for such communities; difference or conflict becomes indistinguishable from subversion.[9]

Thomas Jefferson, of course, was less worried about subversion. He even recommended frequent revolutions, always trusting the democratic practice of the living. It is this spirit that prompted Alexis de Tocqueville to refer to Jefferson as "the most powerful advocate democracy ever had."[10] But however much we are moved, and properly so, by Jefferson's magnificent democratic professions, we must also attend to the theory of society that underlay them. Jefferson could trust democracy because he assumed a societal consensus on values, and he opposed places like New York, calling them "cancers" on the body politic, in part because they would produce citizens whose values and interests would be marked not only by difference but even serious conflict.

It is only since Garry Wills publicized the Scottish influences on Jefferson that the communitarian basis of his social thought has been seriously considered. Jefferson believed men were naturally endowed with a "sense of right and wrong" because they were "destined for society."[11] Yet this "moral sense" was honed by actual social relations, making common sense, as Wills put it in *Inventing America*, actually "communal sense." The approbation of the community provided the basis for assessing virtue.[12] For example, Jefferson granted blacks a moral sense, going on to explain that it was "their situation" that accounted for their evident "disposition to theft."[13]

Jefferson's admiration for Native American tribal cultures has been much remarked. But we must grasp more fully the centrality of such communalism to his general theory of society. It was the basis for his confidence that in the agrarian society he envisioned, Leviathan was not needed.[14] Sociability and affection, not the artifice of government, would make the good society. All of this depended, however, upon shared values. That is why he encouraged territorial expansion, which would endlessly replicate his favored agrarian world. He sought a common experience in a nation of relatively equal yeoman farmers. On the negative side, his commitment to uniformity made Jefferson very hesitant about immigration. Arguing against a policy of encouraging immigration, he explained that "it is for the happiness of those united in society to harmonize as much as possible in matters which they must of necessity transact together."[15] For Jefferson, homogeneity and the duration of the republic seemed closely linked.

His fear of the heterogeneity he associated with immigration provides a clue to his inability to contemplate a republic made up of former masters and former slaves. Historians have long tried to determine the sources of Jefferson's peculiar position on slavery and freedom: he strongly criticized slavery but declined to become publicly identified with any antislavery movement. Even in his private considerations he always assumed that freed blacks would have to be deported. Some Jefferson scholars have focused on his racist language, others upon economic interest, still others on his inability to transcend the worldview of his time, place, and class. Some have even suggested that slavery was fundamental to his republicanism: freedom was defined by slavery. All such explanations contain part of the answer, but no one, to my knowledge, has noted the way in which his theory of society as necessarily conflict-free made an interracial republic of former masters and former slaves impossible.

Jefferson himself gave this kind of explanation. In his *Notes on the State of Virginia* (1784), he explained why freed slaves, if ever there was such a population, must be removed from society:

> Deep-rooted prejudices entertained by whites; ten thousand recollections by the blacks, of the injustices they have sustained; new provocations; the real distinctions which nature has made; and many other circumstances, will divide us into parties and produce convulsions, which will probably never end but in the extermination of the one or the other race.[16]

Writing in 1820, Jefferson observed that "we have a wolf by the ears, and we can neither hold him, nor safely let him go. Justice is in one scale, and self-preservation in the other."[17] When faced with real conflicts of interest and values, the happy revolutionary retreated to the conservative standard of self-preservation.[18] He even feared the divisiveness of public antislavery agitation, hoping, quite unrealistically, for a natural and conflict-free moral progress that would somehow remove the blot of slavery.[19] There was nowhere else for Jefferson to go.

Certain elements in the Jeffersonian tradition may thus appear in a new light. We can now see why Jefferson wanted a happy and undifferentiated yeomanry and why he opposed the development of cities, with their complex social structures, diverse values, and conflicting interests. The great defender of democracy based upon sameness, Jefferson could find no way to accommodate difference. He found himself compelled to discourage immigration, to maintain slavery, and to oppose urbanization. Hardly a democratic theory for our time.

Both the Puritan and the Jeffersonian myths nourish a distrust of democracy—at least any democracy that proceeds from difference, whether of culture or interest. But of course there is no point in democracy if there are no conflicts of values and interests. Democratic practices are worth our investment precisely because they offer a political method, one in principle open to all voices, for allocating societal resources.

New York, marked by diversity and openly conflicting interests, has operated on different premises than those identified with Winthrop's town-based communalism and Jefferson's agrarianism. Very early in the city's history, difference and conflict among interests were acknowledged as not only inevitable, but perhaps of positive value. In anticipation of James Madison's famous tenth and fifty-first Federalist papers, differences and the conflict arising from them were understood as political resources, as a possible foundation for the maintenance of freedom.

Of course, as we have already seen, there have been important episodes in which New Yorkers lost confidence in the potential contribution of a politics of difference. There has been a long historical thread of episodic racial intolerance and, indeed, terrible violence. In praising New York's relative acceptance of difference, one cannot overlook a terrible history that runs from the colonial period, to the infamous Civil War draft riots, to the recent police actions against black residents of the city. And there have been other nativist and antiradical crusades as well.

Democratic politics as well have been repeatedly questioned. We have seen a line from Tocqueville's observations in the 1830s, to former Mayor

Philip Hone in the 1840s, and to E. L. Godkin in the years after the Civil War. And there have been more recent manifestations. For example, Felix Rohaytn, lionized as New York's first citizen for "saving" New York from bankruptcy in the 1975 fiscal crisis, put in place a rescue plan that was very much in the tradition of E. L. Godkin's notion than the city's finances must be protected from democracy. No less than Godkin, Rohaytn distrusted the ways of democracy.

In place of the tumult of a politics of difference, he proposed to rescue the city and even the nation from excessive democracy with an elite council of conciliation that would have been, perhaps, familiar to the leaders of a Puritan church. It was charged with winning the wayward—the spenders on social services, the unions looking to advance their members, those in need who were demanding improved social supports, and the like—to the one true way.

Dealing with the federal government's refusal to provide any aid to the city—recall the *Daily News* headline: FORD TO CITY: DROP DEAD—Rohaytn presumably decided that the only way to make New York City acceptable to the rest of America was to depoliticize it, to effectively disenfranchise the weak who sought social benefits from the city, those who needed public hospitals, public libraries, the free education of the City University, and the like. Such a politics of need was denied a voice with the creation of the Municipal Assistance Corporation and the Financial Control Board, which could override any political claims. It was a supra-political authority, Rohaytn explained, that was "publicly accountable but . . . run outside of politics."[20] This is pretty much what the Tilden Commission, on which Godkin served, had recommended a century earlier.

In the years since the fiscal crisis, there has been a more general marginalization of politics and an inflation of the claims of the market. On this matter, there is not a whole lot of difference between neoconservatives and neoliberals. The triumph of the market—what we now call globalization—is not unrelated to the theme of sameness and difference before us. Myths of sameness not only favor provincialism over cosmopolitanism, but they undermine our capacity or even inclination to bring economic life within the purview of a democratic politics.

If there were fully shared values (and resources) the market need not be an arena of conflict. It would be no more than a mere mechanism of exchange, essentially without implications for power relations. If, however, the assumption of consensus is false, then the market, unless politically moderated, becomes autonomous and self-legitimating. And it thus justifies economic and political inequalities. Whether because of avoidance of confict models of society or other reasons, Americans, more than any other people, have come to accept the market as a law of nature, as a public philosophy.

Although there have certainly been New York intellectuals of both radical and conservative persuasions who have put their faith in the market on the basis of these mythical assumptions, the broader political culture of the city—grounded upon an experience marked by the reality of difference—has energized attempts to bring economic decisions within the sphere of democratic politics. To the extent that modern America is more like New York than it is like Jefferson's America, New York's history may become prophetic. An America—even a world—victimized by the illusion of the market as a public philosophy may well find in New York's history an important alternative theory of America that would sustain a more vital and democratic politics.

The special character of New York was evident from the beginning. If religion inspired the Puritans and if the dream of plantations and wealth drove the Virginians, the practicality of trade engaged the first settlers of New Amsterdam. If churches and regular church service came quickly to both Massachusetts and Virginia, it was the countinghouse, not the church, that represented early New Amsterdam. In fact, the first substantial building in Manhattan was a stone countinghouse. There was little impulse to exclusion; trading partners were sought no matter what their background. Already in the 1640s eighteen languages were spoken in the area that is now New York City.

This very different history became the material for a different understanding of society and politics, one that embraced difference, diversity, and conflict—as well as the dollar. The city was characterized by a divided elite and a rich diversity of groups and cultures. As a result, the city early experienced a continuing contest over the definition of itself. Competitive struggle, initially between competing elites, drew more and more individuals and groups into the political process. Entry into public life was no mere ritual reaffirming established authority as it was in Virginia; often in New York it was in the spirit of challenge or response to challenge. There was a kind of political precocity in New York and the middle colonies generally.[21]

At first no one acknowledged or even recognized that—quite contrary to the prescription Montesquieu or Jean-Jacques Rousseau would offer—they were inventing a new political culture based upon difference and interest. By the middle of the eighteenth century a politics of interest was becoming commonplace in the city. As early as 1733 one can find an argument justifying this novel pattern of politics. Contra Jefferson and the tradition of classical republicanism, New Yorkers began to grasp that liberty and a politics of interest might sustain each other. Writing in the *New York Gazette* in 1733, a political realist whose identity remains unknown acknowledged that "a free government cannot but be subject to parties, cabals, and intrigues." He insisted that this was a benefit, not a problem:

> I have somewhere seen opposition of interests called a curse attending free governments because it is inseparable from them. When it tends to sap the foundations of the constitution then indeed it properly deserves that name, but to pronounce the opposition of those a curse who from a just zeal and jealously for their liberty endeavor to defeat schemes of power and destructive of liberty is the dialect and language of tools of power and sycophants. I may venture to say that some opposition, though it proceed not entirely from a public spirit, is not only necessary in free governments but of great service to the public. Parties are a check upon one another, and by keeping the ambition of one another within bounds, serve to maintain the public liberty. Opposition is the life and soul of public zeal which, without it, would flag and decay for want of an opportunity to exert itself. . . . It may indeed proceed from the wrong motives, but still it is necessary.[22]

Fifteen years later William Livingston, a New Yorker who would later be governor of New Jersey and a signer of the Constitution, developed an even more elaborate rationale for a specifically New York politics that would build upon the city's distinctive cultural diversity.

Born in 1723, Livingston was one of the first of the New York elite to go to college, graduating from Yale College. In 1743, a year before Jefferson's birth, he returned to New York and began the study of law. Several years later the trustees of the proposed King's College (today's Columbia) requested a royal charter of incorporation that privileged one religion at the expense of others. (It prescribed an Anglican president in perpetuity.) Livingston, who had been invited to be one of the trustees, responded with a critical and innovative vision of city culture that was cosmopolitan and pluralistic.

At the time Livingston wrote, one could say that colonial intellectual life was organized within denominational institutions, with each of the major Protestant denominations having a college whose influence touched all the colonies. Harvard and Yale were Congregational, with Harvard coded liberal, and Yale conservative; the Anglicans had the College of William and Mary, where Jefferson would study; and the Presbyterians had just established the College of New Jersey, which would become Princeton. Livingston rejected this intercolonial logic of cultural organization. Rather than a culture premised on religious institutions, he proposed thinking about higher learning institutionalized within the context of a place.

Writing in his own magazine, *The Independent Reflector*, Livingston described a "free" college, one not tied to any religious group or any private group at all. It would be governed by the people in their public character, that is, through public authorities.

> While the Government of the College is in the Hands of the People . . . its Design cannot be perverted. . . . Our College, therefore, if it be incorporated by Act of Assembly, instead of opening a Door to universal Bigotry and Establishment in Church, and Tyranny and Oppression in the State, will secure us in the Enjoyment of our respective Privileges, both Civil and religious. For as we are split into a great Variety of Opinions and Professions; had each Individual his Share in the Government of the Academy, the Jealousy of all Parties combatting each other, would inevitably produce a perfect Freedom for each particular Party.[23]

This sense of city culture and democracy not only tolerated difference but depended upon it. So far from Jefferson, yet so clearly anticipating Madison.

Almost exactly one hundred years later, Walt Whitman transformed these same social materials into a work of art that at once reveled in and reconciled difference. But Whitman's achievement was aesthetic, and its glue was emotion, not ideas. An ideological expression of New York as democratic and cosmopolitan found its best voice another half century later, in the person of Randolph Bourne.[24]

The symbolic leader of the first generation of American writers to call themselves intellectuals, Bourne was in fact the prototype of the later New York intellectual, working at the intersection of politics and culture. He gave articulation to a notion of American culture that was essentially New York (at its best) writ large, a vision that would substitute cosmopolitanism for the provincial values of America. Seeking to liberate himself and his generation from the Anglo-Saxon parochialism of the dominant culture, Bourne embraced the immigrants who were transforming New York City. His essay, "Trans-National America," published in the *Atlantic* in 1916 amid the intolerance of war, combined an acceptance of enduring particularism with a commitment to a common or public culture. He envisioned an America that, like New York City, would be a federation of cultures. Rejecting the Anglo-Saxon tradition as defining of America, he declared that American culture "lies in the future," it "shall be what the immigrant will have a hand in making it."[25]

This was an audacious claim when it was made, and it could have been made only in New York. The editor who published the piece, Boston's Ellery Sedgwick, stood for more traditional and homogeneous American ideals. He had agreed to publish the essay only because of his long-standing relationship with Bourne, a regular contributor since his days as a student at Columbia. He also granted that it was very well written. But he informed Bourne in his letter accepting the article: "I profoundly disagree with your paper." In the incredulous voice of genteel Boston confronted by cosmopolitan New York, he admonished: "You speak as if the last immigrant should have as great an effect upon the determination of our history as the first band of Englishmen." Which is, of course, precisely what Bourne meant. Sedgwick continued, insisting that the United States had neither political nor literary lessons to learn from Eastern Europe, and he bridled at Bourne's equation of an old New Englander and a recent Czech as "equally characteristic of America."[26]

The tradition of New York and America articulated by Livingston, Whitman, Bourne—and many others—is always at risk, and the present moment is no exception. The logic of the present moment of free markets and consumerist definitions of the United States (and perhaps the world) threaten both the particularity of place, the recognition of difference, and the significance of politics. One can talk about the sameness of a suburban consumer's republic, but one must acknowledge that the city is not exempt. New York, always a city of small manufacturers and prolific of shops, is becoming transformed by corporate models of business, the export of manufacturing jobs, and the replacement of local shops with chain stores.

Nothing better represents this than the so-called new Times Square. The redevelopment project there serves two clients: corporate America (particularly finance and communications) and consumer America. What had been a very distinctive public space, recognized in the city, the nation, and the world for its role in both energizing and representing the public culture of New York, disappeared. The convergence of subways lines had made it rich in diverse users, bringing New Yorkers from all the boroughs to the center as a part of their daily lives as well as for special occasions. There was a plethora of small businesses as well as large theatres and eateries that offered both employment and entertainment.

Neither the proponents nor the critics of the redevelopment plan adequately recognized these aspects of Times Square. The new Times Square could be anywhere. The bright signs remind me not of the older New York but rather of the new Seoul, where they are often even bigger and advertise the same international brands. The crowds are visitors, as I was a visitor to Seoul, not New Yorkers, and they shop in stores they could find back home in their suburban malls. If twenty years ago many New Yorkers avoided Times Square because it was dangerous, they do now because it is an alien intrusion of the culture of sameness.

The destruction of the historical Times Square destroyed one of the city's most potent symbols of the peculiarly cosmopolitan politics and culture of the city. Times Square, like Union Square before it, has historically represented the complexity of the city's culture. Here for all to see, for all to experience, the city had in the past represented itself in all its fullness *to itself* and to the world.

When the project to redevelop Times Square commenced, there was not yet much discussion of globalization. That is mostly the rhetoric of the 1990s. But in its basic logic, it constitutes the same kind of threat as the commercial transformation of Times Square. If there is a homogenizing tendency to globalization—and I am not sure there need be—that too poses a risk for New York's culture of difference. Just because the globe's most powerful agents of globalization are headquartered in New York—some in Times Square itself—New Yorkers cannot assume that they will escape the pernicious impact of the utterly uncontrolled capitalist expansion for which globalization is a euphemism and justification. We receive what we give: increasing inequality and the unbounded commercialization of culture.

The highly particular politics of the local warrant attention; such a politics is still relevant. New York would do the world and itself a very good deed by showing that through a democratic politics the benefits of global markets can be enhanced and their unhappy consequences moderated by strategic political interventions. Globalization need not erase the democratic political culture New York has developed. A vigorous politics operating on a metropolitan scale and drawing upon the distinctive political traditions of the city might nudge the new world order that is in the making toward more human and just purposes.

I realize that I am asking a lot of a marginalized New York theory of culture, society, and politics. The theory as I have tried to excavate it from the city's past does not in itself constitute a politics. Nor has it ever been adequately developed or realized in practice. And even if success were achieved in New York, it would still remain uncertain whether the city could make a cosmopolitan culture and democratic politics of difference respectable in America. Yet New York and America would both lose if the lessons of the metropolis were casually abandoned. If New York gives in, if New York abandons engagement with difference, if New York gives up on a politics of challenge, who will be left in America to stand against the rising tide of privatization, residential isolation, intolerance toward difference, and the substitution of consumerism for politics?

12

CITIES AND CITIZENSHIP

Modern citizenship has been attached to the nation. Notions of social politics have mostly worked through the state, as represented by the national welfare state. But such was not always the case. In the late nineteenth century in the United States the city provided a vital platform for men and women to think themselves into politics, to make themselves into citizens, to initiate a social politics. In the decade of the 1890s reformers, journalists, and academic intellectuals (a cluster not so differentiated then as now) thought urban democracy possible, even necessary. They were able to imagine the city, in the words of Frederick C. Howe, a leader of the movement, as "the hope of democracy."[1]

My intention is to recall that moment and movement. Not only is the resurgence of laissez-faire in the 1990s reminiscent of the 1890s, but so is the discussion about the significance and work of the national state in the age of globalization. The debate in the 1890s pointed toward what became the national welfare state during the New Deal era; today the debate is about the dismantling of that version of the nation-state. Such realignments in the relations and powers of nation-states—in this case between cities and nations— invite both historical scholarship and speculation about alternative ways of addressing the social costs of capitalism.

Even if we are skeptical of the talk that envisions the disappearance of the nation-state in our time, it is clear that its role is changing and the meaning of citizenship may be changing as well. In that context I reconsider the city as a site for a politics that addresses the social consequences of the present phase of capitalism on a global scale, for, as in the 1890s, the manifestations of the social cost of laissez-faire capitalism are inscribed most dramatically in the physical form and daily life of cities.

A century ago such inquiry was the work of the fledgling social-science disciplines, particularly political science. Today, political science and the social sciences generally are less attentive to the particularity of time and place or, to be more specific, to the city. Looking backward, however, we discover a generation of academic intellectuals engaged with urban questions. That engagement proved fruitful to their professional agenda of disciplinary development, infusing a formal and abstract discipline with both vitality and realism, while it sustained a sense of civic participation that enriched the political culture of the city and extended urban democracy. I am not proposing that the city is permanently available for such political work; my point is simply that there is a certain mobility of such political sites and that historical circumstances may in any given instance favor cities. Such was the case in the 1890s in the United States, and at the beginning of the twenty-first century cities may again have a special role in defining a social politics.

The emerging social sciences provided a new language for reform, one stressing social connection and interdependence. After experiencing new levels of interdependence during the Civil War and in growing cities, Americans found in the language of the social, upon which the new social sciences were being built, a better way to describe and explain the world around them. The idea of social causation weakened the hold of those notions of individual agency that were articles of faith for Americans in the middle third of the nineteenth century.[2] In Europe and America, the social sciences developed in a dialectical relationship to the massive social transformations driven by industrial capitalism: social explanation was both a product of new experience and a way of understanding that new experience. Indeed, to explain and manage that society was the raison d'être of these new disciplines.[3]

Although one can speak of the social sciences as a single movement of thought in the nineteenth century, there were important distinctions among them, and they approached the task of explanation and management in different ways, with different dialects. Economics was the first of these new social sciences to professionalize in the United States, and in the 1880s economists supplied a method of historical economics that enabled reformers to enter the troubling question of the political economy of labor and capital in a new way. By playing down ideology and shifting the ground from the formal and deductive approach favored by theorists of laissez-faire, the historical economists, relying upon empirical and historicist claims, intervened with significant effect, arguing for historically specific and strategic interventions in the economy.[4]

Gradually, however, the focus and language of reform changed. The new society increasingly became identified with the city, rather than with the conflict between labor and capital, which generally did not have a geographical referent. Sociologists claimed the city, a novel "social aggregation," as their subject. Sociology and social reform were nearly assimilated the one to the other, especially at the University of Chicago, where Albion Small created the first sociology department in the United States. But with their focus on civil society and voluntary action, the sociologists in the end offered little access to politics, a matter of significance because the social concerns of the era were increasingly being understood in terms of a politics, a new social politics.[5]

During the 1890s and 1900s, in the first years of the intellectual and political movement that assumed the name Progressivism, political scientists, following the lead of Columbia's Frank Goodnow, achieved primacy for the language of politics as a means of addressing the social implications of industrial capitalism as they revealed themselves in the city. In the phrasing of Goodnow, "the city must be studied not merely from the sociological point of view, but also from the political point of view: the city is not merely an urban community, a social fact; it is also a political organization."[6]

The challenge for a generation of ambitious political scientists was to bring the city into a general theory of democratic politics.[7] "The city," it seemed to Frederick C. Howe, had "grown more rapidly than social science," and it "is what it is because political thought has not kept pace with changing conditions."[8] The problems of industrial society—standard of living, equality of opportunity, uplifting life—not only presented themselves in the city, but were, according to Howe, "almost all municipal matters."[9] By 1933, as we shall see, these problems would be understood as national problems. This mobility of political perception is part of my subject here, but first we must establish the movement from the nation to the city at the turn of the century.

"While our attention has been fixed upon the national state," observed Delos F. Wilcox in 1897, "the theory and practice of local government have been partially neglected."[10] Wilcox, a recent Ph.D. in political science, urged younger students to follow him into the study of cities. "The student who aspires to be a scholar can devote himself to no richer or inspiring field than the modern city, its government, its institutions, and its tendencies."[11] At this period in American history, he assured his readers, no other area of specialization was of so great importance, for "it is here that the reconstruction of political practice and of social institutions goes on most rapidly."[12] A writer in *The Nation* had recognized this shift in attention two years earlier: "Perhaps there never was time when a deeper interest was felt in the government of cities."[13]

At the heart of a new, activist political science was an aspiration to revitalize a democratic public that had been diminished, especially in cities, by monopoly and privilege.[14] Such a public, reformers believed, would detach power from wealth and empower the people.[15] Cities and the essential character of city life seemed to constitute a challenge to the premises of the laissez-faire market celebrated by the regnant political economy of the Gilded Age. Cities were collective in spirit and in experience. Thus they might be the staging ground for mounting a collectivist challenge to excessive individualism. The "formless" capitalist development of the city, argues Daniel Rodgers, encouraged the development of a countervailing urban political consciousness. The practical work of municipal administration, in fact, had an ideological dimension. When cities assumed the tasks of providing the modern array of municipal services, it represented a "recognition of the de facto collectivity of city life." The municipalization of transportation or utilities, for example, meant a diminution of the exclusive domain of the market, replacing private supply with public provision.[16]

It was a commonplace among reformers that "if socialism ever comes, it will come by way of the city."[17] Charles Beard, in the first college-level textbook on urban politics, argued that "collectivist" responses to the implications of the industrial revolution were being developed first and mainly in the cities. In cities, he pointed out, one could observe a cross-class confluence of political interests pointing to collectivist approaches: working-class organization was taking form in trade unions while there was mounting bourgeois support for municipal services.[18] In *The Modern City*, Frederic C. Howe claimed that in the city Americans are overcoming "the laissez-faire and are acquiring a belief in democracy." The city, he insisted, reveals this "new point of view even more markedly than does the nation."[19]

This new generation of political scientists challenged the philosophic idealism and formalism of the discipline's founding generation.[20] In the city these political scientists and other social scientists found a locale of engagement where theory and practice would be brought closer together in new ways. The city provided a means of rethinking the political in a nonformalist, more pragmatic way, moving from the formal and abstract concept of the state to political experience.[21] Not only the language of the state, but even the language of class was partially displaced by a language of place, or more precisely, relations in space. It was in the particularity of place that the various interests of society converged, and the task of modern political life was to imagine and construct a cooperative relation among these interests.[22]

However, this strategy for reform and professional development posed for political scientists a particular and quite difficult theoretical problem. The object of inquiry that defined the discipline was the state, the supreme political entity, not the city. There was no category of urban politics in American political theory, nor consequently, any concept of urban citizenship. Law was no more helpful. The city has no constitutional standing in the American state. The word *city* does not appear in the Constitution, and American municipal law in the late nineteenth century was controlled by the authoritative Dillon Rule, enunciated by Justice John F. Dillon of the Iowa Supreme Court in *City of Clinton v. Cedar Rapids and Missouri River Railroad* (1868).[23] His long-standing and universally endorsed interpretation insisted that the city was not a political entity. Rather it was merely an administrative agency with strictly enumerated powers.

The timing of this formulation and of the general embrace of it by legal and political elites is explained by a profound fear of urban political mobilization. Under the Dillon Rule, cities—which had always been objects of suspicion in the American political tradition—were to be denied political standing, even disenfranchised. But the target in fact was more specific: it was the specter of the voting power of the urban masses. Political and economic elites, having witnessed the depredations of the Tweed Ring, blurred the mob and the increasingly organized working classes of cities. They feared that these irresponsible classes might initiate a regime of excessive spending and redistributive taxation of the rich.[24] By denying the political character of the city, the Dillon Rule delegitimated urban political movements and limited the power of cities to do damage—and good.

Thus, the first order of business for political scientists was to redefine the status of the city, giving it a political character. They did this by associating themselves with a contemporary urban political movement for "home rule," a demand that state legislatures stop passing special legislation interfering with the cities and that state constitutions give cities the powers necesssary to make policy in those areas that are distinctively local and characteristic of such concentrated settlement. There is, therefore, an important confluence of the theoretical, the professional, and the political, all pointing toward an expansion of the possibilities of urban citizenship. For political scientists and for urban activists, some of whom were the same individuals, achieving home rule created a domain of the political that was essential not only for their own work, but to make city dwellers into citizens. Intellectuals and cities thus needed each other at this moment.

American historiography has been too complacent about the question of citizenship. Historians have assumed that the state-by-state enactment of white male suffrage in the 1820s settled the question and set the terms for future American politics.[25] Some years ago Alan Dawley went so far as to lament that the ballot box was the coffin for American socialism.[26] But as David Quigley has recently demonstrated, the issue of suffrage and citizenship, even for white males, remained highly contested in northern cities in the third quarter of the nineteenth century, especially in New York City.[27]

At mid-century, before the crisis of union, as Mary Ryan has so ably demonstrated, there was an inclusive and robust democracy in the cities.[28] Not only was participation widespread and active—Ryan's point—but urban leaders were also developing a strong sense of the capacity of government to undertake projects of urban development and social improvement, the most notable being the Croton water system and Central Park in New York City. In fact, it was this confidence in positive government among urban elites that had initially helped define the ambitious program of postwar Reconstruction in the South.[29]

The Civil War and the postwar issue of suffrage for freedmen opened a wide-ranging public debate on suffrage and citizenship. Other exclusions were noted, most importantly women.[30] The former slaves were granted the vote, but almost immediately the North weakened in its resolve to provide national support for these rights newly won by the freedmen. Within a dozen years their suffrage and thus citizenship were severely compromised. This retreat from Reconstruction in the South had a complex relation to the politics of northern cities. Working-class political activism in the North produced fear of a state that might empower the lower classes, and this contributed to the federal abandonment of the freedmen with the ending of Reconstruction in 1877. The controversy over the political rights of the former slaves in the South in turn contributed to the worries about urban democracy in the North.[31]

As early as 1868, however, these urban elites were becoming uneasy about positive government. Conflict in the South over suffrage and work for the freedmen as well as political controversy in the North, including working-class agitation for the eight-hour day, the demands by women for the vote, and the activities of the Tweed ring in New York, made the metropolitan gentry increasingly uncomfortable about an expansive urban democracy. Many agreed with Francis Parkman, the great historian, who wrote in the *North American Review* that universal suffrage had been a failure.[32] Samuel Bowles, editor of the *Springfield Republican* and perhaps the nation's most influential newspaper editor among the educated elite, openly worried that the Civil War and the growth of cities had seriously weakened the power of the state governments. That development was worrisome for Bowles and his readers because state, as opposed to city governments, were understood to be supportive of the Victorian values and political agenda of the middle classes. He proposed limiting suffrage in cities to those with a "responsible interest," by which he meant taxpayers. In addition, he strongly supported the creation of state commissions, such as had been developed in New York at the end of the war, to establish state control of certain municipal functions, including police and health.[33]

The attack on urban citizenship in the 1870s pursued two related lines. The first was to challenge universal suffrage, arguing that democracy did not necessarily imply the vote. It was also argued that the city was a corporation, and only those with an interest (stockholder or taxpayer) ought to have a vote. In New York in 1876, as we have seen, the Tilden Commission actually proposed a state constitutional revision that would have disenfranchised the working classes in New York City. Constitutional revision in New York required a vote by two consecutive legislatures, which allowed for a legislative campaign focused on urban citizenship. In an intensely fought campaign, voters elected a legislature that would not repass the measure, and it failed. But in proposing to empower only taxpayers and property-owners the commissions proposal was a powerful challenge to the idea of urban citizenship.[34]

The second approach to disempowering democracy involved a rejection of the idea of positive government. Even if the masses retained the vote, they should know that government was limited. Such was the context for elite celebration of the idea of laissez-faire. There is thus a fit between the dominance of laissez-faire principles at the national level and the Dillon Rule on the local level.

With the political character and autonomy of cities denied, legislatures routinely passed special legislation affecting cities, often motivated by partisan politics at the state level. More often than not, state legislation imposed obligations on cities for which no state funding was supplied. More important yet, state commissions were created to administer vital city services. All of this undermined any notion of urban citizenship.

In the minds of the elites who created this regime, such denial of political standing to the city and its citizens was a means of limiting damage. By the 1890s, however, it was recognized as limiting in another way. It prevented cities from undertaking the development and effective management of vital municipal functions. Home rule became a rallying cry that united urban populations; the need for political authority was great enough to produce a cross-class collaboration.[35] The state legislatures had become so irresponsible in their treatment of cities that the bourgeoisie no longer found security in the disempowerment of cities. More important yet: the city, where the impact of industrial capitalism was most graphically evident, was increasingly understood to be the proper point of political intervention. The manifest needs of urban populations prompted the invention of a social politics.

Life in cities, Howe argued, "is creating a new moral sense, a new conception of the obligations of political life, obligations which, in earlier conditions of society did not and could not exist."[36] The social needs of cities has forced the democratic polity "into activities which have heretofore lain outside of the sphere of government."[37] Here in the city, he prophesized, "the industrial issues" that are "becoming dominant in political life will first be worked out."[38] The city, reformers believed, was the place to face and address modern industrial conditions; it was more promising than the national state, where the laissez-faire ideology seemed unassailable.

When Frederick C. Howe entered graduate school at Johns Hopkins in 1890, the lectures of Albert Shaw—the political scientist, journalist, and social activist—captured his imagination. Unlike so much of the subject matter of the political science he was being taught, which was formal and abstract, cities were concrete, material, a part of daily experience. One could grasp the relations of society and politics in the city.[39] Here he could think himself into politics, his original intention in going to Hopkins. The city, he concluded, "was the place we had to begin."[40]

He was not alone. Frank Goodnow, professor of political science and administrative law at Columbia University, turned to the problem of home rule in the 1890s, and he brought some of his best graduate students with him into the field, including Delos F. Wilcox and Charles A. Beard, whose dissertation was on medieval English municipal law. Woodrow Wilson, whose lectures on state administration Howe attended at Johns Hopkins, was already beginning to rethink the topic from the point of view of cities, and in 1896 he delivered a series of lectures at Johns Hopkins on municipal politics that were open to the public and were widely reported in the local press.[41] For this generation, the city, as Howe put it, was to be "the arena where the social and political forces that are coming to the fore will play."[42]

By the 1890s the new position and role of the city in American political theory had changed so much that E. L. Godkin, a member of the Tilden Commission in 1876 and spokesman for taxpayer suffrage, became an advocate of home rule and urban democracy. The founding editor of *The Nation* magazine and editor of the staid *Evening Post*, Godkin was a powerful political voice for the educated classes of America. He decided that hostility to the city—and a futile hope that somehow the city and its masses would simply go away—had produced undue fear of urban democracy and a distorted urban politics. The modern city, he now recognized, was unlike any previous cities. Cities would be central to society, not peripheral, and in this new era in the history of cities there were no natural limits to their growth. The modern city was global in its reach. "The introduction of steam and electricity," he reflected, enabled them to draw people and resources from "the uttermost ends of the earth."[43] What can one do? "Make the government of cities as good as possible, to meet it as the most solemn, the most difficult, but also the most imperative of all the political duties which our age imposes on modern man."[44] For the conservative Godkin, as well as for the radical Howe, the challenge of modern democracy had become the transformation of the urban dweller into a full citizen and the acceptance of the authority of urban majorities to address the "many wants peculiar to such large collections [of people]."[45]

The theoretical work of creating an urban polity fell mainly to Columbia professor Frank Goodnow. In a series of influential books and articles, he proposed "delimiting a sphere" for municipal politics. In this sphere, there would be local autonomy and freedom from legislative interference. This approach, he argued, recognized the undeniable presence of local political facts, and it empowered urban citizens to act politically for the "satisfaction of local needs."[46]

It was a theoretical claim of significant public importance. "The determination of the proper position of the city," he explained, "is of much more than mere academic interest." It made a difference whether the city was understood as only a "business corporation, as so many have said that it is," for if it is, then "it should be governed in accordance with the principle of business. If, on the other hand, it is a governmental organ, it should be governed in accordance with the principles of government."[47] He acknowledged that cities were in some sense both "politic and corporate," but he insisted that they are "more politic than they are corporate." Historically the city, even after its subordination to the state, had been more than a mere agent. It "became as well an organ for the satisfaction of local needs, needs which while quite distinct from the general governmental needs of the country were still of a social and governmental, and not of a mere business character."[48] He thus rejected the major theoretical argument offered by propertied elites against urban citizenship. By the 1920s, Goodnow's definition of municipal government had established space for a degree of home rule for American cities, but without completely displacing the Dillon Rule.[49] Citizens formed an urban polity, even if it was limited in its sphere of operation.

Goodnow proposed following the European model of municipal government, where cities were recognized as "political corporations," subject to supervision by a central state administration. This approach, he believed, would end the evil of legislative interference with municipalities.[50] In his theoretical framework, central administrative supervision implied that the work of cities was local administration on the basis of local interests and conditions. It is easy to miss the political empowerment embedded in this formulation. Some commentators, with a later understanding of administration as a form of bureaucratic authority guided by expertise rather than by the incorporation of political interests, have misread Goodnow. From their point of view, the word *administrative* suggests a depoliticizing of the city and turning cities over to bureaucratic experts.[51] Such a view, as Michael Frisch explained long ago, seriously distorts Goodnow's theory, even though it does predict later developments.[52] In his own time, however, he legitimated the city as a political entity.

Goodnow's perspective was historical. Much like the historical economists who stressed particular historical conditions rather than relying upon the a priori and formal argumentative style of the proponents of laissez-faire, Goodnow rejected general rules or any a priori specification of the place of the city in American jurisprudence. He insisted that each city must be understood in its historical circumstance. What local needs to be satisfied can be identified? What political authority is required? Over time, and from place to place, answers may differ.[53] The historical approach, again following the economists, had two advantages: first, it lowered the ideological temperature, and second, it provided a permanent need for political scientists able to make such determinations. Here again, we see how new, antiformalist methods in the social sciences invited an urban focus. A new intellectual agenda and professional ambition were both served by the idea of continuous engagement and of the play between theory and practice. Professional interests and the interests of urban citizenship met in this historical conjuncture.

Goodnow, often following the arguments of his colleague, the sociologist Franklin Giddings, held a dim view of the capacity of ethnic and racial minorities. He was skeptical of their capacities as citizens, and this was one reason he strongly supported the notion of a limited sphere of municipal power. "Municipal home rule without limitations," he wrote, "has no place in correct theory."[54] Yet in the end, he declined to challenge universal suffrage in cities. And he observed that more "local autonomy" will prompt "a healthy sense of responsibility."[55]

Woodrow Wilson, who was more democratic than Goodnow, had an even stronger sense of the ways in which the city provided a way for political scientists and American citizens to think themselves into politics and to act politically. In extensive "Notes on Administration," written in 1890, Wilson explored the relation of administration to democracy. He had previously studied and written about this theme from the perspective of the national state, but now he assumed a municipal point of view.[56]

"The modern industrial city," Wilson believed, posed new problems for government and administration, yet it also presented new possibilities for political theory. The "industrial city," in its "recent and rapid growth," had "outstripped . . . the hitherto possible speed of political development."[57] The theorist of modern democracy must turn, therefore, to the city, and Wilson did, addressing the problem of urban politics with a strong commitment to redistributing political power. The "leading classes," as Wilson called them, ruled in their own interest. They would provide police, but they would not support needed sanitary services and education, and they would routinely corrupt the process of urban development. Only if the whole citizenry were empowered would justice and democracy be realized under modern, industrial conditions. Social justice was to be achieved through politics, and home rule was the means of making that politics possible.

Wilson took as his task the legitimation of a participatory urban democracy. "The selfish interests of the wealthy city classes cannot be relied upon to promote the delicate and difficult tasks which come from the masses of men economically dependent. The only wholesome power," Wilson argued, "is the general interest." How might all classes be involved? By creating a sense of urban citizenship. The political scientist must establish that a city is a "body politic" with important functions. Like Goodnow, Wilson insisted that while the city is an organ of the state, it has local political responsibilities and powers.[58]

The Tilden Comission was sharply criticized by Wilson; its proposals made sense, he said, only if "real estate administration is admitted as the basis of municipal function."[59] But in fact the city is a polity, not a public-works corporation.[60] Its political structure must, therefore, represent the totality of the population. "A city is not a group of localities, nor an aggregation of interests, nor an improving (public works) corporation, but an organism, whole and vital only when whole and conscious of its wholeness and identity."[61]

He had great ambition for the city. In time, the work of supplying municipal services—which he construed rather widely to include most of what later would be called the work of the welfare state—would, he thought, yield a modern theory of political administration. In contrast to the medieval city, which he defined as a "locality of trades," granting the "liberty" to conduct trade there, the modern city demanded civic responsibility. The spirit of its constitution would be the political determination of collective "duties."[62] If the city were responsible for "more important, far-reaching and conspicuous functions" under a regime of home rule, a more vital and responsible public would be formed. Such, for Wilson, was the value of home rule and of the municipalization of gas, transit, and charity. How "they are managed affects the whole community" and might nourish a collectivist ethic.[63]

Clearly pointing toward the development of a social politics—or, in our more recent terminology, a welfare state—Wilson argued that the modern city ought to make itself "a humane economic society." The municipality, in Wilson's view, was an "ordinance-making body," meaning an administrative body dealing with all classes of the city, insuring health, safety, education, and aid to those in distress. This vision of democratic administration wedded local need and pragmatic social science. Such municipal administration as Wilson proposed was antiformal and empirical, giving it a pragmatic quality that was for Wilson, as it would later be for Dewey, inherently democratic.[64] "An ordinance lies closer to facts, to practical conditions and details than does law. Its test is its feasibility as shown by direct-experiment."[65] And these policies should "be determined by the representative general voice."[66] The city thus becomes a laboratory for modern democracy.

Wilson, like F. C. Howe, and unlike Goodnow and Beard, had no hesitation about empowering urban immigrants and the lower classes. In a public lecture in Baltimore, he offered the case of Princeton, where, he said, the "management of affairs" by the "poorer classes—mostly Irish and Negroes—has resulted in a better condition of things than if it had been left to the educated classes."[67]

My point, however, is not specifically the democratic qualities of Goodnow or Wilson. It is rather the way in which they gave political legitimacy to the city, and the way Wilson, Howe, and Wilcox, especially, used the city as a point of political engagement as intellectuals and activists seeking to deal with the social implications of industrial capitalism.

Here two points need to be emphasized. The first is the way in which they established the primacy of the language of politics (as opposed to economics or sociology) as the means of addressing the challenge of modernity. The second is their faith that societal problems are best addressed in the city, that, as Wilcox put it, the city "is the center of the complex web of national life."[68] Contrary to the way American liberals have thought about social politics for most of the past century, these early liberals are not asking the nation to rescue the city. They are in fact proposing just the opposite: the city can save the nation. That is the argument of Howe's *The City: The Hope of Democracy*, and it is the point Wilcox made in *The American City*, when he wrote: "The city must face and solve its own problem for its own sake and *for the nation*."[69]

Goodnow, historicist that he was, cautioned that the political standing he proposed for cities at the end of the nineteenth century may not be justified at other times. States eclipsed cities and subordinated them in the eighteenth century. Citizenship became attached exclusively to the nation-state. At that time there was little social need for urban autonomy, according to Goodnow. Moreover, he argued that urban autonomy had tended historically to produce rule by oligarchies. The introduction of state power, Goodnow insisted, was welcomed by cities for advancing the democratic cause. In the nineteenth century, however, with the development of a new kind of society and economy, cities needed limited but real political authority. Goodnow devoted himself to theorizing and justifying that authority. But, he speculated, in time—and perhaps sooner than one might realize—the urbanization of society would no doubt make those issues presently identified with the city into national issues. When that happened, home rule would not be necessary, for there would be no distinctive political work for cities.[70] At that point, should it come, the city would no longer be the focal point for democratic reform of industrial society, nor would it be a place and a concept for thinking one's self into politics or acting politically.

Though Charles Beard was the author of the first college textbook in the field of urban politics, he never granted the city the elevated position that Wilson had given it in the 1890s and that Wilcox and Howe continued to give it at least through World War I. One of the striking qualities of Beard's career as a scholar and activist was the way in which he moved back and forth between the nation and the city as the locale for political inquiry and action. Indeed, he felt compelled to note his different "point of view" in the preface to *American City Government* (1912). "The position is here taken that, strictly speaking, there can be no such thing as 'municipal science,' because the most fundamental concerns of the cities, the underlying economic foundations, are primarily matters of state and national, not local, control."[71] It is fitting, I suppose, that Beard's next two books addressed the national government, particularly the Constitution, conservative readings of which had allowed the courts to strike down so much progressive legislation.[72] Although Beard continued his urban activism—working three afternoons a week at the Bureau of Municipal Research in New York—by the time of World War I, he was convinced that the future of social politics was to be at the national level.

By the 1930s the city had dropped out of the center of social politics. It no longer provided a way to grasp the politics of modern industrial society. The New Deal did not recognize the city as focal point for policy, even if its various policies directed toward labor, families with dependent children, housing, unemployment, occupational safety, and social security, among others, were vastly and intentionally helpful to urban dwellers.

The shift from an urban perspective for social politics had been announced as early as 1909, in Herbert Croly's immensely influential book, *The Promise of American Life*. Interestingly, like Beard, Croly's reputation before 1909 was that of an insightful commentator on cities and editor of *Architectural Record*.[73] Yet one enters a different world of reform thought with Croly's *Promise of American Life*. He explicitly rejected Howe's vision of the city as the hope of democracy. He instead assumed as his task the articulation or rearticulation of the connection between democracy and nationalism. The issue to be addressed, as Croly phrased it in the title of the final chapter, was "the individual and the national purpose." Not the city but the nation was now to be the focus of political identity and engagement for Croly and for *The New Republic*, of which he was the founding editor in 1914.[74]

The Promise of American Life pointed to and inspired the "New Nationalism" of Theodore Roosevelt. In this context it pointed to Wilson as well. Wilson had returned to his earlier nationalism. He never published his work on cities, and he himself moved from municipal concerns to the governorship of New Jersey and then to the presidency. More generally, as Allan Davis has shown, Jane Addams and other social progressives addressing the implications of industrial society shifted their political focus from the city to the nation after World War I.[75] And the National Urban League, which had been urban-based and urban-focused, reorganized itself in 1918 as a national organization with a national program for advancing the interests of African Americans.[76] Another index of this shift reveals itself in the pages of *The Political Science Quarterly*. From 1887 to 1910, rarely was there an issue without at least one article on the city. Over the next twenty years few articles appeared, and there were none in the decade of the 1930s.[77] The address of citizenship in modern, industrial society, whether one refers to the disciplinary agenda of political scientists or the location of political action, had shifted from the city to the nation.

Why? Partly, it was because the cities—though partially empowered by the movement for home rule—were not able adequately to address the problems that so powerfully revealed themselves within the city limits. The city, we might conclude, was a site that vividly represented the crisis of contemporary capitalism and enabled the formulation of a social politics, but it was was in the end too limited a terrain to provide a political solution. But there were other influences that helped to shift the focus of social politics from the city to the nation, and I will suggest four. The emergence of the United States as a world power after 1898 stimulated and invigorated an American nationalism that had been nourished in the 1880s and 1890s as part of the effort to heal the wounds of the Civil War. Massive immigration—which for many threatened to overwhelm American nationality—prompted more nationalist thinking, which culminated in the nationalist (and racist) immigration legislation of the 1920s. The creation of U.S. Steel, the first billion-dollar corporation, in 1901 and other widely discussed mergers, as well as the development of New York City as the headquarters for increasing numbers of national corporations, encouraged a national perspective in theories of social politics. Finally, I suspect that the election of 1912, hard fought by four remarkable candidates (Wilson, Roosevelt, William H. Taft, and Eugene V. Debs) may well have substantially increased expectations for ameliorative policies at the national level.

Lest my argument here be misunderstood, let me say that urban thinking did, of course, continue in the social sciences. But in this thought politics was reduced to city planning and administration, largely under the aegis of Charles Merriam at Chicago. Even the sociologists at Chicago, noted as they have been for the remarkable school of urban studies they created, largely avoided the political, especially after World War I. Following Robert Park, they turned to ecological models and local ethnographies, mapping neighborhoods and real estate markets or describing urban types. Such social science was not a site for democratic discourse or for thinking oneself into politics.

Today one looks in vain in the *Political Science Quarterly* or *The American Political Science Review* for an article dealing with the city.[78] Yet there may now be reasons for a revival of the city as a focal point for a discourse on citizenship and democracy. There is much that is reminiscent of the conditions that prompted such a discussion a century ago.

Both economics and political science then and now were and are trapped in a formalistic mode of analysis that discourages interest in the city and in fact offers little capacity to address the circumstantial facts of time, place, or culture. Both have been focused on the national unit—whether in gathering economic statistics or in examination of the state and its constituents—at a time when the hold of the state on the political imagination and as the primary structure of social, economic, and cultural processes is being questioned and even doubted. Most important of all, a laissez faire political economy is producing a dramatic transformation of metropolitan areas—massive influx of immigrants from a variety of global diasporas, both very rich and, more numerously, very poor; serious levels of inequality; unprecedented (and utterly unplanned and formless) physical extension of the urban areas; a dissolution of public culture; and evident municipal incapacity.

There is a strong awareness by academics and the public that the economic structure of modern society is being transformed—*and* that the spatial relations of everyday life are being radically altered. The implications for the nation-state are not clear, but it is generally anticipated that they will be significant. Likewise, the future of cities is difficult to predict. At first it seemed that the importance of place would be diminished to the vanishing point by cyberspace and an allegedly placeless global economy and culture. Such expectations do not, however, seem to be borne out. The persistence of place in our global age has been striking.

Cities may even be advancing at the expense of nations. Most striking—and like the circumstance in the 1890s—the social impact of global change is most evident in metropolitan areas. Here one witnesses the manifestations of contemporary modernity. Might the city—in its metropolitan form, acknowledging its embeddedness in structures larger than itself—again be the place and means for thinking oneself into politics and acting politically in the social circumstance of our time?

The centrality of metropolitan/regional areas in contemporary economic development has been taken more seriously recently by urban analysts,[79] and the widely read economist Paul Krugman has begun to argue from a geographical perspective the importance of cities and regions. This new thinking about cities and economies has gotten wide distribution and elaboration in a supplement on cities in the *Economist*.[80]

Is political consciousness moving in the same direction? Might it be expected to do so? There is some evidence pointing in this direction. Geographer Peter J. Taylor has argued that "cities are replacing states in the construction of social identities."[81] This development, if accurately identified, alters a pattern of more than 200 years. The great deflation of the political character of cities in the eighteenth century was linked to the creation of a modern, national citizenship. Since then citizens have had primary, even exclusive loyalty to the state, not the city. Social identity and political identity are not exactly the same thing, but the former is the foundation for the latter, and Taylor points out that immigrants to London today do not understand themselves to be English or even British, but rather to be "Londoners."[82] The same pattern of identity formation may be occurring in other global cities—and more and more cities are becoming aware of their having a global dimension.

Understanding globalism as an aspect and not the totality of contemporary metropolitan life brings me to my last point. Our situation is not so different than it was in 1890, and that recognition suggests to me the continuing vitality of turning to the city as a way of thinking oneself into the politics of contemporary social life. Those who lived through the 1890s described their era's transformation much as we describe ours. They had not coined the phrase *globalization*, but it seemed much like globalization to the writers I have discussed. They were intensely aware of a dramatic revolution in technologies of communication. The movement of capital was global, as was the movement of peoples. And anyone who could travel would witness the internationalization of western urban culture, from principles of urban design, to architecture, and to the manifestations of commercial culture—the same domains in which cultural globalization reveals itself most powerfully today.

Aware of these developments, Delos F. Wilcox in 1906 asked some of the questions we are asking ourselves, and I think we would do well to listen closely to his reflections. "The vast expansion of the facilities for transmitting intelligence and goods," he observed, "has seemed of late to be breaking down the barriers of space and diminishing its significance. . . . We think that, space being annihilated, we need no rooms and so will live all in one place." Wilcox challenged that logic. "Locality," he insisted, "persistently reasserts itself, and the faster distance is abolished the more rapidly the price of standing room rises."[83] This observation, based on the remarkable burst of skyscraper development in lower Manhattan between 1895 and 1905, resonates with the Manhattan experience in the 1980s, and especially the 1990s.

Wilcox would not deny, nor would we, that "for industrial society, in considerable degree, distance has been annihilated and space overcome." But his special insight—and one worthy of our consideration today—is that "industrial society and political society are organized on radically different principles. . . . For political society . . . place and territorial limits are fundamental." Citizens experience industrial society in a particular place, and, more important, people become citizens in a place. "It is in this primitive relation to land and locality that citizenship largely consists." The city, therefore, remains—even in an era of global movement of goods, capital, people, and ideas—a place, perhaps *the* place, for thinking oneself into politics. The urban polity, Wilcox declared, "is the most emphatic protest of local interests against the organization of society without reference to place," and as he and the other urban Progressives always insisted, the interest of the city is a democratic social politics. For that reason, according to Wilcox, it is "upon the effectiveness of this protest [that] the life of democracy depends."[84]

Metropolitan dwellers may well have to develop a new political language that "fits" the new social and spatial arrangement of their lives. That work will require an adequate language of metropolitan representation as well as a fuller sense of metropolitan political obligation. Social scientists have an opportunity, as did their predecessors, to contribute to the creation of these new understandings. Such work might again revitalize the disciplines by contact with the texture of local life and at the same time provide the basis for a political definition of the metropolitan citizenship that will, in turn, enable a political mobilization to address the most serious social and economic challenges of our time.

13

THE NEW METROPOLITANISM

It is becoming a commonplace that established representations of city and suburb do not hold. Our capacity to describe or theorize the social and spatial organization of the contemporary metropolis is manifestly inadequate to what we know of the metropolitan experience. About a decade ago, the historian Robert Fishman, an acute student of the history of urban form, wrote that the contemporary city "radically departs" from the historical spatial structure of cities. It "lacks what gave shape and meaning to every urban form of the past: a dominant single core and definable boundaries." And it has attained a heretofore unimaginable scale. If the leading metropolitan centers of a century ago—New York, London, Berlin, for example—covered perhaps one hundred square miles, "the new city routinely encompasses two to three *thousand* square miles." The architect and critic Richard Ingersoll, in an essay on "The Disappearing Suburbs," rightly noted that "cities have become impossible to describe." Their centers, he wrote, are "not as central as they used to be," and their "edges are ambiguous."[1] Moreover, as Fishman remarked in 1990, we do not even have a commonly accepted name for the giant social aggregations that mark our era, and we still do not.[2]

The hold of the traditional notion of the urban center as the city—surrounded by suburbs—remains strong. And this became clear to me on a recent visit to Berlin. Over the past decade, as is well known, Berlin has been at the center of a remarkably prolific local, national, and international discussion of urbanism. The whole world, it seems, knows about Potsdamer Platz and has an opinion concerning its development. Yet I am struck more by what is *not* being discussed in Berlin—or, for that matter, New York, where so much has been written and said about the new Times Square. In both cities, the center has been ceaselessly discussed, but the larger issue of metropolitan development has hardly been noticed.

This general problem struck me in Berlin because there is no major city in the world that is better situated to discuss the outspreading or geographical extension of a city into a metropolitan form. Because of the unique circumstance of Berlin, it did not participate in the postwar geographical expansion so common to cities throughout the world. After 1989, when the barrier to its spatial expansion was removed, this unique history created an extraordinary opportunity to think about and publicly discuss the transformation not only of the center but of the larger metropolis. Berlin's silence is our silence. We talk of the center, or the city and suburb, but the metropolitan question is closer to the heart of the urban dilemma of our time than are the stage sets constructed at Potsdamer Platz and Times Square.

Trying to displace our fascination with the center, Fishman has recalled Frank Lloyd Wright's "Broadacre City," which reduced the center to zero, making each individual the center of the city and able to create his or her own city by their journeys.[3] Such a radical reduction of the center does not ring any truer to our contemporary experience than does the city-suburb binary. And the dissolution of the public city that it implies is a high price to pay.

When Wright wrote about Broadacre City, Lewis Mumford was promoting the idea of regionalism, and we would do well to recover that framing. Further, we might be advised to set aside Jane Jacobs's great classic, *The Death and Life of Great American Cities* (1961), and pick up her less well-known *Cities and the Wealth of Nations* (1984), which claims the metropolitan region as the proper focus for understanding the economy and urban creativity. I want to build upon this notion of metropolitan regionalism, adding to it an argument that widening the lens of urban thinking to the metropolitan scale may, perhaps paradoxically, bring us closer to a revitalized public life and urban democracy. It further offers the possibility, as Peter Calthorpe suggested several years ago, of uniting urban and environmental concerns.[4] And this in turn implies a rich mix of perceptions and institutions that are alternatively metropolitan-wide and decentralized. I am envisioning a metropolitan region that sustains both an extended sense of collective or civic identity and a plurality of local publics and identities.

I have emphasized our inability to describe the contemporary city because my premise is that the political and discursive crises of the city are ones, at least to a signficant degree, of representation. How can the extent of political authority, obligation, and administrative capacity be represented in the context of urban sprawl and globalization? Citizens, Benedict Anderson recently observed, must possess a common imagination of a political territory before politics is thinkable, thus making representational issues central to any notion of urban citizenship and democracy.[5] If, as the poet Wallace Stevens once wrote, people do not live in places but in descriptions of places, our inability to describe the metropolitan agglomerations we inhabit is not only a political failure but a human one as well.

Admittedly, the architectural and popular discussions of Potsdamer Platz and Times Square have been intensely concerned with the issue of visual representation. I can imagine Times Square doing that work for the municipality, as it once did, but can such a singular space do that cultural work for a giant metropolis covering three states that is New York today? The question of representation needs to be pursued on a different geographical scale, or more precisely, on multiple but clearly related or connected scales. And, as we shall see, it must be considered in relation to social practices and institutional forms of power.

Historically, urban spatial representation has been fairly simple. Perhaps it is inevitable that such representation will simplify, a point recently made in a quite critical spirit by James Scott in his *Seeing Like a State*.[6] Yet a bit of simplification may not be a bad thing. It depends upon the content of the simplified image—and its politics. In the case of the medieval and early modern city, the wall defined the city, clearly marking inside and outside and bounding the benefits of city life, something clear in Lorenzetti's famous painting of *Good Government* in Siena. In the nineteenth and early twentieth centuries a different pattern of representation emerged: center and periphery, which sotto voce in the United States described the geography of class and race.

Visual representation of the contemporary city is important, but we must be careful about reducing city to a mere image. Representation is more than an image; the power and usefulness of visual representation of urban life depends upon its capacity for incorporating social history into it. What the new Times Square shares with the towns and suburbs promoted by the "New Urbanism" movement is that they are both little more than scenery, proposing a future fabricated out of nostalgic scenes and consumerist fantasies. Indeed, the foundational and inarticulate assumptions of the New Urbanism share more than is acknowledged with the modernist urbanism to which it is supposed to be an alternative. Like the worst versions of the modernist city, the New Urbanism and Disney's Times Square urbanism seek the same purifying separations and exclusions. It is modernism in costume: retro for one, Halloween for the other. The withering criticisms of nineteenth-century utopian fantasies and nostalgia penned by Walter Benjamin are fairly appropriated in any appraisal of the New Urbanism.

Such urban design produces a remarkably "thin" experience of the modern urban life; I have referred to it elsewhere as "city lite."[7] It is also quite partial; neither the New Urbanism nor any other current urban or suburban, commercial or residential planning technique or theory is presently working with any significant effect at a scale larger than a single subdivision or office park.[8]

The offer made by cities is higher in calories and more complex in structure. Historically and in the present, the gift of urbanism is thickness, texture, partly the result of history, but also produced by the overlapping of activities and uses, the conjuncture of types of people, and the multiplicity of purposes—all located within a sense of a larger whole.

Perhaps no critic has so much influenced our current sense of the visualization of urban life as has Walter Benjamin. Like Georg Simmel before him, he understood modern urban life as peculiarly visual. Simmel's great essay, "The Metropolis and Mental Life," treats the urban experience as almost wholly visual and psychological.[9] Building on Simmel, Karl Marx, and his Frankfurt School colleagues, Benjamin wondered whether he might "conjoin a heightened graphicness to the realization of the Marxist method?"[10] For him the visual representation of the city was inherently related to the social contents of the city. That aspiration, so well captured in the massive and translated *Arcades Project*, remains exciting and important.[11] But we err when we bring Benjamin's perspective to bear on the urban center and ask Times Square or Potsdamer Platz to represent the metropolis.

Neither the Paris of Benjamin nor that of ordinary nineteenth-century travellers to Paris was a centered city. Americans, particularly, were confused. They found no Parisian equivalent of the American "downtown" that had emerged in the United States with the streetcar suburbs and commuter railroad. Urbanism and public life, they discovered, was more widely distributed in Paris, and Benjamin captures this quality of the city. Benjamin's arcades are not centered; nor is one distinctly more important than others. The whole point of his fascination with the arcades was the distribution of dozens of them throughout the city. Rather than being the analyst of a megacenter—meaning here Times Square and Potsdamer Platz—Benjamin was the student of a multicentered city, one in which the most pervasive public space was continually described by him as being like the rooms of a house, possessing important qualities of the private usually associated with interiors. We misappropriate Benjamin when we assimilate his arcades to Times Square, either before or after Disney.

Understood this way—as the restless analyst of the multiple images of a pluralized public culture—Benjamin might be enlisted in the work of understanding the new metropolitanism of our time, though, as I will try to argue in a moment, we must go far beyond him and his focus on space and vision.

If for Benjamin the arcades did not represent the center, how might we characterize them? A term recently adapted by Sophie Body-Gendrot to describe the contemporary city may serve us well. She refers to metropolitan *fractals*—pieces of the city that in microcosm contain the whole.[12] In a more or less Hegelian fashion, Benjamin sought to decode "the whole from the detail."[13] This notion, sans Hegel, leads toward a social history of a complex metropolitan region constituted by replication and difference.

The notion of a highly differentiated modern metropolitan region offers great promise to the urban analyst. But such an approach demands that we abandon four commonplace assumptions. First, we must realize the severe limits of center/periphery understandings of the metropolis. Certainly, there is some centering, even in Houston and Los Angeles, but that does not describe the common experience of the metropolis. Second, we must give up the assumption that cultural and class characteristics can be mapped on a center/periphery or concentric ring conception of the city. Third, it is a mistake to refer to gated communities as strictly suburban or exurban. In fact, Stuyvesant Town in Manhattan is nearer to being an urban gated community than we might want to concede, and I am not sure how a doorman building or a building with an underground garage differs from a suburban gated community. The concerns behind such security practices are scattered through the metropolis. Fourth, we must recognize that *suburb* has become something of a misnomer. What we call suburbs have become, first, more diverse kinds of settlements than we acknowledge, and, second, their relations across the metropolitan region are lateral, not hierarchical.

We must think in metropolitan terms, not city and suburban terms. The spatial expansion of metropolitan areas has been dramatic since World War II, especially in the past two decades. Take Chicago: between 1970 and 1990, the population of Chicago increased by 4 percent, but the physical extension of the city increased by 50 percent. And automobile usage has skyrocketed. Similar figures can be adduced for other American cities, and the story is even more dramatic in places like Mexico City, Jakarta, and São Paulo.

What I am describing is far from the Greek polis. What then happens to the citizen in such a metropolis? What kind of political possibilities, if any, reside in these agglomerations? Can the everyday experience of life in the parts of the metropolis nourish both a sense of individual agency and metropolitan citizenship? Of individual and collective recognition? If we think of a sea of privatized suburban life, isolated and isolating individual houses, soccer and swim clubs, freeways and shopping malls, it does not seem promising.

This rhetorical construction of the metropolitan region flows easily out of our mouths. But it is confounded by facts on the ground. The metroscape, if I may call it that, is far more differentiated than this. The old language may describe the wealthy Westchester suburban town of Rye, New York. But just across the freeway and commuter rail tracks from Rye is Port Chester, a working-class/middle-class town marked by remarkable ethnic and cultural diversity and a rich street life.

A new generation of scholarship is taking a new look at the suburbs. On the basis of close study of New York suburbs on Long Island, the site of the famous Levittown and the less famous but more interesting Freeport, Rosalyn Baxandall and Elizabeth Ewen, two historians identified with the left in the United States and not likely apologists for the suburb, have recently argued that there is more complexity out there than we think.[14] Many of the homogeneous suburbs of the 1940s and 1950s have become integrated, not only by race, but young and old, gay and straight. These places are no longer single-purpose (as in bedroom community); people live, work, and play in these smaller units of the metropolitan region.

The plans for the pretty suburban neighborhoods proposed by the New Urbanists somehow miss these essential aspects of metropolitan life. Life in the metropolis is far more cosmopolitan, even more egalitarian, than the New Urbanists imagine. In their recent book, *Suburban Nation*, which is designed to promote the New Urbanism movement they lead, Andres Duany, Elizabeth Plater-Zyberk, and Jeff Speck talk of commitments to an allocation of affordable housing and mixed or integrated neighborhoods, but they do it in a paternalistic language that turns diversity into "otherness": "When it comes to the integration of different housing types, there is no established formula, but it seems safe to say that a neighborhood can easily absorb a one-in-ten insertion of affordable housing without adverse effects. . . . Such a distribution provides role models for the poor while mitigating against the close-mindedness of the wealthy."[15] The metroscape is not so dichotomous and regulated; it is both more multiform and more democratic, or at least potentially so. The binary language of center/periphery, city/suburb, rich/poor leads these New Urbanists and others to a quite misleading (but consequential) polarization.

What of public life in the metroscape? The argument for a focus on the center emphasizes the importance of creating a diverse public culture, a place where the city represents itself to itself as diverse and tolerant. It is a place where individuals are compelled to locate themselves in a world of difference and perhaps imagine a richer and more democratic urban life. Can local public spaces serve this important function? I think so, but it is useful first to distinguish between types of public spaces and consequent urban publics.

When we think of Times Square or Central Park in New York, we are envisioning a "central" public, one whose benefit is its potential to prompt the imaginary of an urban whole. There are in any metropolis very few sites for such a public. Moreover, as my comments so far suggest, I am not sure that such a central representative place can fairly represent the new scale of metropolitan life and citizenship. I do acknowledge, however, that when it has worked—and might yet again—the result is urban democratic symbolism at its most powerful.

The metropolis is prolific of smaller, local publics. How might we characterize them and their value? At the risk of heresy, I would suggest that they are urban spaces of beneficently modest differentiation. They are not much like our nostalgic image of Times Square as a true peoples' space. Rather they are like the corner of the West Village around Hudson Street so celebrated by Jane Jacobs or like the streets and arcades of Benjamin's Paris.[16] How much difference was celebrated by Jacobs in *The Death and Life of Great American Cities*? Greenwich Village is wonderfully marked by diversity—as we now call it—but it is mostly difference without consequence, which is to say without risk. It is important that we do not overstate the degree of difference Jacobs confronted in her neighborhood. Deeper and more conflicted difference was beyond her ken. She was as baffled by the old Times Square as she must be offended by the new Times Square. When I think of her Village urbanism, I think of Main Street in Port Chester, not Times Square, old or new.

Jacobs stressed visual recognition, and I think that is important. Some spaces facilitate this activity more than others, but in the end, users, not architects, make public space by their appropriation of its possibilities. Moreover, civic life requires more than visual recognition; it is constituted as well by social and institutional mechanisms of connection and, ultimately, deliberation. While we value public space for the visual acquaintance or recognition by sight that it offers, that is a precondition for public life, not the creation of public life. The public is something existential; being a public, as John Dewey argued, is doing the work of the public, which is in the end a form of democratic politics. In *The Public and Its Problems* (1927), Dewey looked to the local as the place where engagement and access to authority is possible. A larger public, what he called "the Great Community," is built upon the habits and accomplishments of local publics.[17]

Urban critics tend to focus on the diversity of public space and publics. That is important, but equally so are questions of *access* to political institutions and the opportunity to give voice to public concerns. Again, I fear that we have slipped into a stage-set notion of the public, one of edifying images of ourselves as cosmopolitan. But I am proposing a public that is a public not because of mere propinquity, however important that is, but because they propose to do something together.[18] The essential quality of what I call the "local" public is not, as we are inclined to think, sameness; it is accessibility to networks of informal power and to institutions of formal politics.

While the "centered" public space offers important symbolic resources, so do local public spaces. In addition and of fundamental importance, local life offers greater opportunity for access, engagement, and voice. This local access, which since the "rights revolution" of the 1960s has been increasingly available to the less powerful, is more and more important as the corporate media and national politics (increasingly mediated and donor driven) become less and less accessible and responsive to those without resources.

I am not seeking to displace centered public spaces; I wish we had more of them. But I am extending the notion of the public to include smaller, more local public spaces and publics in a highly differentiated metropolis.[19] Both are valuable, and they may have some relational impact on each other. But I want to emphasize a point too often lost in our discussion of central symbolic spaces: an important part of making urban citizens, even metropolitan citizens, takes place in local publics.

If I am right so far, the big challenge of the new metropolitanism is to ensure that there are spaces available for the making of local publics. At present, one finds such spaces only in the suburbanized small towns, like Port Chester, that have been swept up in the metropolitan expansion. We need to make new ones, and that may require rethinking issues of urban infrastructure as well as architectural styles. Local publics need centering activities that will bring diverse people together (to see and be seen). This points to an infrastructure issue: commuter railroad stations—dense with shops, public offices, and parkland—are more likely to contribute to this work than do freeways.[20]

Even shopping malls could become more than islands of consumption. If they were willing to be civic they might become the centers of local life. That would mean locating them elsewhere than at freeway exits, and it would mean expanding their self-understanding beyond consumerist fantasies to include useful commerce—groceries, shoemakers, hardware stores—and public services, as in health, employment, and welfare offices. Perhaps even a school!

Does this line of argument point to a "defense" of suburbs? No. In fact, I am arguing that the concept of suburb has been emptied of meaning. Planning and policy must adapt to this development. There is now a possibility of reconceiving localism in a way that combines decentralization, or *devolution* in current language, while heightening the sense of political obligation across the metroscape. A new kind of localism, one not incompatible with metropolitanism, becomes thinkable. Still, one may ask, does not the praise of local publics carry the risk of leading us back to a parochialism that would undermine the very metropolitan-wide sense of political obligation that I am endeavoring to advance?[21] Perhaps, but I think not.

I can explain myself, I hope, by making another distinction. There are two domains for representing the public: public space and public institutions, both of which can be more or less exclusive or inclusive. The public space is the terrain of the public as visual representation, while institutions provide a place for representative political deliberation.

In different ways, major theorists of urban and civic life, from Lewis Mumford to Jane Jacobs, Walter Benjamin to Hannah Arendt, Richard Sennett to Marshall Berman, have been in search of the modern agora. These guides to the city have explicated a public domain in which the individual sees and is seen by the others who make up the city. Seeing and being seen in this view (and it is an intensely visual understanding of city life and human communication) is the central act of being in public and of making a public culture that represents the city to itself.

What, then, is the specific "work" to be done by the public as site of visual representation? I also want to ask what kinds of work it cannot do. In thinking about this, I have benefitted from a recent essay by Richard Sennett, "The Spaces of Democracy."[22] Writing against the grain of much urban theorizing, including his own, he points out that the devotion of urbanists to the mixing of people and activities at the agora in ancient Greece obscures the fullness of Greek public life. Athens, Sennett notes, located its democratic practices in two physical settings: the town square (or *agora*) and the theatre (or *pynx*). Public life thus had two aspects, each with its own work, each with its own "place," one informal and other institutionalized.

The agora stimulated citizens to recognize the presence of others, persons with different needs and rights to be respected. It was a place for representation of difference in a way that implied common affiliation in a collective; its mode of communication was visual inspection and presentation. The work of such a space is to enhance the capacity for tolerance and recognition in a world of difference.

The theatre had different work to do. It enabled citizens to focus their attention and concentrate upon decision-making. There, Sennett writes, "Athenians debated and decided on the city's actions." While the agora is the place of recognizing strangers, the speakers and listeners in the theatre were known—even sitting in assigned seats. Since it was a semicircle, all could see all, and specific arguments could be identified with particular individuals, clans, and tribes—and their interests. This ancient form of public deliberation made citizens responsible for their words. Not only was argument enabled, but this forum established responsibility and resulted in decisions, none of which are well sustained by the Baudelairian notion of public life in the streets.

Again, my intention here is not to favor one version of public life over the other. The work of both is important for a democratic and just city. Visual representation and deliberative (or formal political) representation are complementary aspects of a democratic public.

Understanding this relation reframes a central debate around the work of Jürgen Habermas. From its publication in 1962, his book *The Structural Transformation of the Public Sphere* and its successors have been at the center of a revitalized international discussion of democracy. Beginning with the "invention" of the public sphere in the coffeehouses of eighteenth-century London, Habermas traced the various transformations of the public sphere over the following two centuries, appraising the degree of democratic possibility inherent in each iteration. He was not particularly attentive to the physical spaces of public discourse, focusing rather upon class and institutional issues. Moreover, his work focused very much on formal discourse, on opportunities for rational argument, as in newspapers. Still his vision of a democratic public sphere drew the attention of urban theorists as well as political philosophers. Over time, critics—especially social historians—came to argue that Habermas had too narrow a notion of the public sphere, of the legitimate speakers, of the spatial character of the public sphere, and of the meaning of politics in public. While Habermas had in mind formal discourse and deliberation, the historians focused on an alternative and often disorderly symbolic politics in local streets.[23]

The tendency has been to pose one point of view against the other, but the argument I seek to make is that these positions are complementary. The public has two dimensions: visual representation, including a variety of forms of cultural expression; and formal deliberative representation. It also combines local and central manifestations of each. Different and complementary forms of public representation occur in the agora and in the theatre, in the streets and in institutionalized forms of public deliberation, in neighborhoods and in the center. Each site is a different public space where citizens do different work, and both are essential for a democratic and just city.

Returning from theory to everyday life in the metropolis, an immediate problem confronts us. There are no metropolitan-wide deliberative institutions, and local publics seem to be anything but progressive. Gerald Frug, in his *City Making*, has recently written with great insight on this issue.[24] He points out that the metropolis is broken up into very small political units. The political economy of the metropolis effectively forces competition and conflict to define intra-metropolitan relations. Hence each of these town and village governments turns inward, defending itself from the larger (and external) metropolitan region, thus undermining any enlarged sense of collective political obligation.

For my present purposes two aspects of this parochialism are relevant. As fiscal units, local governments compete with each other for tax base, and this undermines the unity of the metropolis. As cultural units, they seek to protect local "values," as they might call them. One could call this localism the basis of a welcome diversity in the metropolis, but, as we all know, this impulse often leads to exclusionary policies that are driven by racism, class solidarity, and other particularisms that are incompatible with a democratic society.

The nub of the problem must be identified with precision. It is not localism per se. Rather it is the tightness of the association of governing authority and culture, for that makes local values (or claimed local values) official values enforceable by public policy. Localism in fiscal and cultural affairs reinforce each other. It almost makes the maintenance of parochialism the work of government in both the fiscal and cultural domains. Frug, a legal theorist and local government specialist at Harvard Law School, recognizes this problem, and in a clever move he turns to poststructuralist theory to deconstruct the conventional beliefs in internal unity and of boundedness characteristic of local jurisdictions. He proposes to re-represent local governments as other than single subjects, as inherently unstable, multiple in identity, and without clear borders—and thus not in fact local cultures. It is an interesting use of poststructuralist theory that bears some relation to everyday experience, but I doubt that distributing copies of Jacques Derrida's *Of Grammatology* (1974) to local mayors will do the trick.

The power of discourse is real, but here I think one must look beyond linguistic practices to institutional reform. The constitutional politics of local government is to address the functional needs of the jurisdiction. While some of those functions will include cultural activities (the maintenance of adequate libraries and schools, for example), and inevitably the articulation of cultural values, the work of local government ought not be reduced to (or expanded to) the defense of the content of local culture, or of presumptively unified local values. The experience of everyday life prompts value questions, and one hopes that there can be open or inclusive spaces in that domain to address, shape, and continually reshape them, leaving local governments to undertake a variety of functional responsibilities. This work will increasingly include functions—ranging from clean air and water to transportation—that require collaboration with other local governments or with trans-local institutions, whether county governments or special authorities. New Yorkers concerned with a pure and adequate water supply, for example, are increasingly aware of how tightly bound their daily lives are to the environmental policies of upstate counties that are part of the extensive New York water system, and the residents of those counties are increasingly aware of how the concerns of New York may affect their daily lives and livelihoods.

Everyday experience, including traffic flows and concern about watersheds, undermines the assumption of local autonomy and encourages participation in intra-metropolitan governmental institutions. More and more one must recognize that the metropolis is, in the phrasing of Sophie Body-Gendrot, "at once decentered and interdependent."[25] Cultural developments point in the same direction. There are historical processes and shifts in cultural sensibility (notably the positive valuation of diversity) presently at work that may well undermine commitments to local cultural sameness. It is increasingly reasonable to think that with some strategic prompting local jurisdictions might be nudged into acknowledging the need for functional interdependence and intergovernmental cooperation on a metropolitan scale.

More optimistically, but not impossibly, one might anticipate the development of an understanding of culture as something in the making, something made by diverse participants, rather than as a weapon in the arsenal of exclusionary practices. Such a recovery of the cultural theories of Randolph Bourne could encourage more humanly generous policies of inclusion at the local level and collaborative engagement at the metropolitan or regional scale.[26]

The question of local cultural distinctiveness is a delicate one. In our multicultural moment it is difficult to balance the positive claims to difference based on "heritage" against the negative tendencies toward exclusion. The trick, of course, is to create a cosmopolitanism—what Bourne aimed toward—that can enable individuals to live their lives on dual channels, particularistic and cosmopolitan, local and metropolitan. My hope, my claim, is that were we to construct working metropolitan-wide participatory political institutions oriented to function, not culture, they would gradually open closed communities and promote greater cultural cosmopolitanism.

Not only might local political units learn to work with others whose members may have different sociological characteristics, within single localities there will be more and more difference. Such opening is already occurring, frustratingly slow and crab-like along the lines of color, but it is happening. Recent patterns of metropolitan demographic change—not only in the U.S. but everywhere—are making these decentralized units of social and political life more diverse, more city-like, thus working on the level of everyday life to encourage a more cosmopolitan spirit.

Critics like Frug—and his line of analysis goes back at least to Robert C. Wood's study of political fragmentation of the New York region in 1961[27]— emphasize the multiplicity of local governments and the way they undermine representation of the metropolis, both in the imaging sense and in the formal sense of political representation. In one perspective that assertion is surely correct. Yet since the 1920s and 1930s local communities have been willing to empower "special purpose taxing districts." These are functional, not cultural. The cultural worries, so evident in the metroscape and that turn communities defensive, seem to be set aside in this case in order to obtain important and effective service provision by intra-metropolitan administrative bodies that deal with functional issues that transcend single political jurisdictions.[28]

At this stage in the development of the metroscape it may be too much to ask local governments to cooperate with each other directly. Frug's pessimism may on this point be well placed. Yet there is another route: limited purpose trans-local forms of governmental planning and service provision might provide a base upon which to build a new metropolitanism.

Two important tasks immediately present themselves. First, it is necessary to identify those policy areas in which such governmental structures are appropriate. Second, these metropolitan and regional administrative structures, most of which work bureaucratically and invisibly, must be converted into participatory political institutions.

If, as I believe, it is necessary to think both spatially and institutionally to do this work, recent trends in scholarship complicate this task. Under the influence of a reinvigorated geography we have spatialized social analysis, much enriching urban studies. At the same time, largely under the influence of post-structuralist sensibilities in general and more particularly culture studies (American style), both of which have spatialized social inquiry, we have also marginalized institutions and institutional analysis. Indeed, it is fair to say that to a considerable extent recent scholarly practices have dematerialized the social and the architectural by reducing them to texts and discursive practices.

It is important to bring institutions and the material aspects of life (environment, transportation networks, etc.) back into our study of society. In fact, there is a happy convergence between the physical needs of the metropolis and the metropolitan-wide special purpose districts that have been developed to address these material needs.

Historically the governmental institutions that I am calling *special purpose districts*, but which could also be called *public authorities*, have been defined by a functional need, most often very material needs. I emphasize three: environment, transportation, and infrastructure. Each of these requires a metropolitan-wide image of the city, if not more. In even the most difficult instances of tension between jurisdictions (as in the case of Berlin before 1989 or Jerusalem today, where environmental planning and infrastructure involve two hostile nation-states, or in the second and more complicated case a nation-state and the Palestinian authority) urban administrators concerned with vital material and functional issues must collaborate across local borders, usually outside of formal municipal government channels.

In order to move toward a conclusion and specify more precisely the progressive possibilities inherent in present patterns and processes of metropolitan life, it is necessary to pull together several of the themes I have scattered about so far. Then I will conclude by suggesting a crucial role for architecture in creating the metropolitan perception and imaginary of the metroscape necessary to realize such possibilities.

This opportunity will escape us if we keep our eyes on the center of a city-suburb model; if we think of the public and of representation culturally but not institutionally; if we fail to recognize that visual and deliberative representation are complementary; if we do not recognize that many of the theorists we tend to admire referred to what I am calling *local publics* far more than to centered publics. Put more succinctly, the "places of hope" about which David Harvey has recently written,[29] may be more scattered and more a part of the everyday life of ordinary people than we have supposed.

At a series of seminars on urban citizenship sponsored by the Project on Cities and Urban Knowledges at NYU in 1999–2000, I was struck by the difference in attitude revealed by academic experts on urban politics and civic activists in New York. The academics who studied traditional urban politics were deeply pessimistic about the prospects for progressive politics, while Eddie Bautista, a local activist, talked about the cross-class, interracial, metropolitan-wide coalition he was building as director of the Environmental Justice Project of the New York Lawyers for the Public Interest.[30] Bautista's environmental-justice movement discovered places of hope organizing around a metropolitan-wide functional issue that was framed within a commitment to social justice.

Can functional needs be transmuted into a metropolitan politics concerned with social justice as well as the management of material conditions? Can the bureaucratic institutions that deal with these issues—the authorities and the special-purpose tax districts—be reconfigured as participatory political institutions? Such a transformation is neither easy nor impossible. It has been done, however. A recent example, Porto Alegre, has drawn considerable attention. This Brazilian city of 1.3 million people has devolved the management of its capital budget (the source of most transportation and infrastructure policy-making) to local area assemblies. Two results are notable: first, there has been a dramatic increase in citizen engagement, and, second, there

is evidence of growing recognition of common as well as conflicting thematic interests across the metroscape.[31]

I earlier mentioned three material issues that could provide the focus for
the development of a metropolitan imaginary and politics: environment,
transportation, and infrastructure. These thematic and inherently trans-local
or metropolitan elements of urban planning and design deserve vastly more
attention than they get. If environmentalism has moved to incorporate issues
of social justice, so has transportation advocacy (as in the Los Angeles Bus-
Rider's Union, organized by Eric Mann and others, which has forced a reallocation of transit dollars in the region). Increasingly, infrastructure is seen as
a social-justice issue. Michael Cohen, for example, has recently shown that a
very large part of the disadvantage suffered by the poor of Buenos Aires
derives from the cumulative effect of massively unequal investments in urban
infrastructure.[32]

Justice in transportation, infrastructure, and environmental-justice policies link the circumstances of particular groups to the larger metropolis. The
effects of injustice in these three domains are felt locally. Yet local interest can
become wider when many different local publics recognize the commonality
of their interests in service or regulatory failures at the metropolitan scale.
When the trans-local interdependencies are recognized as causes and consequences, there is a basis for broad and diverse coalitions.

Is there reason to expect that this process of reinventing functional tax
and service districts will create spaces of hope? Will the lessons learned
extend to other issues at once general and experienced differently by different places and peoples in the metropolis: education, racial division, health
care, policing.

It is a hard question, one that cannot be answered with certainty. Can a
local and regional politics of transportation, infrastructure, and environmental justice provide a basis for wider and deeper metropolitan democracy? In
fact, many of the social injustices in cities are associated with, even caused by,
environmental, transportation, or infrastructural policies. I think that the
political and social experience of coalition building will have a spillover
impact. Working for environmental justice, for example, will create structures, workaday theories of metropolitan power and responsibility, and personal understandings and relations that might very well be expected to flow

over into other issues that demand cross-class, interracial, and metropolitan-wide politics.

The new metropolis must find ways of effectively representing the myriad interdependencies that make it a collectivity. There are no representative institutions, and the spatial unity of these issues has not found sufficient visual representation. If the challenge before us is representational—both visually and deliberatively—then we must ask whether we can reimagine urban life in terms of transportation, infrastructure, and environment. The capacity to describe the metroscape is a necessary—if not sufficient—basis for the invention of deliberative institutions to make issues of transportation, infrastructure, and environment both metropolitan and political.

A new metropolitan politics, regional yet forged out of a plurality of local publics, requires an image of itself. The focus of architecture on the individual building, the development, or, at most, the dramatic urban center—the Times Square or Potsdamer Platz—does not address this need. The fascinations of both of these central public places is easy to understand, and surely it is legitimate to focus on them, if inadequate. Yet I am struck—whether in Berlin, New York, Buenos Aires, or Mexico City—by how difficult it is to start a conversation about how to enrich local publics and the connections between them.

Again, the ancient Greek experience might help us imagine a new metropolitan democracy. Sennett has enriched our sense of the Greek legacy of public life by looking beyond the agora to the theatre as a place of public deliberation. Now let me add a third aspect of Greek public life: sanctuaries. A recent book on the origin of the Greek city-state by the French classicist François de Polignac reveals the importance of "ex-centric" sanctuaries in shaping urban perception and citizenship. He argues that in archaic Greece—save for the case of Athens—religious sanctuaries were not set mainly on the acropolis, but rather on the edges or thresholds of settlements, marking the extension of the city. They thus promoted everyday awareness of the relation of city and country, commerce and agriculture, and civilization and wilderness. The result was a new and extended sense of "city-territory." A "new civic identity" was born of the "rites of social integration" associated with the sanctuaries and the processions between sanctuaries on the edge and the center. While these activities were religious in purpose (and my concern here is with functional and material aspects of metropolitan life), his conclusion seems to hold in both cases. "These axes of the civic territory," running between the center and an ill-defined edge, "constituted a stage" where the "social body" performed for and represented itself.[33]

Is there some kind of contemporary equivalent to the sanctuaries, some kind of architectural prompt to a larger territorial vision and understanding? I think one finds it in the work of the architect William Moorish. His urban-design practices give visual representation to a city-region that is unified by environmental, infrastructural, and transportation relations that connect nature and humans, humans and humans. His work, as I see it, uses architecture and architectural representation in a genuinely novel way. It is less concerned to represent itself, or even make spaces, public or private. Rather it represents interconnections and interdependencies. And like the Greek sanctuaries, the urban-design principles he offers build upon and enable the needs and aspirations of everyday life.

In an important series of projects for Phoenix, Arizona, Moorish and his late wife and partner, Catherine Brown, designed boulevards and freeways as architectural elements that give form to the city. Infrastructural buildings, such as water treatment and sewerage plants, usually hidden, are brought into public vision as major works of architecture that reveal interdependence and define metropolitan geography. And with various public sculptural gestures they have emphasized that the natural environment is a fundamental part of urban life and that its possibilities and vulnerabilities are of common interest.

Their innovative architecture is only a start—and a primitive one at that. But it is there, to see, to develop further. And with such visual representation, it is easier to develop a popular recognition of metropolitan interdependence and collective interests. That establishes a foundation for the construction of representative deliberative institutions that will address environmental, infrastructural, and transportation concerns. With such institutions, representatives of highly differentiated local publics might come together to deliberate about the metropolitan whole and their own distinctive place in it.

The metropolitan-wide tax and service districts are mostly in place. But they lack an image of themselves as being more important than the political jurisdictions that divide the metropolis, and they do not understand themselves as deliberative institutions that invite participatory decision-making. If it is the work of architecture to provide material bases for representation of the metroscape, it is the work of citizens and their leaders to create participatory, deliberative political institutions on a metropolitan scale, building upon the special tax and service districts.

The metropolis I am envisioning would remain highly differentiated, even fragmented. Such coherence as it achieved would be a "thin coherence."[34] Yet that would be enough to bring together the thickly embedded local publics of the metropolis. In such a metropolis the plurality of local distinctions would be acknowledged. But the sharpness of these local distinctions might well be muted, the sense of otherness moderated, and the imagination of a metropolitan citizenship slowly nourished.

Everyday material needs and the interdependence they imply might nourish forms of culture and politics that bridge divisions and produce on a metropolitan scale a multifaceted and vital public life. It would be a version of the pattern of difference and negotiation that Alexis de Tocqueville long ago saw emerging out of the same sort of practical needs in a small-town America.

14

CITIES, NATIONS,

AND GLOBALIZATION

"World" cities, those cities that claim to organize the processes that we call "globalization," are not wholly novel, nor is the awareness—that seems so fresh to us—that the world is unified. From Roman times to the present there have been repeated recognitions of new levels of integration of the known world. For example, in his 1873 inaugural address President U. S. Grant seems to be describing *our* sense of global transformation, though his language is Victorian and his final observation surely seems a bit optimistic: "As commerce, education, and the rapid transition of thought and matter, by telegraph and steam have changed everything, I rather believe that the great Maker is preparing the world to become one nation, speaking one language, a consummation which will render armies and navies no longer necessary."[1]

By placing the current discussion of world cities and globalization into some historical perspective, we may get a better sense of the present. That, in turn, ought to help us focus our thinking about the political opportunities and limits that will define the structure of possibility for metropolitan regions over the next generation.

Cities were once more important than nations in organizing large parts of the world. In what historians call the "early modern period" of European history, particularly the sixteenth century, the social, economic, and cultural life of the Mediterranean and of the newly invented oceanic world was organized by cities. It is helpful to recover a sense of these urban-focused worlds, for to do so is to achieve an outside perspective from which to examine the relations of cities and nations in our global present.

Those worlds are so distant not only in time but also in concept that they are difficult for us to imagine. But for precisely that reason it is worth the effort required. Twentieth-century Europeans and Americans have known only a world of nations. Nations seem to be natural units of society. Further, one of the great transformations of the past half century has been the movement of the greater part of the remainder of the world's peoples from various forms of local life and colonialism to nationhood. This recent global experience masks the temporal limits of our understanding. We tend to project our experience backward; historians, for example, tend to use the modern nation as the frame for histories that antedate nations. There are historians of medieval French history, an era when there was no French nation. Others specialize in colonial United States history, when there was no United States or even much reason to anticipate such a political entity.

Thus while it is fair to say that nations have organized the most important global relations in the twentieth century—perhaps even the past couple of centuries—we err in assuming that they are, have been, and will be the natural and exclusive units of political life and identity. Talk of national economies, societies, and cultures comes easily to us, too easily.

The origin of the modern nation-state is recent, even in the West. At the moment of European colonization of the Americas, what we now call Europe was a mosaic of more than 500 political units, roughly the same number as existed at that time in North America. One can argue about the precise moment of crystallization for the nation as the dominant unit of society and the polity, but it is hard to date it before the seventeenth century. It is implausible to speak of the "modern nation-state" until after the American and French Revolutions, which invented the modern citizen, the building block of the modern nation and the international system of states.

With this history in mind, can we anticipate, or even imagine, a new geography of citizenship—one characterized by multiple scales and domains of relevance? Can one be at once a citizen of a metropolitan region, a nation, and a transnational, even global, world? Are such multiple sovereignties and identities possible? Likely? It is hard to say, but there have been some movements in this direction. One thinks, of course, of the European Union, which is notable for its adaptation of the federal principle. Even more novel, however, is the seriousness with which it takes border-crossing city-regions. Are these likely to become significant political, economic, and cultural entitities?

Future visions often come from the provocation of historical difference. Such a shock of unfamiliarity is offered by the world in 1700. When we examine a map of that era, we silently fill in the lines indicating the nations that will later give their different colors to that world. If we suppress that impulse, we see another geography, one focused on cities, not nations or proto-nations. For example, there was no Italy, but there were important Italian cities organizing large parts of the Mediterranean. The culture and economies of these cities stretched through southern and northern Europe and eastward into the Ottoman empire. Venice was the "hinge of Europe," connecting Europe with central and east Asia; Rome was the home of the world's largest organization; Genoa was a trading city whose activities reached east to Constantinople—and the Genoese tower in the Galata quarter of today's Istanbul is still a major historical landmark. In the person of Columbus, the city's famous native son who believed he could sail west to Asia, the small Italian city reached the New World, which was named after the Florentine humanist Amerigo Vespucci, who recognized what had been "discovered."

To move beyond Italy, consider Barcelona, still unwilling to be wholly captured by the Spanish nation. It was a power unto itself in the Mediterranean, and it was to Barcelona that Columbus returned to the welcome of Ferdinand and Isabella. Amsterdam, to take another example, was already global in the first quarter of the seventeenth century. Keep in mind that the founding of New Amsterdam (today's New York) was accomplished within a year of the Dutch founding of Batavia, today's Jakarta. The physical layout for both of these quite different overseas trading posts were strikingly similar, so much so that in the old center of Jakarta today one gets a better sense in that tropical city of the architecture and spatial arrangement of Dutch New York than has been possible on Manhattan for two hundred years. Lisbon had achieved a global reach even earlier, with Goa, Macau, and the settlements of Brazil's northeast. One could go on. I emphasize these particular cases because they were unmistakably the work of cities; none had a notably large and powerful nation to back them. As late as the seventeenth century, Europe was still constituted by cities, not nations, though nations were certainly being developed. Even if we can grant that England was precociously developing into a nation in the seventeenth century, it is fair to say that it was the city of London, not the nation of England, that mounted the first colonial plantations in North America and the Caribbean.

Looking toward the age of colonial settlement in the Western Hemisphere, one might fairly ask: Does the urban geography I am proposing work there as well? How might the New World have been mapped in 1700? Again, in retrospect, when we see an outline map of North America circa 1700 we tend to impose the map of the United States, separate the Caribbean from British North America and divide it into its various island nations, and identify Canada and Mexico (using their post-1846 borders).

At the time, however, villages, cities, regions, borderlands, and empires defined the continent for both Europeans and Americans. Mexico City, Havana, New York, and Montreal marked the geography and organized political and economic life; they were the operational centers for empires. Moreover, the Western Hemisphere was part of a global culture, a point recently and wonderfully made by the writer Thomas Pynchon in his novel *Mason & Dixon* (1997).

My purpose in making these comments is not to displace the nation, or to claim it is not or was not important. Indeed, the nation will long be with us, and a good thing that is. The nation-state possesses the power to protect and enforce those rights—namely the rights of citizenship—that helped to bring it into existence. I would not want to see those rights put at risk, even as we increasingly replace talk of citizenship with references to human rights and identity. These are important developments that may extend human freedom. But as yet we have no vehicle other than the nation-state to protect and sustain these rights that, in fact, are corrosive to the sovereignty of the modern nation. Likewise, the global movement of labor and capital is not independent of nations. National borders and national policies still powerfully affect the economies and the movement of people. One of the most obvious rights of national citizenship is the right to stay put. A citizen cannot be deported.

Yet we grant too much to the nation. A case can be made that cities (or, alternatively, corporations) are larger partners in the global economy than we recognize.[2] According to Jane Jacobs, there is no such thing as a national economy. The natural unit of economic life, she argues, is neither the nation nor the globe; rather it is the city-region.[3] She may have overstated the matter, but she has captured something quite important. We must be able to imagine that possibility, for if true there are local resources that can contribute to significant metropolitan politics in our global age.

That nations have dominated cities since the eighteenth century does not preclude other relationships. Even if nations remain important, even in some ways dominant, it does not mean that the nation will be important in the same manner and degree. To recall that cities were once more important than nations allows us to imagine the possibility of another change in the relationship of cities and nations. In other words, my aim here is to use history to relocate cities and nations in our imaginations.

As metropolitan centers and nations renegotiate their relations and roles, metropolises might well recognize new rights and assume new obligations to their citizens. What I am suggesting runs counter to what many see as the logic of globalization (the erosion of locality). Yet that logic is not persuasive. Human agency is rooted in the domain of the accessible, and that is local and concrete, not universal and abstract. The emerging metropolis may well organize our economic and cultural life in ways heavy with political significance. Certainly, as we saw in the previous chapter, they can shape key areas of infrastructure, transportation, and environment. With the 1890s in mind, we might fairly consider the possibility that the city can generate policies to address the social dimensions of the economy. And then there is the urgent challenge of accommodating difference and multiple identities. The distinctive contribution of the metropolis may be its special capacity to organize the heterogeneous social orders so increasingly evident in our highly and self-consciously pluralized world.

To amplify this point, more needs to be said in a definitional way about cities and nations. The novelties introduced by the invention of the nation were two: First, the demarcation of firm boundaries, staunchly defended. Second—and this follows from the first—there was a presumption of uniformity within these boundaries. All national citizens were formally equal—I stress formally, not actually—and the nation would be formally (again) undifferentiated within its firmly bounded territory. It is neither formally nor ideologically possible for the modern nation-state to acknowledge the lived experience of ambiguous solidarities, of multiple identities and affiliations, and of permeable boundaries that are more like borders than barriers. Such experiences are more easily accommodated within the logic and culture of cities than of nations. In fact, the nations forged in the nineteenth century weakened cities and denied the regional values and polyethnic character of the populations captured within the newly demarcated and enforced national boundaries. The idea of a homogeneous or "pure" nation is a modern invention, something very much at odds with the experience of either city life or of the empires that preceded modern nations.[4]

Empires, whatever their various vices, did not worry about either firm boundaries or uniformity of culture. They tended to be concerned with dynastic politics, and they were organized around a collection of cities and regions. Under the Ottomans, for example, there was no word for Egypt; what we know as Egypt today was called Cairo, after the key city of the region. The assumption of territorial homogeneity was the product of the logic of the nation-state, infused first with romanticism, later with scientific racism. The work of the nation—its contribution to modern history—has been the mobilization of populations for social progress as well as war.[5]

Cities work differently than nations. Modern cities, cities without walls, have no passports (passports are an invention of the nineteenth-century nation-state), and their edges are unmarked. Their borders are permeable— and they must be so for the city to work as a city, which is historically a place of exchange of people, money, things, and knowledges. The city is not bounded or pure; mixing is typical. If in a nation one is either a citizen or not, in cities there are a variety of degrees of participation or affiliation. It is more like a continuum of possibilities than the binary relationship so central to the nation. These qualities of the city make it quite adaptable, more so than the nation, to the mobility of people and cultures characteristic of globalization, whether today or in the past. In fact, recent moves by several nations to permit dual citizenship might be interpreted as an important gesture by nations to become more like cities.

Concrete examples of the different relations of cities and nations may help at this point. Shanghai and New York are at once profoundly different cities, yet strikingly similar. From very early in their histories these two cities anticipated the metropolis of our global age. Both cities began their modern histories as the creations of colonial powers. They were developed into trading posts for Europeans: New York in the seventeenth century and Shanghai in the nineteenth. In neither case did the colonial powers—the Dutch in the instance of New Amsterdam, the English, French, Germans, and Americans in the case of Shanghai—have much interest in extensive interior settlement.

Their interests were commercial, and a position on the edge of huge continental landmasses was quite satisfactory to them.

They sought security and autonomy. The Dutch West Indies Company had this in New Amsterdam, and later the municipality of New York had charter privileges that ensured the same. The "concessions" in Shanghai created safe and autonomous European enclaves. Indeed, some of the streets in the French quarter of Shanghai remind one of a provincial French town. The Europeans did not demand control over the Chinese outside of their enclave, and neither did the Dutch propose to rule the Indians in the New York region. In both cases the aim was trade, not political power or control over land. And in neither case did they seek to create a uniform culture, in the city or its region. The British in New York later moved more in this direction; likewise the Japanese in China. When they forced themselves on Shanghai (and other parts of China) in the twentieth century, the Japanese sought forms and degrees of political and cultural authority that the Europeans had not. And by the time the Japanese invaded Indonesia, the Dutch had transformed its earlier colonial trading center into an extraordinarily vicious and controlling economic and political regime. Why the change? Beginning in the eighteenth century and continuing into the twentieth, colonial regimes were transformed by the rise of a global plantation economy, committed to control of the land and sustained by slavery that represented the ultimate control of labor.[6]

Shanghai and New York remained trading cities. Neither was wholly separate from the new regime, and New York, especially, profited from the plantation economy in the Atlantic world, but it profited from it without hosting it— though slavery was important in New York. As trading cities, Shanghai and New York were open to whomever would trade, and both became cosmopolitan cities. This was particularly true of New Amsterdam, where, it is reported, eighteen languages were spoken in 1640. That number is especially interesting: it is not clear that nineteen *European* languages were spoken. The witness who was listening on the streets of New Amsterdam apparently chose to credit and include Indian and African languages, and perhaps the Creole language formed out of African and European roots. There was without doubt a remarkable cosmopolitanism in the public culture of the city and, perhaps, in the whole Atlantic littoral, where the peoples of Europe, Africa, and America interacted in an Atlantic-wide interracial world of slave and free, sailor and merchant. Not only were Europeans settled in America and Africa, but Africans, both free and slave, were to be found throughout this world. Indeed, ten thousand Africans lived in Lisbon in the sixteenth century.

Both New York and Shanghai, global from the point of their founding, had and still have peculiar relationships to their host nations. Both are thought to be not quite like the rest of the nation, not really American in the one case, or Chinese in the other. In both cases the cities tend to think of themselves as better than the nation, assuming that the nation would be better off being New York or Shanghai writ large. One imagines—though I have not heard of it—that there is a Shanghaiese equivalent of the poet W. H. Auden's famous quip to his worried English friends: he was not going to America, but rather to New York.

What might have happened if New York or Shanghai had been national capitals? Would either the city or the nation have benefited? I think not. The world cities are perhaps better able to realize themselves when free of the burden of being a national city. As everyone knows, New York City was only briefly the national capital, and the city at the mouth of the Yangtze was never capital of China, though Suzhou, nearby—very different and thought to represent *guji* or "national essence"—was.

Some commentators on New York City have lamented the antiurbanism that cost the United States a real city for its capital. They have suggested that were cosmopolitan New York the national capital, its commitment to world standards of excellence and ambition would ramify through the land. The whole nation would somehow be centered and uplifted by a New York playing Paris.[7] Perhaps. But I am wary of too close an association of cities and nations, for the balance can swing in the other direction and undermine metropolitan possibilities.

The contrasting case of Budapest is in this regard illuminating.[8] One could argue that at the beginning of the twentieth century Budapest suffered by being the national capital and having to represent the Hungarian nation. Ironically, the nation's embrace crippled Budapest's metropolitan ambitions. At the same time, New York, denied both that honor and burden, was able to become the quintessential modern metropolis, somewhat loosed from its national moorings and freer to be cosmopolitan. New York and Shanghai might have gone the way of Budapest, trapped by the heavy hand of national history and agendas. This did happen to Shanghai under the Communist regime; the city was subordinated to the nation politically and culturally and then liberated again in the 1980s. It would be foolish to presume that New York as capital would have been captured by the nation, but it is equally foolish to deny the possibility. Metropolitan cities and nations are quite different, and they have different interests and legacies.

What we today call globalization, with its weakening of the boundary-making capacity of the nation in cultural and economic life, may make possible more New Yorks and Shanghais. But the emergence of New Yorks and Shanghais might equally prompt a nationalist counterattack on cosmopolitanism. This is what happened in Budapest after 1919, as it became identified with cosmopolitan values. It is also a way to interpret the recent tragedy of Sarajevo. Was what happened there a revolt against that city's historical cosmopolitanism? The weakening of nations and the rise of a particular kind of urban cosmopolitanism offer two very different future scenarios: cosmopolitan urbanism that sustains a rich metropolitan life or a reactive parochial nationalism. The twentieth-century history of Shanghai shows both developments, and the character of the twenty-first century world is not yet clear.

There is a good deal of commentary on the growth of nationalist intolerance in our global era. There is less said about the possible extension of metropolitan values. Are metropolitan values becoming more general? I advance a hypothesis quite tentatively: what I describe as the logic and experience of great cities is being extended beyond the city limits. I make this point partly because of unprecedented levels of urbanization on a global scale, but also because a communications revolution nearly a century in the making is producing a kind of "urban culture" on a global scale. Urban modernity (knowledge of others, mobility, and multiple identities) is becoming more general; it is no longer geographically specific or at least not wholly geographically determined and bounded.

What is the relation of cities and globalization? Can we get a tighter fix on their present and likely relations? How should we locate the present process of globalization and urban transformation? Most directly, we can ask: Is globalization, as we understand it today, a phenomenon that begins only in the 1970s or, perhaps, even after 1989? Has it weakened urban autonomy?

What is new, I would argue, is the *ideology* of globalization. It has justified the Thatcherite version of the world, a relentless economism, denying culture or any alternative value. Most important, of course, is Margaret Thatcher's insistence—not challenged by liberals—that there is no alternative.[9] Never has capitalism been so crude. The specter of global competition is deployed to justify the dismantling of the welfare and regulatory state as well as a neocolonialism that uses finance and investment (through the IMF) rather than the political structures of nineteenth-century imperialism to organize the global economy. The substitution of markets for imperial bureaucracies is a major change that may in fact strengthen the relative position of city-regions—a development that would place on them new responsibilities to act in behalf of their populations.

The commitment to act may depend upon a belief in the significance of the local in a global age. Have I got it exactly backward? Is not the city and the particularity of place (and thus urban citizenship and politics) being dissolved by the processes of globalization and virtual worlds? Discussions of the new globalization refer to the seemingly irresistible flow of capital and people. One hears constantly that cities are growing more similar across the globe. It is easy—perhaps too easy—to point out the proliferation of postmodern skyscrapers and gated communities, McDonald's and Armani stores, American popular culture, from basketball shoes to rock music, from Buenos Aires to Shanghai, from Budapest to Johannesburg.

Are cities becoming mere placeholders rather than places—nodes in a global flow and without political agency? History may help focus this question. There is more historical continuity than we usually acknowledge when we make these lists. Let me give one example. One of the nicest McDonald's stores anywhere is in Budapest. McDonald's renovated the waiting room in one of Budapest's major railway stations, one designed at the turn of the century by Gustave Eiffel, better known as the designer and builder of the Eiffel Tower in Paris. Thus that building, now retrofitted with a McDonald's, represents not the first modern extension of global capital and knowledge, but the second. We have been there before. And recall: a century ago the physical, administrative, and social reform of cities was an international phenomenon.

If one focuses—as is usually done—on those immediately visible aspects of globalization—architecture and urban design, popular culture, chain stores, fashion or style, urban technologies (telephone, subway, and the like)—it is clear that the globe's major cities were in some sense already global a century ago. In Buenos Aires, El Retiro, the great centrally located and highly visible railroad station, was designed by a British architect and financed by British capital, as was much in the city. One of the more fashionable restaurants in Budapest at the turn of the century and more recently, was the Café Hungaria, founded at the turn of the century as the New York Café in the building of the New York Life Insurance Company. Nearby was an Astor Hotel, long before Hilton Hotels were even imagined there or anywhere else in the world. The Bund in Shanghai, the banking center of East Asia until 1949, is called the Bund because it was the center of German banks and other international businesses.

One cannot visit the major cities of Europe, Asia, the Middle East, and Latin America without being struck by the historical markings of the globalism of the 1890s, in architecture, in schools, in Western museums and symphony halls, in urban technologies, in particular neighborhoods. Cities as different as Cairo and São Paulo, for example, have "Garden City" neighborhoods from early in the century. I could go on, but so can anyone who has visited almost any of the world's major cities.

The rate of urbanization (on a global scale) was greater in the 1890s than it is today, and so was the percentage of foreign investment. Clearly there was a globalization of capital as well as diasporic movements of populations from east and west, north and south, and all around the globe. The city and its stock in trade—money, people, knowledges, and things—was open.

Thinking about the first and second rounds of globalization in the 1890s and 1990s raises the issue of the in-between. The logic of current discussion presumes a natural progress of scales in history generally or in the history of capitalism. Yet history shows a retreat from the global scale of the 1890s. That raises inevitable follow-up questions. What happened in the middle? How do we account for the dampening, even the reversal of globalization? When or why did the process stop? Why did it resume? I do not pretend to have answers to these crucial questions. But some obvious factors come to mind. World War I and the Great Depression, both of which were worldwide, encouraged a resurgence of economic and cultural nationalism. After World War II, and partly because of the war, the colonial system was undermined. One of the large achievements of the UN that we forget was the work of the Trusteeship Council, which oversaw the dismantling of the old colonial system. But that—along with the Bretton Woods Conference and later revisions of the international monetary system—opened the way to a market colonialism that we now call globalization.

We must not think there is no difference between then and now. Still, there are two lessons we might draw from remembering that history. First, we are not the first generation to notice the seeming devaluing of place by modern economic and cultural developments. Second, one should always beware of assumptions of unilinear narratives.

With those caveats, we can look to our predecessors who confronted a version of what we face. They understood something of the relation of cities and globalization. We in fact share much with the generation of urban theorists who wrote at the turn of the century. Those who lived through the 1890s described their era's transformation much as we describe ours. They were intensely aware of the dramatic revolution in technologies of communication, which were surely more dramatic in their historical context than is the internet today. They were alert to the movement on a global scale of both capital and people. And they saw Western culture, denominated modern, expanding well beyond the Euro-American point of concentration.

Our present, in other words, may have begun not in recent decades, but more than a century ago. And even this century may not be so utterly unprecedented as we tend to think. Since the 1890s, we may be witnessing a repeat, on a vaster scale, of the urbanization that Rome brought to the Mediterranean and the regions more or less contiguous. With Rome itself as the metropolis, Romans extended the culture of cities by a process of city building. They extended Roman urban culture, as Polybius put it, through "nearly the whole inhabited world . . . a thing unique in history."[10] Perhaps unique then, but not now. If they extended their urban culture in the form of the theater, forum, and baths in every town, we replicate the McDonald's, the convention center, and the hotel with the American standard bathroom.

Even granting that the Romans built famously good roads, the degree to which they exported and unified an urban culture is astonishing. Remember: no message could travel faster than the human being carrying it; this limitation was not overcome until the 1840s, when New York's Samuel F. B. Morse successfully demonstrated the telegraph. The subsequent century and a half has experienced the possibility of a radically new level of trans-local cultural unity. Communication vastly extends cultural markets, and I refer to art as well as commodified culture. But we make a large mistake if we presume too much solidity in that culture. Communication and culture—many academic departments so named not withstanding—are not the same thing.

Notions, of a global economy and, even more, a global culture are highly abstract. They look much less complete on the ground. Economists may be able to model a global economy that seems to have some predictive power, but its virtue is pragmatic, not descriptive, not even rigorously theoretical. To the ethnographer, the economy is much more fractured, much less unified than the economists propose. The closer to everyday experience one gets, the wiser Jane Jacobs is, with her view of city life from the street. We live in a semi-integrated global economy and culture. Certainly, it is no more integrated than it was during the age of colonialism—indeed, many of the current lines of financial and cultural extension follow paths initially established in the age of high imperialism.

The extension of city life around the world does not necessarily homogenize. The geographer David Clark writes that "the interaction between the global and local results in a range of hybrid cultural forms. Just as living in a city does not create a homogeneous urban lifestyle in a single society . . . [likewise] the worldwide transmission of information produces richness and variety of urban responses on a global scale."[11] More important and more worrisome are the constraints on culture, politics, and economy established by history and by position in the hierarchy of cities. Urban hierarchies are a much more serious problem than homogeneity.

Situating oneself in the world, as Arjun Appadurai has argued, will involve selective appropriation, irony, and sometimes resistance.[12] If there are unprecedented levels of trans-local, even delocalized cultural connections, it turns out that people still live in particular places. Local cultures continue to flourish. Yes, the items sold on the streets near tourist sites seem to be made in a single great factory somewhere in the center of the earth, but who can say that the culture, material and otherwise, of Beijing and New York, Jakarta and Mexico City, Budapest and Vancouver are not profoundly different—and likely to continue so. Instead of arguing whether globalization is homogenizing or not, we should be exploring with sensitivity the complex, continuing, and ever-changing relations between our local and our trans-local selves, between the vernacular in our culture and the cosmopolitan, between the claims of justice and those of the market.

Marx was right and remains right in his insistence that we are first of all material beings, who require space and material sustenance to live. Emerson, Marx's contemporary, was equally right to explain that he had a dual consciousness: one aspect of his life was in a trans-local world of ideas, beyond place and particularistic identity, while there was another material and local aspect to his life that provided him with nurture, intimate sociability, and physical pleasure—and pain. These relations are not fixed, and the one continually inflects the experience of the other.

Each metropolitan region must assert its agency. It can in a civic way imagine itself and its place in the larger global imaginary, openly constructing a distinctive way of life. And it can act in behalf of that political aspiration. A concrete, civic life can incorporate history; indeed, the principal local resource of a city is its connection with the past. Whatever novel global culture we devise in the next millennium will be marked locally by the precipitate of past human dwelling in particular places.

And this brings me to my final historical point. I note a difference between then and now that is striking but difficult to explain. When the generation of the 1890s observed the trans-local movements of capital, people, things, and knowledges including technologies, architecture, cultural forms, and model governmental and social reforms, they were inspirited. Even a certain degree of homogeneity appealed, if it represented a borrowing that produced a pattern of modernity that was associated with global "progress." These changes often seemed to invite democratic possibilities and richer lives. Today, we observe these developments with dread; they threaten cities, they threaten urban distinction, they threaten democracy.

Are we simply a generation of little faith, or are we wiser? Are there identifiable and very problematic differences between then and now? It does seem that culture and politics, the resources that make us human, are both being undercut by the extraordinary celebration of the market—a process driven by New York, the capital of capital. The metropolitan-led global capitalism we have witnessed—especially since 1989—may be undoing itself. These cities (or corporate elites within them)—partially freed from the now wrecked welfare states and state socialist experiments—are causes of their own misfortunes as well as of their successes. Market-driven metropolitan life on all continents provides manifold evidence of political disempowerment, cultural commodification, and increasing social inequality.

Extreme pressure is being placed upon the world's great cities; the failures as well as the successes of the current phase of capitalism is manifest in them, sometimes in appalling ways. Given that circumstance and recalling the similar circumstance in the 1890s, when such visibility prompted reform, one might (hopefully) predict that the social politics of the future is likely to be grounded in the everyday life of the world's metropolitan centers. Such a politics would doubtless be founded upon the historical resources that identify and make cities and their regions distinctive.[13] The task will be one of mobilizing urban history to confront the present and reinvent a metropolitan public that will in and of itself sustain a vital culture of creativity and a politics of justice.

CREDITS

I wish to thank the various publishers of earlier versions of several of these essays, all of which had different titles in their original publication:

Chapter 1: Rick Beard and Leslie Berlowitz, eds., *Greenwich Village: Culture and Counterculture* (New Brunswick: Rutgers University Press, 1993) and another version in: Mindy Cantor, ed., *Around the Square* (New York: New York University, 1981)

Chapter 2: *Annals of the New York Academy of Science* 424 (1984)

Chapter 3: (with William R. Taylor) William Sharpe and Leonard Wallock, eds., *Visions of the Modern City* (Baltimore: Johns Hopkins University Press, 1987) and an earlier version (with William R. Taylor) in: William Sharpe and Leonard Wallock, eds., *Visions of the Modern City* (New York: Columbia University Society of Fellows in the Humanities, 1983)

Chapter 4: *Rivista di studi Anglo-Americani* 8 (1990)

Chapter 6: Joyce Bedi, ed., *The Inventor and the Innovative Society* (Baltimore: Johns Hopkins University Press, forthcoming)

Chapter 7: Steven Spier, ed., *Urban Visions* (Liverpool, U.K.: Liverpool University Press, forthcoming)

Chapter 8: Lynn Garafola, with Eric Foner, eds., *Dance for a City* (New York: Columbia University Press, 1999)

Chapter 9: Herman van der Wusten, ed., *The Urban University and its Identity* (Dordrecht, The Netherlands: Kluwer Academic Publishers, 1998)

Chapter 10: *Culturefront* 1 (1992)

Chapter 11: *Dissent* (1987) and another version in: Leslie Berlowitz, Denis Donohogue, and Louis Menand, eds., *America in Theory* (New York: Oxford University Press, 1988)

Chapter 12: *Citizenship Studies* 3 (1999) and another version in: James Holston, ed., *Cities and Citizenship* (Durham, N.C.: Duke University Press, 1999)

Chapter 13: *Harvard Design Magazine* (2001)

NOTES

Introduction: The Incomplete Metropolis

1. Herbert Croly, "New York as the American Metropolis," *Architectural Record* 13 (1903): 193–206.
2. Edmund Wilson, *Shores of Light* (New York, 1952), 477.
3. In addition to the essay on New York as a metropolis, see Herbert Croly, "Civic Improvement: The Case of New York," *Architectural Record* 21 (1907): 347–52.
4. I here adapt the phrase *pragmatic pluralism* from Blair Ruble's excellent book, *Second Metropolis: Pragmatic Pluralism in Gilded Age Chicago, Silver Age Moscow, and Meiji Japan* (New York, 2001).
5. Georg Simmel, "The Metropolis and Mental Life," in Kurt H. Wolff, *The Sociology of Georg Simmel* (New York, 1950): 409–24.

Chapter Two: Brooklyn Bridge

1. J. Hardie, *A Census of the New Buildings Erected in this City, in the Year 1824* (New York, 1825).
2. Frederick Law Olmsted, "The Future of New-York," *New York Daily Tribune*, December 28, 1879.
3. Quoted in *The New York Times*, May 25, 1883.
4. Quoted in D. Hammack, *Power and Society: Greater New York at the Turn of the Century* (New York, 1982), 192.
5. Peter Derrick, "The Dual System of Rapid Transit: The Role of Politics and City Planning in the Second Stage of Subway Construction in New York, 1902–1913" (New York: Ph.D. dissertation, New York University, 1979).
6. *A Close-up of the Regional Plan of New York and Its Environs* (New York, 1929), 4.
7. *Ibid.*, 6.
8. Lewis Mumford, "The Plan of New York," *The New Republic* 71 (June 15, 22, 1932): 121–20, 146–54.

CHAPTER THREE: SKYSCRAPER AND SKYLINE

1. See Thomas Bender, "Ruining Times Square," *The New York Times* (March 3, 1984).

2. The Disney Plan, developed in consultation with architect and Disney Board member Robert A. M. Stern, who also published a gigantic history of New York architecture, claimed with some legitimacy that they too were evoking history, the architecture of the commercial culture that characterized Times Square in the interwar years.

3. For a recent book that celebrates New York modernism in all the arts, see William B. Scott and Peter Rutkoff, *New York Modern: The Arts and the City* (Baltimore, 1999).

4. Sigfried Giedion, *Space, Time and Architecture: The Growth of a New Tradition* (Cambridge, 1967), 780.

5. Montgomery Schuyler noticed the increased presence—both because of numbers and because of their growing self-confidence and aggressiveness—of Beaux Arts–oriented architects in New York in the 1890s. Montgomery Schuyler, *American Architecture*, ed. William H. Jordy and Ralph Coe, 2 vols. (Cambridge, 1961), I, 575–78.

This is not the place to identify all Beaux Arts influences in New York, but it may be useful to say a bit about the leading architects, mostly born in the 1850s, who came of age professionally in New York in the 1890s. These architects were either trained directly at the Ecole des Beaux Arts or they studied in New York offices of Ecole graduates. The first American trained at the Ecole was Richard Morris Hunt (b. 1827), and his New York office provided training on the Ecole model for many men who later became leaders in the profession in New York, most notably George B. Post (b. 1837) and William Ware (b. 1832), the latter having decisively shaped the training programs of the architecture schools at MIT and, later in the 1880s and 1890s, Columbia. Charles McKim (b. 1847), who was trained at the Ecole, in turn trained one of New York's most important architects, Cass Gilbert (b. 1859), who had very little other study beyond his experience in the McKim, Mead, and White firm. McKim's later partner Stanford White (b. 1853) studied in the New York office of Beaux Arts–trained Henry Hobson Richardson (b. 1838). John Carrère (b. 1858) and Thomas Hastings (b. 1860), architects of the New York Public Library, were both trained at the Ecole, as was Ernest Flagg (b. 1857). Whitney Warren (b. 1864) who was primarily responsible for the architectural design work of Grand Central Terminal studied at the Ecole des Beaux Arts, returning to New York City in 1896, after an extended residence in Paris. Finally, Henry Hardenberg (b. 1847), architect of the Plaza Hotel and the Dakota, studied in New York with Beaux Arts–trained Detlef Lienau.

6. On the Ecole des Beaux Arts and urban planning, see Gwendolyn Wright, *The Politics of Design in French Colonial Urbonim* (Chicago, 1991), chap. 1.

7. While we worked on this paper—developing this notion of the progressivist side of the Beaux Arts tradition—Domenico Cecchini shared a brief and helpful paper developing the notion of conservative and progressive sides of classicism ("The Meanings of Classicism and the Image of the City," 1981).

8. Louis Sullivan, *The Autobiography of an Idea* (1924; rpt. New York, 1956), 324–25.

9. Giedion, 393–95.

10. Schuyler, II, 559–60; *Architectural Record* (July 1916): 3–4. It should be noted that Schuyler in the essay cited above also saw (and quite rightly) certain dangers in mis-

reading the urbanistic lesson of the Fair, pointing out that it was unreal, that it was not fitted into the dense fabric of the city.

11. On Charles McKim's special influence at the Fair and at Washington, see John Reps, *Planning Monumental Washington* (Princeton, 1967), 93 (on the Fair) and *passim* for Washington.

12. "New York Daguerrotyped," *Putnam's Magazine* I (1853): 13.

13. Schuyler, II, 424–28.

14. *Ibid.*, II, 595–96. Schuyler is cited frequently in part for convenience's sake, but also because he is a contemporary observer of the evolution of modern architecture generally appreciated by modernists.

15. Dorothy Norman, *Alfred Stieglitz: An American Seer* (New York, 1973), 45.

16. Le Corbusier, *When Cathedrals Were White* (New York, 1947), 59–60.

17. Louis Sullivan, *Kindergarten Chats and Other Essays*, ed. Isabella Athey (New York, 1947), 206.

18. Hugh Ferriss, *The Metropolis of Tomorrow* (New York, 1929), 109.

19. Harvey Wiley Corbett, "New Heights in American Architecture," *Yale Review* 17 (July 1928): 692–93.

20. Lewis Mumford, *From the Ground Up* (New York, 1956), 20–60.

21. They may be seen in New York Regional Plan, *Building the City* (New York, 1931), 69–70.

CHAPTER FIVE: DEMOCRACY AND CULTURAL AUTHORITY

1. Alexis de Tocqueville, *Democracy in America*, ed. Thomas Bender (New York, 1982), 299.

2. On Clinton, see Evan Cornog, *The Birth of Empire: De Witt Clinton and the American Experience, 1769–1828* (New York, 1998).

3. [De Witt Clinton], *An Account of Abimelech Coody and Other Celebrated Writers of New York* (New York, 1815), 15–16.

4. *National Advocate*, March 21, 1818. On this conflict, see Thomas Bender, *New York Intellect: A History of Intellectual Life in New York City, from 1750 to the Beginnings of Our Own Time* (New York, 1987), 68–72, 126–27.

5. Quoted in Thomas S. Cummings, *Historic Annals of the National Academy of Design* (Philadelphia, 1865), 34, 29.

6. Tocqueville, *Democracy*, 296.

7. James F. Beard, ed., *The Letters and Journals of James Fenimore Cooper* (6 vols.; Cambridge, 1960–68), III, 220.

8. On Barnum, see Neil Harris, *Humbug: The Art of P. T. Barnum* (Boston, 1973).

9. Robert H. Wiebe, *The Opening of American Society* (New York, 1984).

10. On this group, whom I characterize as a "metropolitan gentry," see Bender, *New York Intellect*, 130–40.

11. Walt Whitman, "Democratic Vistas," in Walt Whitman, *Leaves of Grass and Selected Prose*, ed. Lawrence Buell (New York, 1981), 468–524.

12. See John Sproat, *"The Best Men": Liberal Reformers in the Gilded Age* (New York, 1968).

13. E. L. Godkin, *Reflections and Comments, 1865–1895* (New York, 1895), 203–4.

14. On these developments, see Bender, *Intellect and Public Life* (Baltimore, 1993), chap. 3.

15. See Casey Blake, "Richard Serra, *Tilted Arc*, and the Crisis of Public Art," in Richard W. Fox and T. J. Jackson Lears, eds., *The Power of Culture* (Chicago, 1993), 247–89.

CHAPTER SIX: METROPOLITANISM AND THE SPIRIT OF INVENTION

1. Edward E. Pratt, *Industrial Causes of Congestion of Population in New York City* (New York, 1911), 41; Sam Bass Warner, *The Urban Wilderness* (New York, 1972), 93.
2. Edgar M. Hoover and Raymond Vernon, *Anatomy of a Metropolis* (Garden City, NY, 1962), 29.
3. Pratt, 94–95.
4. This first known published use of the phrase *skyline* to describe lower Manhattan was in 1894, in William Randoph Heart's *Journal*. Three years later, *Harper's* not only ran the illustration here (Figure 19) but also carried a critical discussion by the architecture critic Montgomery Schuyler.
5. Hoover and Vernon, 41; Carl Condit, *The Port of New York* (2 vols.; Chicago, 1980).
6. Michael Pupin, *From Immigrant to Inventor* (New York, 1923), 38.
7. Huxley is quoted in Albert Fein, "Centennial New York, 1876," in Milton M. Klein, ed., *New York: The Centennial Years, 1676–1976* (Port Washington, NY, 1976), 76.
8. Jane Jacobs, *Cities and the Wealth of Nations* (New York, 1984).
9. One can track this historical development in Alfred D. Chandler, *Visible Hand* (Cambridge, 1977).
10. Annalee Saxenian, *Regional Advantage: Culture and Competition in Silicon Valley and Route 128* (Cambridge, 1994). See also S. W. Leslie, R. H. Kingdon, and E. Schoenberger, "Imagined Geographies: Princeton, Stanford, and the Spatial Dimensions of Knowledge in Postwar America" (unpublished manuscript, Johns Hopkins University, 1993).
11. David Hammack, *Power and Society: Greater New York at the Turn of the Century* (New York, 1982), 41.
12. On the proportion of the labor force in manufacturing, see Susan E. Hirsch, *The Roots of the American Working Class: The Industrialization of Crafts in Newark, 1800–1860* (Philadelphia, 1978); on their ambition, see André Millard, *Edison and the Business of Innovation* (Baltimore, 1990), 26–27.
13. Reese V. Jenkins et al., eds. *The Papers of Thomas A. Edison* (3 vols.; Baltimore, 1989–), I, 642.
14. *Ibid.*, I, 55n.
15. Quotes are from Matthew Josephson, *Edison: A Biography* (New York, 1992, orig. ed., 1959), 131.
16. Jenkins, ed., II, 72.
17. Millard, 33.
18. Millard, 180–85; Josephson, 315–16. This parallels developments at Bell, with similar dating. See Lillian Hoddeson, "The Emergence of Basic Research in the Bell Telephone System, 1875–1915," *Technology and Culture* 22 (1981): 512–44.
19. Josephson, 339–40.
20. Millard, 6, 15.
21. For a discussion of the difference between this form of knowledge and academic knowledge, see Monte Calvert, *The Mechancial Engineer in America, 1830–1910* (Cambridge, 1967). See also Mary L. Walshok, *Knowledge Without Boundaries* (San Francisco, 1995); and Michael Gibbons, Camille Limoges, Helga Nowotny, Simon

Schwartzman, Peter Scott, and Martin Trow, *The New Production of Knowledge* (London, 1994).

22. See Daniel Calhoun, *The Intelligence of a People* (Princeton, 1973).

23. Josephson, 136.

24. George S. Bryan, *Edison: The Man and His Work* (New York, 1926), 126.

25. Thomas Bender, "The Culture of the Metropolis," *The Journal of Urban History* 14 (1988): 499; *Idem.*, *New York Intellect: Intellectual Life in New York, from 1750 to the Beginnings of Our Own Time* (New York, 1987), chap. 9. This visual orientation is evident in classic writers on the city; for example, Walter Benjamin and Georg Simmel.

26. See Brooke Hindle, *Emulation and Invention* (New York, 1981), chaps. 4 and 5. More generally, see the brilliant analysis of American intellectual styles in Daniel Calhoun, *The Intelligence of a People* (Princeton, 1973).

27. Bryan, 113, 115, 145.

28. On this transition in academic culture, see Thomas Bender, *Intellect and Public Life* (Baltimore, 1993), chap. 3. See also chapter 10, below.

29. See Wanda Corn, "The Artist's New York," in Thomas Bender and Carl Schorske, eds., *Budapest and New York: Studies in Metropolitan Transformation, 1870–1930* (New York, 1994), 275–308; and Wanda Corn, *The Great American Thing: Modern Art and National Identity, 1915–1935* (Berkeley, 1999), part 1.

30. This excursion came about one month after Duchamp's arrival, and it seems to have been the first place Quinn brought him. See Marcel Duchamp to Walter Pach, July 28, 1915, in *Affectionately Marcel: The Selected Correspondence of Marcel Duchamp*, trans. Jill Taylor, ed. F. M. Nauman and Hector Obalk (Ghent, 2000), 40–41.

31. Quoted in Barbara Haskell, *Joseph Stella* (New York, 1994), 213.

32. Lewis Mumford, "The Metropolitan Milieu," in Waldo Frank et al., eds., *America & Alfred Stieglitz* (Garden City, NY, 1934), 45.

33. Leon Edel, ed., *Henry James: Selected Letters* (Cambridge, 1987), 15–16.

34. See Thomas Bender, *New York Intellect* (New York, 1987), 248–49; Ross Posnock, *The Trial of Curiosity: Henry James, William James, and the Challenge of Modernity* (New York, 1991).

35. See Jerrold Seigel, *Bohemian Paris* (New York, 1986); Roger Shattuck, *The Banquet Years* (rev. ed., New York, 1968).

36. See Martin Green, *The Problem of Boston* (New York, 1966).

37. The phrase, used by a French visitor to New York (Georges Duhamel) is used by Jean-Louis Cohen as the title for his exhibition catalogue, *Scenes of the World to Come: European Architecture and the American Challenge, 1893–1960* (English Edition; Paris, 1995). For the importance of New York in South America, see Margarita Gutman, "Buenos Aires-New York: 1880–1925: Itinerant Images of Metropolitan Futures," paper presented at the International Center for Advanced Studies, NYU, 2001.

38. Stieglitz did, however, mount a genuine avant-garde movement with the Photo Secession and the 291 Gallery. See William Inness Homer, *Alfred Stieglitz and the American Avant-Garde* (Boston, 1977).

39. See William R. Taylor, ed., *Inventing Times Square* (New York, 1991); Lewis Erenberg, *Steppin' Out: New York Nightlife and the Transformation of American Culture, 1890–1930* (Westport, CT, 1981); Kathy Peiss, *Cheap Amusements: Working Women and Leisure in Turn-of-the-Century New York* (Philadelphia, 1986); Lary May, *Screening Out the Past: The Birth of Mass Culture and the Motion Picture Industry* (New York, 1980).

40. John Kasson, *Amusing the Million: Coney Island at the Turn of the Century* (New York, 1978), 6.

41. David Hammack, "Developing for Commercial Culture," in Taylor, ed., 48.

42. Federal Writers Project, *New York Panorama* (New York: Pantheon Books, 1984, orig. ed. 1938), 155; William R. Taylor, *In Pursuit of Gotham: Culture and Commerce in New York* (New York, 1992), chap. 10; Taylor, ed., xi–xxvi.

43. See Elizabeth Kendall, *Where She Danced* (New York, 1979).

44. Adam Gopnik, "The Genius of George Herriman," *New York Review of Books* 33 (December 18, 1986), 19ff. See also Adam Gopnik and Kirk Varnedoe, *High & Low* (New York, 1990).

45. Lawrence Levine, *Highbrow/Lowbrow: The Emergence of Cultural Hierarchy in America* (Cambridge, 1988).

46. On Huneker, see Arnold T. Schwab, *James Gibbons Huneker* (Stanford, 1963).

47. Joseph Horowitz, *Wagner Nights* (Berkeley, 1994).

48. Quoted in *ibid.*, 323.

49. *Ibid.*, 326.

50. I would very much disagree with Ann Douglas, *Terrible Honesty: Mongrel Manhattan in the 1920s* (New York, 1995), a book widely praised in the general press, that praises and exaggerates a "terrible honesty" across the racial divide. Compare her admittedly lively but rather irresponsible history with the carefully researched and well-argued work of George Hutchinson, *The Harlem Renaissance in Black and White* (Cambridge, 1995).

51. Bender, *New York Intellect*, 337.

52. Philip Fisher, "The Novel as Newspaper and Gallery of Voices: The American Novel in New York City, 1890–1930," in Thomas Bender and Carl E. Schorske, eds., 332–51.

53. See Elizabeth Milroy, *Painters of a New Century: The Eight and American Art* (Milwaukee, 1991). See also Bruce St. John, ed., *John Sloan's New York Scene, from the Diaries, Notes, and Correspondence, 1906–1913* (New York, 1965).

54. Lois M. Fink and Joshua Taylor, *Academy: The Academic Tradition in American Art* (Washington, 1975), 50–89; Milroy, 15, 17.

55. Charles Musser, *Before the Nickelodeon: Edwin S. Porter and the Edison Manufacturing Company* (Berkeley, 1991), 1,3.

56. Musser, 10. On the press, see Neil Harris, "Covering New York: Journalism and Civic Identity in the Twentieth Century," in Bender and Schorske, eds., 248–68.

57. Musser, 10; David Bordwell, Janet Staiger, and Kristin Thompson, *The Classical Hollywood Cinema* (New York, 1985).

58. Musser, 34.

59. For an intentionally upbeat but less encouraging reading of the new geography of California urbanism, see Rob Kling, Spencer Olin, and Mark Poster, eds., *Postsuburban California* (Berkeley, 1995).

CHAPTER SEVEN: MODERNIST AESTHETICS AND URBAN POLITICS

1. See Walter Benjamin, *Charles Baudelaire: A Lyric Poet in the Era of High Capitalism* (London, 1983); Georg Simmel, "The Metropolis and Mental Life," in Kurt H. Wolff, ed., *The Sociology of Georg Simmel* (New York, 1950), 409-24; Carl Schorske, *Fin-de-Siècle Vienna: Politics and Culture* (New York, 1980); Richard Sennett, *The Conscience of the Eye* (New York, 1990).

2. Meyer Schapiro, "The Introduction of Modern Art in America: The Armory Show," in his *Modern Art* (New York, 1978), 135–78; Irving Sandler, *The Triumph of American Painting: A History of Abstract Expressionism* (New York, 1971).

3. See, for example, Gail Levin, *Catalogue Raisonné of Edward Hopper* (New York, 1995); Serge Guilbaut, *How New York Stole the Idea of Modern Art* (Chicago, 1983); Robert Storr, "No Joy in Mudville: Greenberg's Modernism Then and Now," in Kirk Varnedoe and Adam Gopnik, eds., *Modern Art and Popular Culture* (New York, 1990), 160–90.

4. Duchamp is discussed more fully in chapter 8.

5. I refer to his notion of the "structure of feeling." Raymond Williams, *The Country and the City* (New York, 1973).

6. Michel de Certeau, *The Practice of Everyday Life*, trans. Steven Rendell (Berkeley, 1984), xxi, 92–93.

7. Edward Bryant, *Pennell's New York Etchings* (New York, 1980), notes for illustration #35.

8. See especially Glackens's *Far From the Fresh Air Farm* (1911).

9. Theodore Dreiser, *Sister Carrie* (Boston, 1959 [orig. 1900]), 275, 245.

10. For a pioneering exploration of these alternative representations of the city, see Sidney H. Bremer, *Urban Intersections: Meetings of Life and Literature in American Cities* (Urbana, IL, 1992).

11. Useful discussions of each of these circles may be found in William Innes Homer, *Alfred Stieglitz and the American Avant Garde* (Boston, 1977); Merrill Schleier, *The Skyscraper in American Art, 1890–1931* (New York, 1986), esp. chap. 3; Elizabeth Milroy, *Painters of a New Century: The Eight and American Art* (Milwaukee, 1991); and Rebecca Zurier, Robert W. Snyder, and Virginia M. Mecklenburg, *Metropolitan Lives: The Ashcan Artists and Their New York* (New York, 1995).

12. Clement Greenberg, *Art and Culture* (Boston, 1961), 50.

13. This print was last exhibited in 1977; it is now presumed to be in the possession of an anonymous private collector.

14. Norman Podhoretz, *Making It* (New York, 1967), 3.

15. Theodore Dreiser, *The Color of a Great City* (New York, 1923), 284–85.

16. Quoted in Samella Lewis, *African American Art and Artists* (Berkeley, 1990), 62. The mural is now in the reading room of Harlem's Schomberg Library on 135th Street.

17. Dorothy Norman, *Alfred Stieglitz: An American Seer* (New York, 1973), 45.

18. See, for a photographic history of the Flatiron Building, Peter Kreitler, *Flatiron* (Washington, 1990).

19. Quoted in Casey Blake, *Beloved Community: The Cultural Criticism of Randolph Bourne, Van Wyck Brooks, Waldo Frank and Lewis Mumford* (Chapel Hill, NC, 1990), 144.

20. Some critics have argued that this picture was intended to be political, even suggesting the *later* anarchist bombing of the building realized its political content. Strand's comments are in fact ambiguous. See Maria Morris Hambourg, *Paul Strand: Circa 1916* (New York, 1998), 29.

21. Two other Luks paintings of the same neighborhood could be used here to make the same point: *Allen Street* (Hunter Museum, Chattanooga, Tennessee) and *Houston Street* (St. Louis Art Museum).

22. And the same can be said of his *Men of the Docks* (1912) (Maier Museum of Art, Randolph Macon Women's College).

23. Both quoted in Schleier, 64.

24. Quoted in Ruth E. Fine, *John Marin* (New York, 1990), 126.

25. On the meaning of monumentality and history suggested here, see Hans-Georg Gadamer, *Truth and Meaning* (New York, 1982), 138.

26. By extended Village, I expand the boundaries of the Village to include an indeterminate area between East Fourteenth Street and East Twentieth or Twenty-first streets, where Bellows lived, and where some others of "the Eight" lived at one point or another in their careers. Sloan lived in the Village "proper" during the whole of the period under consideration.

27. Quoted in Sara Greenough and Jane Hamilton, *Alfred Stieglitz* (Washington, D.C., 1983), 214.

28. Dreiser, *The Color of a Great City*, 1.

29. Lewis W. Hine, *Men at Work* (New York, 1977).

30. Her 1939 text was republished as *New York in the Thirties* (New York, 1973). The whole project has recently been documented in Bonnie Yochelson, *Berenice Abbott: Changing New York: The Complete WPA Project* (New York, 1997).

31. Similarly, Stieglitz could do Abbott's thing. His *Old and New New York*, done in the same year as his *City of Ambition*, was conceptually (and even formally) very close to Abbott's picture of Washington Square to be discussed later in this chapter: it portrayed nineteenth-century buildings in the foreground with a very large modern skyscraper rising in the background. After 1910, Stieglitz largely stopped addressing this theme.

32. Abbott, *New York in the Thirties*, text by Elizabeth McCausland accompanying figure 40.

33. See Michael Denning, *The Cultural Front* (London, 1997).

34. There is some context for this picture. During the 1920s, Marin became as interested in the streets as in the buildings, but beginning in 1931, human figures begin to emerge. See his *Bryant Square* (1931), a preliminary drawing, and *Bryant Park* (1932), the finished picture, both at the Phillips Gallery, Washington, D.C. See also *Pertaining to Fifth Avenue and Forty-Second Street* (1933) (Phillips Gallery, Washington, D.C.).

35. Particularly informative in connection with the argument made here is the volume entitled *Building the City* (New York, 1931).

36. Lewis Mumford, "The Plan of New York," *The New Republic* (June 15, 22, 1932): 121–26, 146–54.

37. Hugh Ferriss, *The Metropolis of Tomorrow* (Princeton, 1986, orig. 1929).

38. See Robert Fitch, "Planning New York," in Roger E. Alcaly and David E. Mermelstein, eds., *Fiscal Crisis of American Cities* (New York, 1977), 246–84. He complicates (and softens?) this interpretation in Robert Fitch, *The Assassination of New York* (London, 1993). On Moses and the urban politics he represented, see Robert Caro, *The Power Broker: Robert Moses and the Fall of New York* (New York, 1974).

39. Jane Jacobs, *The Death and Life of Great American Cities* (New York, 1961).

40. Marshall Berman, *All That Is Solid Melts Into Air* (New York, 1982), 315.

41. It was such a vision of the city that Lewis Mumford tried, without success, to define in much of his writing in the interwar years. This theme would require a whole study, but see Thomas Bender, "The Making of Lewis Mumford," *Skyline* (December 1982): 12–14.

CHAPTER EIGHT: THE ARTS AND THE WORLD OF INTELLECT

1. Irving Howe, "Ballet for the Man Who Enjoys Wallace Stevens," *Harper's* (May 1971): 102. On Wilson as the "gold standard" for *Partisan Review* critics, see Thomas Bender, *New York Intellect* (New York, 1987), 255.
2. Virgil Thomson, *Virgil Thomson* (London, 1967), 313. This division could, in fact, be tracked through the whole of the twentieth century, with the relative weight of each shifting.
3. On the importance of the ballet for Cornell, especially Romantic ballets and the ballets of Balanchine, which offered Cornell—who, with an open invitation from Kirstein, regularly dropped by rehearsals—representations of "female purity" safely out of reach, see Deborah Solomon, *Utopia Parkway: The Life and Work of Joseph Cornell* (New York, 1997), 110, 112, 155, and *passim*.
4. See Clement Greenberg, *The Collected Essays and Criticism*, ed. John O'Brian (4 vols, Chicago, 1986), II, 288.
5. *Ibid.*, I, 124–25.
6. Humphrey Carpenter, *W. H. Auden: A Biography* (Boston, 1981), 393; Richard Davenport-Hines, *Auden* (London, 1995), 219.
7. Quote from Michael Leja, *Reframing Abstract Expressionism: Subjectivity and Painting in the 1940s* (New Haven, CT 1993), 47.
8. Brad Gooch, *City Poet: The Life and Times of Frank O'Hara* (New York, 1993), 192.
9. See Daniel Bell, *The Winding Passage* (New York, 1980), 127–28.
10. On Levy, see Russell Lynes, *Good Old Modern: An Intimate Portrait of the Museum of Modern Art* (New York, 1973), 78, 98. Levy was a college friend of Askew. See Solomon, 155.
11. Lincoln Kirstein, *Mosaic: Memoirs* (New York, 1994), 177–78; Lincoln Kirstein, *By With To and From*, ed. Nicholas Jenkins (New York, 1991), 31, 34.
12. Nicholas Fox Weber, *Patron Saints: Five Rebels Who Opened America to a New Art* (New Haven, CT, 1995), 179.
13. Virgil Thomson, *Virgil Thomson* (London, 1967), 215–16.
14. Nicholas Jenkins, "The Great Impressario," *The New Yorker* (April 13, 1998): 56.
15. Though the phrase is identified with Johnson and Hitchcock, it was Barr who coined it.
16. On the initial importance of MOMA for Cage, see Thomas Hines, "Then Not Yet 'Cage': The Los Angeles Years, 1912-1938," in Marjorie Perloff and Charles Junkerman, eds., *John Cage* (Chicago, 1994), 65–99.
17. On the way Greenberg's dominance as a critic obscured the persistence of surrealist influences in Abstract Expressionism, see Leja; and Stephen Polcari, *Abstract Expressionism and the Modern Experience* (New York, 1991); and Martica Sawin, *Surrealism in Exile and the Beginning of the New York School* (Cambridge, 1995).
18. Dan Wakefield, *New York in the Fifties* (Boston, 1992), 111.
19. Quoted in Wakefield, 112.
20. *Time* (December 16, 1957): 67.
21. Gooch, 427.
22. Amiri Baraka, *The Autobiography of LeRoi Jones* (Chicago, 1997), 235.
23. For a revealing sampling, from the perspective of MOMA, see Riva Castleman, ed., *Art of the Forties* (New York, 1991).
24. Reprinted in Greenberg, I, 5–22.

25. Greenberg, I, 23, 28, 32. For a good, brief overview of Greenberg's ideas and role, see Robert Storr, "No Joy in Mudville: Greenberg's Modernism Then and Now," in Kirk Varnedoe and Adam Gopnik, eds., *Modern Art and Popular Culture* (New York, 1990), 160–90. The larger context of Greenberg's worry about contamination is developed by Andreas Huyssen, *After the Great Divide: Modernism, Mass Culture, Postmodernism* (Bloomington, 1986).
26. Lincoln Kirstein, "The State of Modern Art," *Harper's* (October, 1948): 51.
27. Irving Howe, "Ballet for the Man Who Enjoys Wallace Stevens," 105–6.
28. Guy Davenport, "Civilization and Its Opposite in the Nineteen Forties," in Castleman, ed., *The Art of the Forties*, 31.
29. Interesting in this context is the argument of Philip Fisher about the cultural work done by sentimental novels, another lower-order artistic form. See Philip Fisher, *Hard Facts: Setting and Form in the American Novel* (New York, 1987).
30. Greenberg, II, 38.
31. On Duchamp, see Jerrold Seigel, *The Private Worlds of Marcel Duchamp: Desire, Liberation, and the Self in Modern Culture* (Berkeley, 1995).
32. Elisabeth Sussman, "Florine Stettheimer: A 1990s Perspective," in *Florine Stettheimer: Manhattan Fantastica* (New York, 1995), 56. That this is a catalogue for a recent show on Stettheimer at the Whitney Museum reinforces my point.
33. Solomon, 98.
34. Stettheimer, incidentally, had her own way of playing with the American flag, particularly in *New York, 1918* (1918), *Fourth of July* (1927), and *Wall Street* (1939).
35. Sussman, 62.
36. Kirk Varnedoe, "Philip Johnson as Donor to the Museum Collections: An Overview," in *Philip Johnson and the Museum of Modern Art* (Studies in Modern Art, volume 6; New York, 1998), 12. Varnedoe points out that Johnson's donations in the 1960s literally created the Museum's collection of Pop and minimal art by donating works by Warhol, Donald Judd, Robert Morris, Frank Stella, and Claes Oldenburg.
37. Solomon, 269.
38. Sussman, 66. I should note that credit for the scholarly rediscovery of Stettheimer belongs to Linda Nochlin's "Florine Stettheimer: Rococco Subversive," *Art in America* (September 1980): 64–83.
39. Sally Banes, *Greenwich Village, 1963* (Durham, 1993).
40. For a broad survey of twentieth-century performance art, see Rose Lee Goldberg, *Performance Art: From Futurism to the Present* (revised ed.; New York, 1988). For an account more sharply focused on New York in the 1960s, see Banes.
41. See Banes, 54, 10.
42. Denby, *Dance Writings*, ed. Robert Cornfield (New York, 1986), 32; Bane, 55.

CHAPTER NINE: THE UNIVERSITY AND THE CITY

1. "Talk of the Town," *The New Yorker* (November 13, 1978): 41–2.
2. Clark Kerr, *The Uses of the University* (4th ed., Cambridge, 1995); Paul V. Turner, *Campus: An American Planning Tradition* (Cambridge, 1984); J. W. Goethe, *Conversations with Eckermann*, trans. John Oxenford (London, 1909), 252.
3. Daniel Coit Gilman, *University Problems in the United States* (New York, 1898), 99.
4. Adam Ferguson, *An Essay on the History of Civil Society* (3rd. ed., London, 1768), 296.
5. For an important example, see Richard Rorty, "Intellectuals in Politics," *Dissent*

(1991): 483–90. For a rather different formulation, but one embedded in this worry, see Margorie Garber, *Academic Instincts* (Princeton, 2001).

6. M. Gibbons, C. Limoges, H. Nowotny, S. Schwartzman, P. Scott, and M. Trow, *The New Production of Knowledge* (London, 1994).

7. *Ibid.*, 4.

8. For changes in academic culture and the disciplines in the past half century, see Thomas Bender and Carl E. Schorske, eds., *American Academic Culture in Transformation* (Princeton, 1998).

9. On this withdrawal, see Thomas Bender, *Intellect and Public Life* (Baltimore, 1994); Bender, "Locality and Worldliness," in Bender, et al., *The Transformation of Humanities Studies in the Twenty-First Century: Opportunities and Perils* (New York, 1998), 1–10; Bender, "Then and Now: The Disciplines and Civic Engagement," *Liberal Education* (Winter, 2001): 6–17.

10. On Edinburgh and Leiden, see Nicholas Phillipson, "Commerce and Culture: Edinburgh, Edinburgh University, and the Scottish Enlightenment," in Thomas Bender, ed., *The University and the City: From Medieval Origins to the Present* (New York, 1988), 100–16; Anthony Grafton, "Civic Humanism and Scientific Scholarship at Leiden," in *ibid.*, 59–78.

11. Gibbons, et al., *The New Production of Knowledge*, 109.

12. Edward Said, "Opponents, audiences, constituencies, and community," in Hal Foster, ed., *The Anti-Aesthetic: Essays on Postmodern Culture* (Port Townsend, WA, 1983), 147.

13. Bender, *Intellect and Public Life*, chap. 8.

14. John Dewey, *Experience and Nature* (La Salle, IL, 1929), 9–10.

15. Mary L. Walshok, *Knowledge Without Boundaries* (San Francisco, 1995), 13.

16. *Ibid.*, 19.

17. See Chapter 6.

18. On Low at Columbia, see Bender, *New York Intellect: Intellectual Life in New York City, from 1750 to the Beginnings of Our Own Time* (New York, 1987), 279–93.

19. Seth Low, "The University and the Working Man," *Social Economist* (1891): 7–9. My italics.

20. C. E. McClelland, *State, Society, and University in Germany, 1700–1914* (New York, 1980); C. E. McClelland, " 'To Live for Science': Ideals and Realities at the University of Berlin," in Bender, *The University and the City*, 281–97.

21. S. W. Leslie, R. H. Kingdon, and E. Schoenberger, "Imagined Geographies: Princeton, Stanford, and the Spatial Dimensions of Knowledge in Postwar America," unpublished manuscript, Johns Hopkins University, 1993.

22. On the origin of the public sphere, see Jürgen Habermas, *The Structural Transformation of the Public Sphere* (Cambridge, 1990).

23. Paul Tillich, "The Metropolis: Centralizing and Inclusive," in R. M. Fisher, ed., *The Metropolis in Modern Life* (New York, 1955), 546.

24. Habermas, *The Structural Transformation of the Public Sphere*; Steven Shapin, *A Social History of Truth: Civility and Science in Seventeenth Century England* (Chicago, 1994).

25. The nation-state suffers from the assumption that homogeneity is natural, which it is not. See William H. McNeill, *Poly-ethnicity and National Unity in World History* (Toronto, 1986).

26. For important works that suggest this way of looking at history, see Jacobs, *Cities and the Wealth of Nations* (New York, 1984).

CHAPTER TEN: CITIES AND AMERICAN POLITICAL CULTURE

1. David Ramsay, *The History of the American Revolution* (2 vols.; Philadelphia, 1789), 2:666–67.

2. Charles A. Beard and Mary R. Beard, *The Rise of American Civilization* (2 vols. in one; New York, 1930), 1:543 (Washington); and Alexander Hamilton, *The Papers of Alexander Hamilton*, ed. Harold C. Syrett (27 vols., New York, 1961–1987), 10:236.

3. Thomas Jefferson, *Notes on the State of Virginia*, ed. Thomas P. Abernethy (New York, 1964), 157, 158; Thomas Jefferson to John Adams, Monticello, October 28, 1813, in *Adams-Jefferson Letters*, ed. Lester J. Cappon (2 vols., Chapel Hill, 1959), 2:391.

4. Adrienne Koch and William Peden, eds., *The Selected Writings of John and John Quincy Adams* (New York, 1946), 105.

5. Benjamin Franklin to Benjamin Vaughan, Passy, July 26, 1784, *The Writings of Benjamin Franklin*, ed. Albert H. Smyth (10 vols., New York, 1905–07), 9:245–46.

6. Thomas Jefferson to Mr. Pictet, Washington, February 5, 1803, in *The Writings of Thomas Jefferson*, ed. A. E. Bergh (20 vols., Washington D.C., 1907), 10:356.

7. Thomas Cole to Luman Reed, Catskill, September 18, 1933, in Louis Legrand Noble, *The Life and Early Works of Thomas Cole*, ed. Elliot S. Vessell (Cambridge, 1964), 129–31.

8. Letter reprinted in *ibid.*, 167.

9. Alexis de Tocqueville, *Democracy in America*, ed. Phillips Bradley (New York, 1945), I, 298–301.

10. Quoted in Edward K. Spann, *The New Metropolis: New York City, 1840–1957* (New York, 1981), 40.

11. Actually, for a brief period there were two contending police forces in the city during the 1850s.

12. On this episode, see David Quigley, "Reconstructing Democracy: Politics and Ideas in New York City, 1865–1880" (Ph.D. dissertation, New York University, 1997).

13. This continues well into the twentieth century. See Thomas Bender, "A Nation of Immigrants to the Sunbelt," *The Nation* (March 28, 1981), 359–61.

14. Samuel Miller, *The Difficulties and Temptations Which Attend Preaching of the Gospel in Great Cities* (Baltimore, 1820), 32.

15. James Fenimore Cooper, *New York*, with an introduction by Dixon Ryan Fox (New York, 1930), 56–57. For a fuller treatment of Cooper's changing views, see Bender, "James Fenimore Cooper and the City," *New York History* 51 (1970): 287–305.

16. Ebenezer Platt Rogers, *The Glory of New York: A Discourse Delivered in the South Reformed Church on Thanksgiving Day* (New York, 1874), 5.

17. Leonard Kip, "The Building of Our Cities," *Hours at Home*, 11 (1870), 206.

18. Frederick Law Olmsted, "The Beginning of Central Park: A Fragment of Autobiography," in *Landscape into Cityscape: Frederick Law Olmsted's Plans for a Greater New York City*, ed. Albert Fein (Ithaca, 1967), 52.

19. Quoted in Broadus Mitchell, *Frederick Law Olmsted: A Critic of the Old South* (Baltimore, 1924), 39.

20. The modern recognition of the achievements of Olmsted began with Mumford's section on him in *The Brown Decades: A Study of the Arts in America, 1865–1895* (New York, 1931), 79–96.

21. For more on Olmsted and Brace, see Bender, *Toward an Urban Vision: Ideas and Institutions in Nineteenth Century America* (Baltimore, 1982), chaps. 5–6. For a more

critical account of Olmsted, see Roy Rosenzweig and Elizabeth Blackmar, *The Park and the People: A History of Central Park* (Ithaca,1992); for one of Brace, see Christine Stansell, *City of Women: Sex and Class in New York, 1789–1860* (New York, 1986), chap. 10.

22. See Thomas Sugrue, *The Origins of the Urban Crisis: Race and Inequality in Postwar Detroit* (Princeton, 1996).
23. See chapter 12.

CHAPTER ELEVEN: NEW YORK AS A CENTER OF DIFFERENCE

1. See, for example, William R. Taylor, *Cavalier and Yankee: The Old South and American National Character* (New York, 1961).
2. See especially the pioneering book by Henry Nash Smith, *Virgin Land: The American West as Symbol and Myth* (Cambridge, 1950). See also Page Smith, *As a City Upon a Hill* (New York, 1966).
3. Again, as I remarked in the previous chapter, the immediate national response to the tragedy of September 11, 2001, might signal a new accommodation to, even acceptance of, the idea that New York City is continuous with America.
4. Edmund Morgan, ed., *Puritan Political Ideas* (New York, 1965), 92–93, 139.
5. Michael Zuckerman, *Peaceable Kingdoms* (New York, 1970), 4–5.
6. Quoted in *Ibid.*, 51.
7. Smith, *As A City Upon a Hill*, esp. chap. 3.
8. See Thomas Bender, "One for the Books," *New York Times* (February 20, 1982). See also Bender, *Community and Social Change in America* (New Brunswick, 1978), esp. chaps. 3–5.
9. See the powerful argument in Christine Leigh Heyrman, *Commerce and Culture* (New York, 1984).
10. Alexis de Tocqueville, *Democracy in America*, ed. Phillips Bradley (2 vols., New York, 1945), 1:280.
11. Adrienne Koch and William Peden, eds., *The Life and Selected Writings of Thomas Jefferson* (New York, 1944), 430.
12. Garry Wills, *Inventing America* (New York, 1978), 197.
13. Koch and Peden, eds., *Selected Writings of Thomas Jefferson*, 261.
14. Richard K. Matthews, *The Radical Politics of Thomas Jefferson* (Lawrence, KN, 1984), 17–18.
15. Koch and Peden, eds., *Selected Writings of Thomas Jefferson*, 216–17.
16. *Ibid.*, 256.
17. Quoted in David B. Davis, *The Problem of Slavery in the Age of Revolution, 1770–1823* (Ithaca, NY, 1975), 183.
18. On the racial limits of Jefferson's embrace of revolution, see Thomas Bender, "The Age of Revolution," *The New York Times* (July 1, 2001).
19. Koch and Peden, eds., *Selected Writings of Thomas Jefferson*, 641–42.
20. Felix Rohaytn, "Reconstructing America," *The New York Review of Books* (March 5, 1981): 16–20.
21. See Patricia Bonomi, "The Middle Colonies: Embryo of the New Political Order," in Alden Vaughn and George A. Billias, eds., *Perspectives on Early American History* (New York, 1973), 63–92; Gary Nash, "The Transformation of Urban Politics, 1700–1765," *The Journal of American History* 60 (1974): 605–32.

22. Quoted in Bernard Bailyn, *The Origins of American Politics* (New York, 1968), 126. Bailyn suggests that this perception had little continuing implication (p. 127), but Patricia Bonomi, the principal student of politics in colonial New York, challenges Bailyn and insists that there is a strong pattern of interest-based politics practiced and justified. See Bonomi, "The Middle Colonies," 88.

23. Milton Klein, ed., *The Independent Reflector* (Cambridge, 1963), 194–95.

24. Bourne was at this point a follower of Dewey; Dewey might well be the closest thing, as I have previously written, to "democracy's intellect." See Bender, *New York Intellect* (New York, 1987), 309–16.

25. Randolph S. Bourne, *War and the Intellectuals*, ed. Carl Resek, (New York, 1964), 114, 108.

26. Ellery Sedgwick to Randolph Bourne, Randolph S. Bourne Papers, Special Collections, Columbia University.

CHAPTER TWELVE: CITIES AND CITIZENSHIP

I wish to acknowledge the research assistance of John Baick, a graduate student in history at New York University. He skillfully located the literature on home rule for me, and in addition counted urban articles in the *Political Science Quarterly* (1986–1995) and the *American Political Science Review* (1906–1995).

1. Frederick C. Howe, *The City: The Hope of Democracy* (New York, 1905). See the positive reference to Howe's aspiration in the more hard-hearted Charles A. Beard's pioneering textbook on municipal government, *American City Government* (New York, 1912), 38. However, Beard's position, as will be seen, was in fact more nation-centered than Howe's.

2. See Thomas L. Haskell, *The Emergence of Professional Social Science* (Urbana, IL, 1977).

3. See Nathan Glazer, "The Rise of Social Research in Europe," in Daniel Lerner, ed., *The Human Meaning of the Social Sciences* (Cleveland, 1959), 43–72; Thomas Bender, *Intellect and Public Life* (Baltimore, 1993), esp. chap. 3; Haskell, *Emergence*.

4. See Mary O. Furner, *Advocacy and Objectivity: A Crisis in the Professionalization of American Social Science* (Lexington, 1975); Bender, *Intellect and Public Life*, chap. 4.

5. See Daniel Rodgers, *Atlantic Crossings: Social Politics in a Progressive Age* (Cambridge, 1998), esp. chap. 4.

6. Frank J. Goodnow, *City Government in the United States* (New York, 1910, orig. ed. 1904), 21. See also Frank J. Goodnow and Frank G. Bates, *Municipal Government* (New York, 1919, orig. ed. 1909), 3.

7. See Delos F. Wilcox, *The Study of City Government* (New York, 1897), 12.

8. Frederick C. Howe, *The Modern City and Its Problems* (New York, 1915), 6.

9. Howe, *The City*, 302.

10. Wilcox, *Study of Municipal Government*, 3. The preoccupation with the nation is a legacy of the Civil War, which was the focus of inquiry by both historians and political scientists who sought to understand the constitutional and political aspects of disunion and reunion, mostly in the interest of strengthening the state.

11. *Ibid.*, vii.

12. *Ibid.*, 235.

13. Rev. of Goodnow, *Home Rule*, in *Nation* 61 (October 31, 1895): 316.

14. See Robert Wiebe, *Self-Rule* (Chicago, 1995), Part 2.
15. A generation of sensitivity to elite strategies of social control has made historians insensitive to the intensity of Progressive faith in a revitalized and empowered public. Some worried about empowering immigrants, but in the end there was remarkable faith in an empowered urban citizenry. The strongest arguments are in Howe, but see more broadly the study by Kevin Mattson, *Creating a Democratic Public: The Struggle for Urban Participatory Democracy During the Progressive Era* (University Park, PA, 1998).
16. Rodgers, *Atlantic Crossings*, 114.
17. Wilcox, *The Study of City Government*, 238.
18. Beard, *American City Government*, 28–29. See also Delos F. Wilcox, *The American City: A Problem in Democracy* (New York, 1906), 13–14.
19. Howe, *The Modern City*, 367.
20. See Daniel Rodgers, *Contested Truths* (New York, 1987), chaps. 5–6; and James T. Kloppenberg, *Uncertain Victory: Social Democracy and Progressivism in European and American Thought, 1870–1920* (New York, 1986).
21. Charles Beard was a leader in theorizing and practicing this new political science. See his *Politics* (New York, 1908); and the introduction to his classic, *An Economic Interpretation of the Constitution* (New York, 1913). For a broader discussion of Beard and the city, see Bender, *Intellect and Public Life*, chap. 6.
22. Wilcox, *The American City*, 7–14.
23. *Iowa Law Review* 455 (1868). The "rule" became part of standard American jurisprudence largely through Dillon's *Municipal Corporations* (New York, 1873).
24. For a good account of the Dillon Rule, see John G. Grumm and Russell D. Murphy, "Dillon's Rule Reconsidered," *Annals of the American Academy of Political and Social Science* 416 (1974): 120–32.
25. On this development, see Chilton Williamson, *American Suffrage: From Property to Democracy, 1760–1860* (Princeton, 1960). For an important revision of this assumption, see Alexander Keyssar, *The Right to Vote: The Contested History of Democracy in the United States* (New York, 2000).
26. See Alan Dawley, *Class and Community: The Industrial Revolution in Lynn* (Cambridge, 1976).
27. See David Quigley, "Reconstructing Democracy: Politics and Ideas in New York City, 1865–1880" (Ph.D. Dissertation, New York University, 1997).
28. Mary P. Ryan, *Civic Wars: Democracy and Public Life in the American City During the Nineteenth Century* (Berkeley, 1997), esp. p. 128.
29. See Bender, *New York Intellect* (New York, 1987), 184.
30. Besides Quigley, "Reconstructing Democracy;" see Eric Foner, *Reconstruction* (New York, 1988); and Judith Shklar, *American Citizenship* (Cambridge, 1991). See also Rogers M. Smith, *Civic Ideals: Conflicting Visions of Citizenship in U.S. History* (New Haven, 1977).
31. See Bender, *New York Intellect*, 184–91.
32. Francis Parkman, "The Failure of Universal Suffrage," *North American Review* 127 (1878): 1–20. Note also that Thomas Carlyle, in an essay that had prompted Walt Whitman to write his *Democratic Vistas* (1871), had earlier pronounced universal suffrage in America a failure.
33. Samuel Bowles, "The Relation of City and State Governments," *Journal of Social Science* 9 (1878): 140–46.

34. See Quigley, "Reconstructing Democracy."
35. There was still some middle-class fear of fiscal irresposibility by non-taxpaying voters, but they felt that various mechanisms of review at the state level could prevent such abuse.
36. Howe, *The City*, 27–28.
37. *Ibid.*, 30.
38. *Ibid.*, 7.
39. Howe, *The Confessions of a Reformer* (New York, 1925), 5–6.
40. *Ibid.*, 236. See also Frederic C. Howe, *The British City* (New York, 1907), 336.
41. For Wilson's notes of 1890, see Arthur Link, ed., *The Papers of Woodrow Wilson* (vol. 6; Princeton, 1969), 484–521.
42. Howe, *The City*, 23.
43. E. L. Godkin, "The Problem of Municipal Government," *Annals of the American Academy of Political and Social Science* 4 (1894): 877.
44. *Ibid.*, 878–79.
45. The quote is from E. L. Godkin, "Pecularities of American Municipal Government," *Atlantic Monthy* 80 (November 1897): 633. Cf. Howe, *The City*, 47.
46. Goodnow, *City Government in the United States*; Frank J. Goodnow and Frank G. Bates, *Municipal Government*; Frank J. Goodnow, "Municipal Home Rule," *Political Science Quarterly* 21 (1906): 77–90; *Idem.*, "Municipal Home Rule," *Ibid.*, 10 (1895), 1–21; *Idem.*, *Municipal Home Rule: A Study in Administration* (New York, 1895); *Idem.*, *Municipal Problems* (New York, 1911, orig. pub. 1897); *Idem.*, "The Relation of City and State," *Municipal Affairs* 1 (1897): 689–704.
47. Goodnow, *Municipal Problems*, 24.
48. *Ibid.*, 25.
49. See John C. Teaford, "State Administrative Agencies and the Cities, 1890–1920," *The American Journal of Legal History* 25 (1981): 225–48.
50. Goodnow, "The Relation of City and State," 699.
51. Contemporary with Goodnow, there were early proposals for such expertise in cities, and this became the dominant pattern in American cities after World War I. For an early proposal of this sort, see C. W. Eliot, "One Remedy for Municipal Mismanagement," *The Forum* 12 (October 1891), 153–58. For a later one, see Charles Merriam, "The Place of Politics, Civic Education, and Science in City Government," *American City Magazine* 32 (February 1925): 192–93.
52. Michael H. Frisch, "Urban Theorists, Urban Reform, and American Political Culture in the Progressive Period," *Political Science Quarterly* 97 (1982): 295–316. Frisch argues persuasively that it was not his intention to depoliticize the administration of cities. Admitting that point, it remains likely that theory he developed may well have enabled developments that reduced political authority and increased the authority of functional state bureaucracies over cities. On later developments, see Grumm and Murphy, esp. 130–31; and Teaford, "State Administrative Agencies and the Cities."
53. Goodnow, *City Government in the United States*, 35–36.
54. Goodnow and Bates, *Municipal Government*, 109.
55. Goodnow, "Municipal Home Rule" (1895), 9.
56. These extensive notes are found in Link, ed., *The Papers of Woodrow Wilson*, 6:484–521.

57. *Ibid.*, 487–88.
58. *Ibid.*, 490.
59. *Ibid.*, 501.
60. *Ibid.*, 499.
61. *Ibid.*, 492.
62. *Ibid.*, 499.
63. *Ibid.*, 450. Howe, in *The City*, 123, makes the same point: "municipal ownership will create a public sense, a social conscience, a belief in the city and an interest in it."
64. For Dewey's most concise theorization of the relation of pragmatism to democracy, see his "Philosophy and Democracy," in Jo Ann Boydston, ed., *The Middle Works of John Dewey, 1899–1914* (14 vols.; Carbondale, 1982), 11:41–53. See more broadly, Robert Westbook, *John Dewey and American Democracy* (Ithaca, 1991).
65. Link, ed., *The Papers of Woodrow Wilson*, 9:450.
66. *Ibid.*, 470.
67. *Ibid.*, 471. F. C. Howe is at least as strong in his affirmation of the political capacity of the poor and the immigrant. See Howe, *The City*, 2–3.
68. Wilcox, *The American City*, 14.
69. *Ibid.*, 22. Emphasis mine.
70. Goodnow, *Municipal Government in the United States*, 106–7.
71. Beard, *American City Government*, ix.
72. See *The Supreme Court and the Constitution* (New York, 1912) and *An Economic Interpretation of the Constitution.*
73. See esp. Herbert Croly, "New York as the American Metropolis," *Architectural Record*, 13 (1903), 193–206.
74. Herbert Croly, *The Promise of American Life* (New York, 1909). For the specific reference to Howe's phrase, see 349.
75. Allan Davis, *Spearheads for Reform: The Social Settlements and the Progressive Movement, 1890–1914* (New York, 1967). The nationalizing impact of World War I has been noted by historians, but its role in this shift seems likely to have been quite important and worth exploration. See the interesting essay of William E. Leuchterg, "The New Deal and the Analogue of War," in John Braeman, Robert Bremner, and David Brody, eds., *Change and Continuity in Twentieth-Century America: The 1920s* (Columbus, 1964), 81–143.
76. Nancy Weiss, *The National Urban League, 1910–1940* (New York, 1974).
77. This is based on a survey of the journal by John Baick, then a graduate student in history at New York University.
78. John Baick, a graduate student in history at NYU, examined issues of both journals at five-year intervals for me, and he found no articles on cities in 1980, 1985, 1990, and 1995. This contrasts sharply with the case between 1890 and 1910, but it is similar to the 1930s, when no articles on cities were published.
79. See Jane Jacobs, *Cities and the Wealth of Nations* (New York, 1984).
80. Paul Krugman, *Geography and Trade* (Cambridge, 1991); *Idem.*, "On the Number and Location of Cities," *European Economic Review* 37 (1993): 293–98; *Idem.*, "First Nature, Second Nature, and Metropolitan Location," *Journal of Regional Science* 33 (1993): 129–44; *Idem.*, *Development, Geography, and Economic Theory* (Cambridge, 1995); "Cities," *Economist* (July 29, 1995): survey supplement, 1–18.

81. See Peter Taylor, "World Cities and Territorial State: the Rise and Fall of their Mutuality," in Paul L. Knox and Peter J. Taylor, eds., *World Cities in a World-System* (Cambridge, 1995), 58.

82. *Ibid.*

83. Wilcox, *The American City*, 201.

84. *Ibid.*, 200, 6, 226–27.

CHAPTER THIRTEEN: THE NEW METROPOLITANISM

1. Robert Fishman, "Metropolis Unbound," *The Wilson Quarterly* (1990), reprinted in Philip Kasinitz, ed., *Metropolis: Center and Symbol of Our Times* (New York, 1995), 398; Richard Ingersoll, "The Disappearing Suburb," *Design Book Review* 26 (1992): 5.

2. Fishman, "Metropolis Unbound," 400. An interesting beginning effort at rethinking may be found in Rob Kling, Spencer Olin, and Mark Poster, eds., *Postsuburban California: The Transformation of Orange County Since World War II* (Berkeley, 1991), while Allen J. Scott and Edward W. Soja, eds., *The City: Los Angeles and Urban Theory at the End of the Twentieth Century* (Berkeley, 1996) promises much but delivers little descriptive or theoretical help.

3. Fishman, "Metropolis Unbound," 408–9.

4. Peter Calthorpe, *The Next American Metropolis: Ecology, Community, and the American Dream* (Princeton, 1993), 36.

5. Benedict Anderson, "Nationalisms, Identity, and the World in Motion: On the Logics of Seriality," in Bruce Robbins and Pheng Cheah, eds., *Cosmopolitics* (Minneapolis, 1998), 120.

6. James Scott, *Seeing Like a State* (New Haven, 1998).

7. Thomas Bender, "City Lite," *Los Angeles Times* (December 22, 1996): M1,3.

8. James Russell, "Privatized Lives: On the Embattled 'Burbs," *Harvard Design Magazine* 12 (Fall 2000).

9. See Georg Simmel, "The Metropolis and Mental Life" (1904), in Kurt Wolff, ed., *The Sociology of Georg Simmel* (New York, 1950), 409–24.

10. Walter Benjamin, *The Arcades Project*, ed. Rolf Tiedemann, translated by Howard Eiland and Kevin McLaughlin (Cambridge, 1999), 461.

11. *Ibid.*

12. Sophie Body-Gendrot, *The Social Control of Cities? A Comparative Perspective* (Oxford, 2000), 21.

13. Rolf Tiedemann, "Dialectics at a Standstill," in Benjamin, *Arcades Project*, 940.

14. Rosalyn Baxandall and Elizabeth Ewen, *Picture Windows: How the Suburbs Happened* (New York, 2000). For an account of partly successful efforts in the 1960s to build suburbs that were diverse and marked by an active political life, see also Nicholas Dagen Bloom, *Suburban Alchemy: 1960s, the New Towns, and the Transformation of the American Dream* (Columbus, 2001).

15. Andres Duany, Elizabeth Plater-Zyberk, and Jeff Speck, *Suburban Nation: The Rise of Sprawl and the Decline of the American Dream* (New York, 2000), 53–54.

16. Jane Jacobs, *The Death and Life of Great American Cities* (New York, 1961); Benjamin, *Arcades*.

17. John Dewey, *The Public and Its Problems* [1927] (Athens, Ohio, 1988). Alexis de Tocqueville made the same point in his analysis of American democracy a century before.

18. Here I refer to José Ortega y Gasset: "People do not live together merely to be together. They live together to do something together." Quoted in Robert A. Nisbet, *The Quest for Community* (New York, 1953), 61.
19. Although she does not address public space, Nancy Fraser offers some stimulating comments on multiple publics in "Rethinking the Public Sphere: A Contribution to the Critique of Actually Existing Democracy," in Craig Calhoun, ed., *Habermas and the Public Sphere* (Cambridge, 1992), 109–42.
20. For a modest but valuable contribution to this point, see Michael Bernick and Robert Cervero, *Transit Villages in the 21st Century* (New York, 1997), esp. p. 6. Nearly a century and a half ago (1866), Frederick Law Olmsted brilliantly grasped this point, particularly the role of public sites of natural beauty in overcoming suburban privatization, in his plan for Berkeley, California.
21. For the real dangers here, see my own critique of one version of defending local communalism in reference to school library censorship on Long Island: Thomas Bender, "One for the Books," *The New York Times* (February 19, 1982): Op-Ed Page.
22. Richard Sennett, "The Spaces of Democracy," *The Harvard Design Magazine* (Summer 1999): 68–72.
23. See Mary P. Ryan, "Gender and Public Access: Women's Politics in Nineteenth Century America," in Calhoun, ed., *Habermas*, 259–88; *Id.*, *Civic Wars: Democracy and Public Life in the American City in the Nineteenth Century* (Berkeley, 1997); Geoff Eley, "Nations, Publics, and Political Culture: Placing Habermas in the Nineteenth Century," in Calhoun, ed., *Habermas*, 289–339.
24. Gerald Frug, *City Making* (Cambridge, 1998).
25. Sophie Body-Gendrot, 24.
26. I refer to Randolph Bourne, "Trans-National America," *Atlantic* (July 1916): 86–97. See also chapter 11.
27. Robert C. Wood, *1400 Governments: The Political Economy of the New York Metropolitan Region* (Cambridge, 1961).
28. Jon Teaford, *Post-Suburbia: Government and Politics in the Edge Cities* (Baltimore, 1997), 25, 208.
29. David Harvey, *Spaces of Hope* (Berkeley, 2000).
30. A week after he made this claim, it was at least partially validated by the Guiliani administration's announcement that the city would abandon the waste transfer plan that Bautista's coalition opposed. The plan would have had a devastating impact on poor and working-class neighborhoods.
31. See Boaventura de Sousa Santos, "Participatory Budgeting in Porto Alegre: Toward Redistributive Democracy," *Politics and Society* 26 (1998): 461–510; Rebecca Abers, "Learning Democratic Practice: Distributing Government Resources through Popular Participation in Porto Alegre, Brazil," in Mike Douglas and John Friedman, eds., *Cities and Citizens: Planning and the Rise of Civil Society in a Global Age* (Chicester, UK and New York, 1998), 39–65.
32. Michael Cohen, "The Five Cities of Buenos Aires: An Essay on Poverty and Inequality in Urban Argentina," paper presented at Project on Cities and Urban Knowledge Seminar, International Center for Advanced Studies at NYU, March 1, 2000.
33. François de Polignac, *Cults, Territory, and the Origin of The Greek City-State*, trans. Janet Lloyd, (Chicago, 1995), quotes from pp. 33, 9, 40. I am indebted to Christopher Ratté for this reference. The archeological museum in Siracusa (ancient

Syracuse), which has a remarkable regional collection, displays much archeological evidence in support of this thesis, and intentionally or unintentionally connecting these findings to the present uses the word *suburban* to describe territory being connected by the sanctuaries and rituals surrounding them.

34. I adapt this phrase and concept from William Sewell, "The Concept(s) of Culture," in Victoria E. Bonnell and Lynn Hunt, eds., *Beyond the Cultural Turn* (Berkeley, 1999), 35–61.

CHAPTER FOURTEEN: CITIES, NATIONS, AND GLOBALIZATION

1. Quoted in Eric Hobsbawm, *The Age of Capital, 1848–1875* (London, 1962), 48.
2. See "Cities," *The Economist* (July 29, 1995): survey supplement, 1–18.
3. Jane Jacobs, *Cities and the Wealth of Nations* (New York, 1984).
4. William H. McNeill, *Polyethnicity and National Unity in World History* (Toronto, 1986).
5. For an illuminating, if overstated, characterization of the modern state, see James C. Scott, *Seeing Like a State* (New Haven, 1998).
6. See Philip Curtin, *The Rise and Fall of the Plantation Complex* (2nd ed., New York, 1998).
7. See Stanley Elkins and Eric McKitrick, *The Federalist Age* (New York, 1993), chap. 4.
8. See Thomas Bender and Carl E. Schorske, "Budapest and New York Compared," in Thomas Bender and Carl E. Schorske, eds. *Budapest and New York: Studies in Metropolitan Transformation, 1870–1930* (New York, 1993), 1–28.
9. This has been forcefully challenged by David Harvey in *Spaces of Hope* (Berkeley, 2000).
10. Quoted in Diane Favro, *The Urban Image in Augustan Rome* (New York, 1996), 47–48.
11. David Clark, *Urban World/Global City* (London, 1996), 134.
12. See Arjun Appadurai, "Disjuncture and Difference in the Global Cultural Economy," *Public Culture* 2 (1990): 1–32; Arjun Appadurai, *Modernity at Large: Dimensions of Globalization* (Minneapolis, 1996).
13. Thomas Bender, "La historia urbana y el futuro de la urbe," *Medio Ambiente y Urbanizacion* (Argentina) 16 (2000): 17–26.

INDEX

ABOUT THE AUTHOR

Thomas Bender has lived in New York City since 1974, when he joined the faculty of New York University. He has been chair of the history department and dean for the humanities at NYU, and he is presently university professor of the humanities and professor of history. He is the author or editor of thirteen books, including *Toward an Urban Vision* (1975), *Community and Social Change in America* (1978), *New York Intellect* (1987), *Intellect and Public Life* (1993) (with Carl Schorske), *Budapest and New York* (1994) (with Carl Schorske), *American Academic Culture in Transformation* (1998) (with Michael Peter Smith), *City and Nation* (2001), and *Rethinking American History in a Global Age* (2002).

He has been engaged in the public culture of New York—both as a contributor to newspapers and magazines, including the *New York Times, The Nation, Dissent, Grand Street,* and through such civic organizations as the Municipal Art Society, where he was on the board of directors, and the New York Council for the Humanities, where he was a member and chair.

His honors include a Guggenheim fellowship and a Rockefeller humanities fellowship. He was also a Getty scholar, and he has been elected to membership in the American Academy of Arts and Sciences.